Celtic
the Bri... ...nage

MANCHESTER
UNIVERSITY PRESS

Celtic identity and the British image

Murray G. H. Pittock

Manchester University Press

Manchester and New York

distributed exclusively in the USA by St. Martin's Press

Published by Manchester University Press
Oxford Road, Manchester M13 9NR, UK
and Room 400, 175 Fifth Avenue, New York, NY 10010, USA
http://www.man.ac.uk/mup

Distributed exclusively in the USA by
St. Martin's Press, Inc., 175 Fifth Avenue, New York, NY 10010, USA

Distributed exclusively in Canada by
UBC Press, University of British Columbia, 6344 Memorial Road, Vancouver, BC,
Canada V6T 1Z2

British Library Cataloguing-in-Publication Data
A catalogue record for this book is available from the British Library

Library on Congress Cataloging-in-Publication Data applied for

ISBN 0 7190 5266 1 *hardback*
0 7190 5826 0 *paperback*

First published 1999

06 05 04 03 02 01 00 99   10 9 8 7 6 5 4 3 2 1

Typeset in Great Britain in Minion
by Northern Phototypesetting Co Ltd, Bolton

Printed in Great Britain
by Bookcraft (Bath) Ltd, Midsomer Norton

for Cairns Craig and Owen Dudley Edwards

Contents

	List of figures	*page* viii
	Acknowledgements	xi
Introduction	Defining terms	1
Chapter 1	Self and other	20
Chapter 2	Gendering the Celt	61
Chapter 3	Nationality, identity and language	94
Chapter 4	The 'imagined community'	129
	Notes	145
	Bibliography	159
	Index	173

List of figures

1 Van Guzzel, *The Highland Visitors*, 1746. Courtesy of the Print
   Collection, Lewis Walpole Library, Yale University.   26

2 *Sawney Discoverd or the Scotch Intruders*, 1760. Courtesy of the Print
   Collection, Lewis Walpole Library, Yale University.   27

3 *The Flying MACHINE from EDINBURGH in one Day*. By kind
   permission of the National Galleries of Scotland.   28

4 Hogarth, *Sawney on the Boghouse*, 1745. Courtesy of the Print
   Collection, Lewis Walpole Library, Yale University.   32

5 *The Caledonians Arrival, in Money-Land*, 1762. Courtesy of the
   Print Collection, Lewis Walpole Library, Yale University.   33

6 *The Scrubbing Post*, early 1760s. Courtesy of the Print Collection,
   Lewis Walpole Library, Yale University.   34

7 *The Whipping Post*, early 1760s. Courtesy of the Print Collection,
   Lewis Walpole Library, Yale University.   35

8 *The First Laird in Aw Scotia*, 1822. By kind permission of the
   National Galleries of Scotland.   38

9 *The Chevaliers Market, Or Highland Fair*, 1745. Courtesy of the Print
   Collection, Lewis Walpole Library, Yale University.   53

10 *Scotch Collops*, early 1760s. Courtesy of the Print Collection, Lewis
   Walpole Library, Yale University.   55

11 *This is the Butcher beware of your Sheep*, late 1740s. By kind
   permission of the Trustees of the National Library of Scotland.   59

12 *Lord Lovat a Spinning*, 1746. By kind permission of the National
   Galleries of Scotland.   67

13 J. Williams, Prince Charles as Betty Burke, late 1740s. By kind
   permission of the National Galleries of Scotland.   68

14 Henry Mayo Bateman, *Sir Harry Lauder*, 1915. By kind permission
   of the Scottish National Portrait Gallery.   88

15 John Duncan, *Saint Bride*, 1913. By kind permission of the National
    Gallery of Scotland and the Design and Artists Copyright Society.
    Copyright Estate of John Duncan, 1999. All Rights Reserved, DACS.   91

16 *Famine*, 1763. Courtesy of the Print Collection, Lewis Walpole
    Library, Yale University.   114

Acknowledgements

The blossoming interest in Celticism and its associated culture and politics which has been visible throughout the 1990s has made this a particularly exciting time to write at length on the subject. Specifically, the University of Strathclyde's involvement in Scots-Irish studies through the Irish-Scottish Academic Initiative and the Scots-Irish Research Network has made it a particularly suitable location to write such a book, on which both the writing and conversation of my colleagues have had significant influence. In particular I must mention the work of Dr Richard Finlay, Director of the Research Centre in Scottish History, Mr Mark Sheridan, head of Music and co-organizer of the annual Celtic Connections festival, and Professor Tom Devine, now of the University of Aberdeen. Their ideas, and the climate in which they flourish, have had an important influence on the direction this book has taken, as has the new scholarly common ground in Scottish and Irish studies, where I must particularly thank Mícheál MacCraith of Galway, Breandàn Ó Buachalla of UCD, and Eavan Boland, whose insights into the feminized Celt were shared in a memorable evening with my family in 1997. I am conscious too of the support which the Irish Government has given to these joint initiatives, and most particularly to Daniel Mulhall, scholar of the Irish Renaissance, who is now the new Consul-General in Edinburgh. My debt is also more generally to the University of Strathclyde, whose grant of leave in the first half of 1997 made possible the research for this book,

As the dedication suggests, however, there are other deep and older debts at work. The research of Owen Dudley Edwards and Cairns Craig has helped change the dimension of our understanding of the 'Celtic' in Scotland and Ireland, and made it less possible than ever to reduce it to the dimensions of traditional stereotyping. Both of these considerable figures have not only commented on but participated in the cultural and political milieux in Scotland in significant fashion in the last twenty-five years; I have been privileged to know them both from childhood up and also as colleagues at the University of Edinburgh, where so much of the most remarkable work on Scotland and Scottish identity has been carried out. Here I am indebted also to the conversation and ideas of Ronnie Jack, David McCrone, Lindsay Paterson (who will yet be proved right over the Scottish Six), Alex Murdoch and Michael Lynch, whose distinguished and careful mind it is a pleasure to hear in the act of critical judgement.

It has been a privilege also to be part of a society where much of the book's subject-matter is being continuously discussed and debated at large. Here I owe much to a range of personalities too numerous to name, for which synechdochally must stand Robert Crawford, Alexander Broadie, Angus Calder, Ted Cowan, David Ellis, Miles Glendinning, Allan Macinnes, Aonghas MacKechnie, Ross Mackenzie, Duncan Macmillan, Jamie Reid-Baxter, Sandy Stoddart, Neil MacCormick, David Stenhouse and Paul Scott. Excellent external perspectives have been provided by the wise heads of Jeremy Black and Frank McLynn. I am grateful for Helen Watson, Helen Nicoll and Susannah Kerr's help at the National Portrait Gallery and for the SNPG, National Gallery and National Library of Scotland's agreement to give permission to reproduce prints from their collections. At Yale, I likewise benefited from the kindness and good offices of Gordon Turnbull, Claude Rawson and the staff of the Lewis Walpole Library, first and foremost the Librarian, Richard Williams, who came to work on a Labor Day Saturday to allow me to select prints for this book. I am grateful to the Library for permission to reproduce material from its collections and to the Design and Artist Copyright Society for permission to reproduce John Duncan's *Saint Bride*.

Lastly and mostly, I owe a great debt to the help and affectionate support of Anne, Vinnie and Lexie – but most of all to Velox.

Bearsden, February 1999

Introduction

Defining terms

In books, the press, television and speech, Britain is often said to be skirted by a 'Celtic fringe'. The word conjures up an image of a decorative but indefinite edge, a place where the substance of a carpet, a head of hair or a country begins to thin out and fray. 'Celtic fringe' is a term true to this picture, for it expresses both a thinning of population density and a fraying of British identity, though the former renders the latter barely relevant, and in no sense a serious object of concern within the terms in which this dismissive phrase is used. This lack of seriousness is reflected in the indefinite geography of the 'fringe', which usually encompasses Wales, Scotland and Ireland, though seldom Cornwall and Man, while remaining imprecise about whether industrialized Central Belt Scotland or South Wales are to be included. Sometimes, indeed, the term is used to refer principally to those areas which speak or recently spoke a Celtic language, or, more usually, a vague western area in Wales and Scotland associated with the survival of such languages. This lack of definition in its turn reflects the complex assumptions underlying the 'Celtic' label, politico-cultural, ethno-cultural and linguistic. Few who use simple territorial borders to denominate the 'fringe' wish to confer national consequence on its inhabitants by doing so: rather their approach exemplifies the phenomenon of the 'cultural gradients sloping steadily downhill from the Himalayan peaks of … Hyde Park Corner' to the 'Celtic fringe … Scotch mist … Irish bogs', identified by Norman Davies,[1] in which the importance of cultural boundaries and identities is in inverse proportion to their distance from London. At the same time, the retreat of Gaelic and to a lesser extent Welsh renders linguistic boundaries less important, and more infrequently used as a definition of 'fringe'. As a result, perhaps the main assumption underlying the 'Celtic fringe' is an ethnic one. The manner in which ethnicity differs from the civic assumptions of a participative multicultural modern democracy is important: it suggests, rather, tribalism, local peculiarity and a jealous distinctiveness. The

ethnic premiss underlying attitudes to the 'Celtic fringe' is frequently evident. One outstanding recent example surfaced during the 1997 Scottish
referendum debate, when there were many and serious calls for 'Scots'
(such a term was not defined) living outside Scotland to be able to vote
on the constitutional future of their 'home' country. This measure was
both politically impracticable (queues outside polling stations in
Lewisham with evidence of Scots parentage?), and obliquely insulting to
non-ethnic Scots living in Scotland: its premiss was that political deci-
sion-making was dependent on tribalism rather than residence. Such a
view would no doubt have horrified its proponents had it led to Irish-
Americans shipping their votes into Northern Ireland for Sinn Fein, but
then it was never intended as rational politics. Rather, it was an emotive
spasm against the sudden realization that Scotland was about to vote to
define itself politically, within a definite parliamentary political border, in
violation of the common assumption in Britain that Celticism is tamely
ethno-cultural (bony cheeks and Burns Nights) rather than threateningly
territorial. This dominant characterization of the Celt in ethnic terms has
long been critically important in the images and expression of British
identity; the impact of these and the resistance offered them by their
objects will be a key theme addressed in this book.

Before proceeding further, it is important to recognize that many principally academic commentators feel uneasy with the use of the term
'Celtic' to define the diverse experiences of different peoples and cultures
in the British Isles in post-Roman times. The term suggests a homoge-
nizing ethnic idealism, more in tune with the Romantic era than with the
particularized history of Scotland, Ireland or Wales. This point of view is
recognized throughout this book, but it is not adopted for three main reasons. First, the current author to an extent accepts Hechter's (1975) argument that the 'Celtic fringe' has a common experience (reinforced by its
physical geography) deriving from its interaction with the English core;
secondly and more importantly, the term 'Celtic' is justified in this book's
remit because of the manner in which British literature and propaganda
have portrayed Celts and the 'Celtic fringe' in a stereotypical and undifferentiated way, particularly when they have been identified as a political
threat. Thirdly, whatever concessions have been made from the com-
manding heights of British ideology to perceived ethnic particularisms,
there has been a history (in the case of Ireland, Scotland and Wales) of
rigid opposition to claims of territorial or national integrity from the
'fringe', in stark contrast to the early grant of self-government concessions
to the major colonies. This resistance is (as I shall argue) derived from a

sense of ownership of the Celt, whose emotional instability and taste for violence (see the cover of the *Spectator* for 14 August 1998, with its return to the caricatures of a quarter of a millennium before) renders him unfit for self-rule. These ideas of Celtic common experience, common depiction and role as common property will be repeatedly revisited in what follows. The depiction of Ireland, Irishmen and Irishness has been amply dealt with in many books, most notably perhaps Perry Curtis's *Apes and Angels* (1971); this book concentrates on depictions of the Scottish Celt which emphasize the commonality of dehumanizing portrayals of both Scot and Irishman, while noting the shift in satirical attention from one to the other that coincided with ebbing fears of Scottish and rising concern at Irish political violence at the end of the eighteenth century.

There are of course many positive representations of ethno-cultural Celticism, with its identification of 'peoples' by stereotypical artefacts rather than contemporary socio-politics. Celtic lettering (admittedly largely a factitious marketing concept) adorns Irish pubs; Celtic design, often in the form of brooches or jewellery, extends the range of many gift shops; the kilt and tartan in general are primary denominators of ethnic Scottishness; Celtic music is celebrated at Gaelic Mod and Welsh Eisteddfod, as well as in the annual 'Celtic Connections' festival at Glasgow's Royal Concert Hall and its Breton equivalent in Brest. Highland Games and festivals, largely a nineteenth-century development, range across the world in summer and early autumn, from the Lonach Gathering on Royal Deeside to the gigantic fests of Colorado, while North Americans scour the world in search of Celtic roots, and find them in their own Deep South. The popularity of 'Celtic' paraphernalia is itself an interesting feature of the global marketplace, where in the 1960s and 1970s 'the Celts once again became included in a very generalised and multinational package of anti-materialist values'.[2] This renewal of fashion renewed the popularity of the Celtic and, as so often, reified its desirable anti-materialism as artefact. As in the Romantic period, the connection of 'Celtic' ethnicity with simple pleasures, rural pursuits and a certain primitive addiction to partying provides an undeniable appeal.

This commercial presentation of Celtic culture is similar to its Romantic precursor in rarely possessing much relevance to the past or present realities of life in the Celtic countries (Scotland, Ireland, Wales, Man, Brittany and by courtesy Cornwall). It is dominated by nostalgic projections of primitivism, through which the positive and negative characterizations of the Celtic in ethno-cultural terms are related: both are focusings of the inherited Anglo-American interest in the 'Noble Savage', whose mystique of antiquity is comprised of elements of both majesty and horror, key ingredients in the eighteenth-century Sublime. The virtues of primitive simplicity, unimproved rurality, bravery, loyalty, elemental courtesy and honour (cf. the portrayal of the film *Rob Roy* (1994), with its obsession with 'honour', a quality in which the historic Rob was somewhat deficient) are exalted on the one hand: these are admirable, if largely pre- and anti-social virtues, given to conflict rather than compromise. On the other, these virtues become vices: simplicity transmutes into indolence, bravery into folly and violence, honour into intractability and loyalty into untrustworthiness, because of its tribal rather than social nature. Much the same duality can be observed in British characterizations of India in the imperial age; and indeed, Edward Said explicitly includes Ireland's case among such oriental parallels in his study of *Culture and Imperialism* (1993). Whether he was altogether right to do so is a question discussed in Chapter 3 below, where it is argued that the key distinction in the idea of the 'Celtic' is that it has pursued a long dialogue with ideas of 'Britain' and 'Britishness' in a manner markedly different from that found in the overseas colonies. Hence the folly and tragic intransigence of the governing classes towards Ireland in the nineteenth century (in contrast to the granting of self-government to other 'white' colonies), and its feeble but uneasy echo in diehard Tory opposition to limited political autonomy in Scotland (and Wales) a century later: the 'Celtic fringe' is felt to be part and heart of Britain in a proprietorial and intensely emotive way. The debate over what Britain and Britishness are and have been is one in which these attachments underlie key premises of organic unity, not least because the original 'Britons' are the Welsh, 'Britain' was a term developed by Scots and Welshmen, and Scottish monarchical symbolism, born out of one of Europe's oldest monarchies (one founded by Irish kings), is of great importance in the portrayal of a fully 'British' monarchy.

The topos of the Noble Savage as one of the few legitimate discourses of Celtic difference continues to be revisited. *Braveheart* (1995), instead of being a film of war between medieval states, presented a Caledonian version of *Dances with Wolves* (1990), with Edinburgh depicted as a collection of muddy wigwams. US 'Scottish interest' magazines in the 1980s might print no article which dealt with modern Scotland, while the films and TV series spawned from the original *Highlander* film of 1984 again envisaged northern Scotland as the breeding-ground of a homely and primitive virtue, richly laced with fey supernatural gifts. Even domestic productions such as Angus Campbell's 1988 Channel 4 series *The Blood is Strong* or Lorne Campbell's 1996 exequy on Jacobitism in *Rebellion!* continue to emphasize a chauvinistically intense ethnicity, Celtic by language and blood rather than Scottish by politics and territory, which finds itself compromised and defeated by the modern and progressive currents of general European culture. Save to some extent in the case of Northern Ireland, with its virulent politics, Celticism remains a concept marketed at an ahistorical and depoliticized distance from the contemporary.

There are some very unwelcome aspects to this, which far transcend concern over cultural packaging. The invocation of the 'spirit of Wallace and Bruce' by 'American militiamen' and their educated allies makes explicit the racist tendencies always implicit in any dominantly ethnic account of cultural identity. The Ku-Klux-Klan's longstanding adoption of the 'crostarie' or fiery cross from Highland warfare is well known, and indeed the Klan has tried to recruit in Scotland in modern times. Other US groups see the Scots and Irish as the 'most pure' of the Aryan peoples: in such contexts, the heroic and primitive virtue projected onto the Celt as the mark of a free people uncorrupted by government takes on the tones of American survivalism, cults and the relics of 'states rights' in Southern culture, which in their turn seek to emblemize the primitive republican virtue associated with the American Revolution. The 'Celtic connection', conceived in this way, can be regarded as 'a touchstone ... of the true white race'. On the Internet, the webpage 'Nationalism, Guns, God and The Fight for Freedom' indicates the consequences which can flow from such beliefs. This obsession with ancestry as the mark of authenticity is the dark side of ethnic tourism: the characterization of Celticism becomes in such cases the projection of an existential goal for self, the desire to be part of a 'race' with whose alleged virtues of upright, heroic and violent simplicity one seeks to identify.[3] Even in the perfectly respectable context of *Braveheart* itself, anti-governmentalism is associated with heroic virtue. The Bruces represent the governmentalist interest, politics as the art of the possible, while Wallace is portrayed in American survivalist terms: living in the open, a man of integrity and a foe to both English and Scottish 'big government', which in their turn seek only to destroy him.

The manifest growth of Celticism in the cultural marketplace has naturally attracted some scepticism. Since the 1970s, Malcolm Chapman has ploughed a lonely furrow in alleging the fictional status of the ethnically Celtic, and suggesting that the 'Celt' is a construct based on oppositions such as wild/tame, savage/civilized or idealist/utilitarian, all recognizably Romantic projections of ethno-cultural Celtic identity.[4] More recently, he has been joined by others such as Simon James, who argues 'that forcing blanket Celticity on past peoples has probably consigned their own, diverse identities into oblivion', concluding that the 'Ancient Celtic' race is a 'chimera'.[5] Such doubts are revealingly directed at the more positive images of contemporary Celtic ethnicity rather than towards the negative assumptions of primitive tribalism which arguably underlie them. Writers such as James and Chapman appear to be more concerned by the way in which the term 'Celtic' is associated by its apologists with certain virtues (albeit that some of these are espoused for doubtful ends) rather than with certain vices: hence there is an emplaced hostility to the idea of Celtic apologetics in their premisses. Their arguments, moreover, remain strongly linked to ethnic characterizations of the Celtic, rather than politico-cultural ones: both Chapman and James neglect the idea of the Celts as an 'imagined community' in Benedict Anderson's terms.[6] As I shall argue in Chapter 4, such projections of collective community work best from a real substratum of shared experience, and here the identification of a collective 'Celtic fringe' in the expression of British identity is both an acceptance of Celtic commonality and a repudiation of Celtic otherness. Those sceptical of the reality of the Celt must face the problem that commonality (of perceived inadequacy) between the Celtic countries has been a historic premiss for the expression of British identity. Celticism is at least in part a construct of those who wished to alienize it. Writers such as Perry Curtis who deal with the vices of indolence, mendacity and subhuman violence through which the 'Celtic fringe' (in common with gypsies and black Africans) was once characterized, appear far less doubtful of the reality of the group they are discussing.[7] Similarly, Said points out that 'imperialism and resistance to it' are 'inextricably linked': identity is born out of opposition.[8] This book, while accepting the widely differing histories of the so-called 'Celtic countries', will treat them in a unified way on the understanding that questions of identity are primarily to be discussed through the history of the dialogue between their own experiences and imaginings and those by which they have been characterized, rather than through the shadowy ethnicity of Bronze Age genetics or one-sided accounts of the Romantic Noble Savage. Indeed, the insistent ethnicization of the Celt in the British imagination has itself acted as a strategy which serves to deny political or cultural territoriality to Celtic *countries*, rather than *fringes*. Rather than exploding myths, James and Chapman may be their inheritors.

This is not to argue that there is no ethnic or ethno-cultural dimension to the identities under discussion, or to suggest that such identities are 'false', while territorial, national ones are 'true'. Indeed, any sophisticated examination of national identity uncovers both ethnic and civic elements in different proportions, with some concepts, like that of the 'people-nation', embracing both: this will be discussed further in the chapters that follow. Rather, what this book draws attention to is the manner in which characterizations of the Celt from *outside* have been primarily ethno-cultural, while internal self-definition has dominantly emphasized the civic and territorial, even while appearing to stress the ethnic: such was particularly true in the Ireland of the Celtic Revival, where many of the fiercest Republicans had somewhat tenuous claims to Irishness by birth or blood: Padraig Pearse, James Connolly, Maud Gonne and Erskine Childers, to name but four examples. On a broader stage than a merely British one, ethnic identities are used as presumptions of inferiority in the language of established and powerful states everywhere, who see themselves as 'inclusive' and progressive (e.g. Russia includes Ukraine) rather than 'exclusive' and ethno-tribal (e.g. Chechens). Sometimes this outlook is largely true; sometimes it is a self-fulfilling prophecy (Latvian nationalism becoming more ethnic in response to Russian settlement in Latvia); sometimes it is false. Always, however, it has a tendency to portray emerging or submerged nations as backward-looking (tribal) and inferior (sectarian, exclusive). This is a visible tendency on the world stage; in the British Isles, it has a long history.

Simplistic and populist as many contemporary manifestations of the 'Celtic' may be, therefore, they are not merely designer flotsam, but the latest descendants of questions deeply lodged in history. This study cannot do justice to every aspect of these themes through time, but it seeks to provide a broad framework for discussion of the 'Celtic' phenomenon, as seen from outside and inside the group to which it refers. It will concentrate on the contestation of political and ethnic priorities through pro- and anti-British expressions of Celticism which between them affect so much representation of the 'Celtic' by distorting the terms of normative historical, political and sociological discussion.

In order to understand the place of Celtic identities within a larger argument about Britain and the nature of Britishness, it is requisite to survey briefly the two main discourses of English identity, and their current manifestations. In recent years, there has been a growing consensus, found in books as diverse as Raymond Williams's *The Country and the City* (1973) and John Osmond's *The Divided Kingdom* (1988), that expressions of English identity in modern times have been strongly bound up with concepts of essential national worth inhering in an idealized and well-ordered rurality, 'the cottage small / Beside a field of grain' of the song 'There'll always be an England', or the more sensitized tones of Ivor Gurney's 'Do not forget me quite / O Severn meadows' or Rudyard Kipling's *Puck of Pook's Hill*.[9] The continuity of such images in the political process is borne witness to in the manner in which John Major's 1993 Mansion House speech, with its invocation of 'long shadows on county grounds, warm beer, invincible green suburbs … old maids bicycling to Holy Communion through the morning mist' echoes not only Orwell but also Stanley Baldwin's 1926 depiction of 'the tinkle of the hammer on the anvil in a country smithy … the sound of the scythe against the whetstone, and the sight of a plough team coming over the brow of a hill … the one eternal sight of England!'[10] As has been well recognized, such imagery tends towards a portrayal of England as rural or small-town, agricultural, quiet and overwhelmingly south midland or southern: *The Archers* has expressed it to millions since 1953, with its sly nominal reference back to the longbow practice at the butts of every village green which once made an earlier England great. This ruralist/organicist envisioning, steeped in agrarian nostalgia, implicitly accuses the city of bringing the criminal and uncouth, unsteady and immoral, into a life of rich, peaceful and cyclical order: this is the role of London in Wordsworth or Jane Austen. Shakespeare (who, appropriately enough, largely ignored the dominant contemporary taste for *city* comedy) is its central literary icon. In more sophisticated forms, ruralism's emphasis on a gentility dependent on country pursuits has been seen as resistant to industrialization and modernization, as in Martin Wiener's *English Culture and the Decline of the Industrial Spirit* (1981). Like Russian nationalism, this southern ruralism fuels a paradoxical inferiority complex, whereby the richest area of the country is seen as an ideal victimized by parasitical outsiders (cf. Philip Larkin's 'Going, Going', with its rank social deprecation of the urban predator ('first slum of Europe … with a cast of crooks and tarts') who intends to make sure that 'that will be England gone'.)[11]

Although such organic and ruralist ideas of England have a long history, they came into their own in the nineteenth century: 'domestication and reconciliation were persistent elements … in exhibitions from 1851', in a pattern which presaged a return to the values of 'Olde Englande'. One example of this was the Tudor revival, which projected 'an image of the indigenous population' in historicized, rural terms. Another was the idealization of the 'Home Counties' in the wake of the late Victorian agricultural crisis.[12] Such developments in domestic idealization were accentuated by increasing anxieties over the future of the Empire as it reached its zenith: indeed Baldwin's 1926 apostrophe to England evokes a time 'long after the Empire has perished', while Kipling's *Puck of Pook's Hill* envisions essential Englishness as unchanged by a series of foreign invasions.[13]

Ruralism benefited from such anxieties to become an increasingly important component of discourses of Englishness (if not indeed their mainstay) from the end of the nineteenth century. The imperial/international/institutional theme of parliamentary sovereignty and Protestant destiny which had dominated the representation of England in a previous age was still powerful, but began increasingly to be used for export, to confirm the 'Britishness' of disparate colonies and their societies, by emphasizing the provision of a visible and also metaphorical framework of common law, diplomacy, government and military authority as the binding skein in a patchwork of colourful localisms. The idea of British identity as primarily a reflection of public school officer caste values (stiff upper lip, pluck, amateurism, love for games) which proved influential far into the twentieth century, took root in this imperial context. This phenomenon can be seen most clearly in Sir Henry Newbolt's famous 'Vitai Lampada', where the 'breathless hush in the Close' with 'Ten to make and the match to win' of cricketing youth gives way to

> The sand of the desert is sodden red, –
> 　　Red with the wreck of a square that broke; –
> The Gatling's jammed and the Colonel's dead …
> But the voice of a schoolboy rallies the ranks:
> 　　'Play up! Play up! and play the game!'

The 'game' is the Anglo-British spirit: it is the unifying frame of Empire in this rhetoric, available not only to the 'English heart' of the Gordon Highlanders but even to 'The Guides at Cabul, 1879':

> SONS of the Island Race, wherever ye dwell,
> 　　Who speak of your fathers' battles with lips that burn,
> The deed of an alien legion hear me tell,
> 　　And think not shame from the hearts ye tamed to learn …
> To fight with a joyful courage, a passionate pride,
> To die at the last as the Guides at Cabul died.[14]

It was an important feature of this discourse of identity that it was Empire-wide, available 'wherever ye dwell': Lawson Walton in 1899 saw this 'period ideology' as 'a formula for interpreting the duties of government in relation to Empire'. The 'morally bracing' effect of British 'character', mediated through 'the compelling influence of … destiny', gave

Britishness to the world. This kind of Britishness was found, as Newbolt indicates, in the schools, with their Empire Tours, Cadet Corps and, latterly, Boy Scouts, and in wider society through the Empire Day and other movements. Britishness consolidated around the ideals nourished through these media, with their focal emphasis on Crown and Country, and the sense they gave that no matter how feebly, the British spirit was emplaced among all its subjects:

> Now all de black men lub de British name,
> Look on de white man-den work de same
> Lib on cornpatch, merrily sing
> Playing on de Banjo, God Sabe de King![15]

This imperial register was, however, in its very internationalism, increasingly focused on a few selected strands of Anglo-British prowess, primarily those realized through dominance, either of character, weapons systems or both. It had lost its intimate connection to Protestant selfhood, instead displaying the self-consciousness of an underlying anxiety, the external correlative to the rise of domestic ruralism. It was no coincidence that the period 1870–1930 witnessed some of the leading apologetics for the antiquity and essentially unchangeable status of parliamentary sovereignty and the institutions in which it is encapsulated. Following the decline of Empire, the imperial discourse of identity dissolved into unfocused totemic insistences on a now far less evident international significance: the Polaris and Trident nuclear deterrents, English football violence on the Continent and Euroscepticism are arguably all manifestations of this crisis. Far from seeing British values disseminated across the globe, right-wing media in particular are far more likely to identify foreigners as 'not playing fair', 'cheating' on the Euro convergence criteria, not implementing EU directives as rule-following Britain loyally does: in short, abandoning the 'game'. In its diminishing life, this discourse remains proud of inherited modes of government, while being prompt to credit tales of corruption and venality in other countries, particularly Catholic or Oriental ones; it also remains jingoistic, finding in England's heritage and institutions 'those strong qualities which shine through our history'. This 'our' is, as Oxford University still put it in 1997–8, 'The History of England (including the History of Scotland, Ireland, and Wales, and of British India and of British Colonies and Dependencies as far as they are connected with the History of England.'[16]

As the above suggests, both rural and imperial/institutional registers of identity are frequently conflated with Britishness, while remaining essentially totally English, and often southern English at that. Internal differences in Britain are not acknowledged by them: the phrase 'island race', derived from the imperial lexicon, apparently excludes the very presence of a 'Celtic fringe', unless its inhabitants are to be viewed as alien to the body politic. Where such difference is recognized at all, the Celtic 'other' is often presented as an inferior being: in this context, Marina Vaizey's verdict in *The Sunday Times* on the 1990 Edinburgh Festival, 'Nothing to show for going native', is of a piece with the same newspaper's 1866 verdict on the exhibition of Welsh art and industry at Chester: 'all the progress and civilisation in Wales has come from England, and a sensible Welshman would direct all his endeavours towards inducing his countrymen to appreciate their neighbours, instead of themselves'.[17] And who are these neighbours ? The 'reserve, respect for privacy … modesty, fair play' attributed to the 'British' character by Daniel Jenkins or Norman Tebbit's notorious 'cricket test', alike promote the 'nominal dissolution of all distinctions' in British identity, while covertly promoting those of a certain group.[18]

Both imperial and organic registers of English identity are, especially when labelled 'British', themselves at least partly ethno-cultural (e.g. island race/British reserve). Yet they have long posed as inclusive terms of unitary political and cultural allegiance throughout the British Isles. This has made the tendency to label the 'Celtic' in ethno-cultural terms more understandable, especially when such labelling is dismissive or marginalizing. Since a partial account of 'Britishness' synecdochally stands for the whole, usurping as it does so both political institutions and the climate and scenery of southern England as features of 'Britain', it has not allowed a contesting variant any political houseroom: the part must stand for the whole, and anything different lies outside that whole, beyond the envelope of Britishness, 'beyond the Pale', to cite a phrase which once described the physical aspect of this process, as later the metaphorical. The Celtic must thus be 'other', and be also disallowed access to political identity within the British Isles: such access threatens Britain and Britishness, by contesting its political space. This was the reason why opposition to Home Rule for Ireland was so futilely and tragically prolonged, and why even today many find it hard to understand the reasons behind the profound anti-Britishness to be found in that country. At the same time, ethnic Celticism, 'a touch of the Celt' in one's ancestry has, at least since the eighteenth century, been a frequently desirable designer accessory of Britishness, and one which is totally unthreatening, as not only is the 'Celt' confined in the body

politic: it is imprisoned in the body itself, the British body whose integrated genetic inheritance parallels its integrative polity. Only one group
in the United Kingdom has resisted the appeal of the Celt in these romantic terms: the Unionist community of Northern Ireland, for whom it represented a political threat. The injunction to 'Kill all Irish' (normally
encrypted as 'KAI') could still be found in Unionist murals in the 1970s:
one cannot make the Gaelic Celt more 'other' than that.[19]

There are of course (at least) two cultures in Ireland, and it is notable
that only in the last thirty years, and often not then, has the tribalism of
Protestant Ulster been characterized as 'other' and unwanted in Britishness. Hitherto it had been acceptable, and indeed was defended by fair
means or foul, because it contested no political space, and made obei-
sance before Britain's Empire and institutions: for this reason, Stormont
was long acceptable while a Scottish Parliament was not. In recent years,
growing British alienation from Northern Unionism has led to a movement towards independent political expression for that tradition. Some
writers, notably Ian Adamson, in two books, *The Cruithin* (1974) and *The
Identity of Ulster* (1982), have sought to create a 'national' identity for
Ulstermen: one which arguably is constructed more in terms of Irish than
British political referents. For example, in a neat reversal of the role of the
Irish hero Cuchulain in the sacrificial nationalist tradition, Adamson
argues for a revisionist image of Pearse's exemplar as a representative of
'the struggle of Ulster against the invading Gael'. The implications of this
will be discussed in Chapters 2 and 4.[20]

Such remarkable reversals in the use of cultural symbolism can be seen
as suggestive of an artificiality about what is or what is not 'Celtic', since
the Republican 'other' of Cuchulain appeared in Unionist murals. If the
signs of cultural identity can be so arbitrarily used, are they not mere ges-
tures of an invented solidarity? Such a view will be considered in the
chapters that follow, but it is hard to give it unqualified support. Not only
does it (as mentioned above) tend to be invoked to vitiate positive features in Celticism and Celtic revivalism; it also focuses exclusively on the
ethnic characterization of the Celt. Linguistic and territorial identities are
ignored: for these reasons among others, much of the sceptical demythologizing of those who prefer to regard provincial or Celtic identities as
'invented traditions' is too trite.[21] 'Invention' is a term one degree stronger
than 'imagination' when describing the process of ideological consolidation in national communities: its overtones of the factitious often betray-
ing a self-interested and unsympathetic evaluation of what indeed makes
'self' and 'other' national.

As early as 1316, 'the Welsh leader Sir Griffudd Llwyd' sent a clandestine letter to Edward Bruce, the King of Scots' brother, which stated that 'the intention of the English' was 'to try to delete our name and memory from the land': that is to destroy the linguistic and territorial identity of Wales, itself defined as a territorial space as early as Offa's Dyke in the eighth century.[22] In their turn, fourteenth-century Scots recognized and understood the process of colonization in Ireland and Wales as bent on destroying 'name and nobility', the language and culture of these areas. Ethnic aliens the Irish and Welsh might be to medieval England: but their ethnicity was understood in linguistic and territorial terms. For example, Englishmen on trial in Wales were only to be convicted by other Englishmen: a neat conflation of ethnic and territorial/institutional jurisdictions.[23]

One ideological element in the concept of Britain nonetheless benefited from the political resistance to English rule in Wales. In 1401, Owain Glyn Dŵr wrote for help to both the Irish chiefs and Robert III of Scots, appealing 'on the score of a common descent from Brutus'.[24] Brutus was in tradition the great-grandson of Aeneas, hero of Virgil's *Aeneid* and the Trojan exile who had founded Rome. Brutus was in turn supposed by medieval legend to have landed in Britain. As the northern romance *Gawain and the Green Knight* put it in the fourteenth century:

> And fer over the French flod Felix Brutus
> On mony bonkkes ful brode Bretayn he settegh wyth wynne, *[joy]*
> > Where werre and wrake and wonder
> > Bi sythegh *[at times]* hatgh wont *[dwelt]* therinne
> > And oft both blysse and blunder
> > Ful skete *[quickly]* hatgh skyfted *[shifted, alternated]* synne *[since]*.[25]

There were two main forms of the legend: one where Brutus and Albanus (Scotland) were brothers, and one in which all Britain was subsequently divided between Brutus's three sons, Locrinus (England), Camber or Kamber (Wales) and Albanactus (Scotland), Locrinus as the eldest having an implicit claim to suzerainty of the whole, a claim which would prove potentially explosive in Anglo-Scottish politics.[26] Brutus was the ancestor of Arthur, King of the Britons, of whom it was said that he would come again to deliver his people when danger threatened them. But there was a fundamental ambivalence in the story, one which would both powerfully contribute to Welsh territorial identity and also in the end vitiate it through the opportunity it offered for a single British monarch to claim the unifying inheritance of Arthur: and this opportunity in turn rested on the semantic ambivalence of the term 'Britain'. The Britons whom Arthur is credited with reigning over were Celts, driven in the end by the Saxons beyond Offa's Dyke and the Tamar into Cornwall and Wales. So was Arthur a Welsh hero? Not exactly, because Britons were also found in Lowland Scotland, in the Kingdom of Strathclyde round Dumbarton and in the eastern Lowlands, source of the first piece of Scottish or Welsh literature (according to taste), *The Gododdin*, which tells the tale of a Celtic warband's heroic and futile attack on their Anglic foes. Arthur belonged to this tradition too: he was supposed buried under the Eildon Hills (rather than Avalon) by one tradition, while Arthur's Seat in Edinburgh was by medieval times to become the Scottish royal park it still remains.[27]

The fact that legends of Arthur as royal deliverer were not confined to a definitive territorial area was an ambiguity which was early exploited by English kings wishing, by virtue of a claimed descent from Brutus' eldest son, to be recognized as suzerains of the whole island. Geoffrey of Monmouth's *Historia Regum Britanniae* (1136), gave 'a precedent for the dominions and ambitions of the Norman kings' through its genealogies, which unsurprisingly adopted the three sons version of the Brutus myth. Geoffrey made Arthur the centrepiece of his history, showing him overthrowing the Scots and Picts, who together with the Irish (and some Saxons) fought against him in the army of the traitor Mordred at the last battle of Camblam/Camlann, 'filled with hatred' against their king. The precedents for Plantagenet sovereignty and Scots-Irish treachery were obvious.[28]. Henry II (1154–89) was the first king to pursue Geoffrey's implicit agenda: the 'discovery' of Arthur's tomb at Glastonbury underlined Plantagenet claims to British overlordship, which were being materially developed by Henry's commencement of the Norman Pale in Ireland and the homage of William the Lion under the terms of the 1174 Treaty of Falaise. Henry's grandson was suitably named Arthur, and it was he who should have succeeded Richard I in 1199, had not John usurped the throne. Edward I's actions in subjugating Wales and attempting a similar policy in Scotland bore out the same ambitions, but it was the Tudors who began to develop the English monarchy as a key unifying symbol for a future British polity. Henry VII's army at Bosworth flew 'the red dragon banner of Wales',[29] and in doing so laid claim to the 'desire for a Deliverer … vigorously expressed … in … numerous prophetic poems' in Wales after the death of Owain Glyn Dŵr. This 'Deliverer' was to be a Welshman who 'would wear the Crown of England', 'fulfilling Merlin's words'. Henry VII presented himself as the fulfilment of the prophecy.[30] On his accession to the throne, he 'declared that he was restoring the kingdom of Arthur',[31] and both Henry and his successors continued to emphasize 'the founding of the nation by Brutus' and 'the historicity of Arthur' as his descendant: Henry gave the name Arthur to his eldest son, who like his predecessor did not survive to rule. Arthurianism was further bolstered by Caxton's printing of Malory's *Morte d'Arthure* in 1485: Caxton himself was a supporter of Henry VII.[32] In the 1540s, Henry VIII once again invoked claims of overlordship over Scotland constructed in similar terms.[33]

Owain Glyn Dŵr's ostensibly pan-Celtic appeal of 1401 to British descent was thus more ambivalent than at first appears. The 'common descent from Brutus', which Glyn Dŵr cites, was part of the core of Welsh monarchical identity, but it had already been conscripted by the Plantagenets to bolster their own pan-British suzerainty claims: to this extent Glyn Dŵr's appeal to it is unintentionally ironic. But as an appeal to Scots or Irish supporters, Brutus also had his limitations. Scotland had developed (it is a keynote in the 1320 Declaration of Arbroath) an alternative origin-myth, which conferred on the country Graeco-Egyptian rather than Trojan roots, in the person of 'Scota, the daughter of Pharaoh'. This was compatible with the monarchy's Irish ancestry, as Skene observes: 'in the Irish form Gathelas or Gaudeglas, the *eponymus* of the Gael, marries Scota ... by which the settlement of the Gael in Scotia or Ireland is prefigured'. Until at least the twelfth century, 'Scotus' was a term indicative of either Scots or Irish nationality: in 1004, for example, the Irish hero Brian Boru was described as 'imperator Scotorum'.[34] The Scots repaid this compliment by deriving their royal line from Irish roots: the Scottish crown's descent from Irish kings, though less emphasized as the Middle Ages progressed, was an important indicator of difference from England and Wales, and indeed betokened a continuing consciousness of cultural alliance with Ireland: the Scottish kingdom was born of Irish immigration. When Bruce appealed to Irish leaders as representatives of 'our common people', *'nostra nacio'*, he was simply recognizing the continuing political and cultural significance of this fact. North of the Forth, Scotland also shared with Ireland the heroic cycle of the Fenians: 'Fionn and his men ... were ... accorded what practically amounted to a religious veneration' in the country, and the Fenian heroes were associated with a number of sites in Perthshire, Invernesshire and elsewhere. Fionn, like Arthur, was a 'sleeping warrior who will one day reappear to restore the Gaels of Scotland to their former greatness'.[35]

It was to prove of great importance to the future development of both Celtic and British identity, that while the central monarchy absorbed and developed the idea of Arthur of the Britons as a unifying national symbol, that of Fionn continued to remain Hiberno-Scottish property. Fionn and the Fianna were ineluctably 'other': part of British culture geographically, but beyond the Pale of its core expression. It was thus no coincidence that the Jacobite risings in eighteenth-century Scotland drew on Fenian typology, or that the idea of a heroic Celtic civilization was elegized by James Macpherson (1736/8–96) writing in the persona of Oisin/Ossian, and utilizing the stories of the Fenian cycle. Nor should the power of the image and very name of Fenian in nineteenth- and twentieth-century Ireland surprise us. The Arthurian appeals of Owain Glyn Dŵr were domesticated into common British property (Geoffrey Ashe, the most prominent contemporary popularizer of Arthur, indeed calls them 'the English national legend'[36]); the stories of Fionn were not. No one by the end of the nineteenth century could write of Arthur in the terms in which Yeats writes of Fionn's son, Oisin, imagined in *The Wanderings of Oisin* (1889; subsequently revised) as a figure from a heroic past trapped in a petty present of Unionism and lower-middle-class Catholic provincialism, symbolized under Oisin's resistance to St Patrick's demands for Christian conformity:

> Put the staff in my hands; for I go to the Fenians, O cleric, to chaunt
> The war-songs that roused them of old; they will rise, making clouds with
>   their breath,
> Innumerable, singing, exultant; the clay underneath them shall pant,
> And demons be broken in pieces, and trampled beneath them in death.
> And demons afraid in their darkness; deep horror of eyes and of wings,
> Afraid, their ears on the earth laid, shall listen and rise up and weep;
> Hearing the shaking of shields and the quiver of stretched bowstrings,
> Hearing Hell loud with a murmur, as shouting and mocking we sweep.[37]

In the context of twentieth-century Irish politics, this verse has a chilling vitality inaccessible to an Arthurianism long overlaid with British sentiment and imperial allegory, as in Tennyson's *Idylls of the King*. The barely disguised use of violence as a metaphor for redemption in Yeats's poem foreshadows the sacrificial blood-cult of Irish Republicanism, an influence of which Yeats himself was not unaware.

By contrast, Bosworth (1485) witnessed the beginning of a long and continuous process of integration for Arthurianism into the ideology of a pan-British suzerainty. In rendering Henry VII 'heir of Cadwallader's vision of a restored British monarchy',[38] the Tudors both neutralized Welsh patriotism and used their clear (and destined) incorporation of

Wales, confirmed by Act of Union in 1536, as a reinforcement of their pan-British claims. Owain Glyn Dŵr's reputation as a *Welsh* patriot hero went into decline in high culture, to re-emerge only under the safe cover of Primitivist nostalgia in Thomas Pennant's *A Tour in Wales* (1778).[39] Meanwhile, the Arthurian role established by the Tudors was extended in 1603, when James VI of Scots became the first King (since Arthur, as was thought) of the whole island of Britain. The opportunity to compare James with his legendary predecessors was too good to miss. William Herbert of Glamorgan, in *A Prophesie of Cadwallader* (1604), termed James 'our second Brute' who 'shall three in one, and one in three unite', giving sacred Trinitarian overtones to the language in which the restored British kingdoms are described. Anthony Munday, in *The Triumphs of Re-United Britaine*, chimed in with his praises of 'our Second Brute (Royall King James)'. The Arthurian ethic was strongly linked to Wales and Corn-wall in James's reign, thus reinforcing a centralized British identity expressed through praise of and interest in its peripheries.[40] Some even termed James 'Arthur returned'. This enthusiasm (often nurtured by Welshmen, who liked to claim that Arthur's was the original British church as well as monarchy, and that they (of course) were the original Britons) even reached the ears of foreign dignitaries. The Venetian Ambassador remarked that James's naming himself king of 'Britain' was in accord with 'the decision of the famous and ancient King Arthur, to embrace under one name the entire kingdom'.[41]

Such language continued to be applied to James's successor. Robert Jegon, in 'A Supplement to the Faery Queene' of 1635, stated that King Charles 'sitt'st in Arthur's seate and dost maintaine / The antique glory of the Britains strong'.[42] Not everyone felt so positively. In the struggles of the War of Three Kingdoms which followed, anti-Stuart ideologues tended to articulate a more specifically English identity, one expressed through 'the laws and custom of the Anglo-Saxons' rather than the pan-British royal claims of Arthur.[43] Extremists even regarded British monarchical ideol-ogy as an imposition, a burden of the Norman Yoke which suppressed the natural liberties of Englishmen. In these terms it may be no coincidence that in the conflicts of the time the King drew considerable support from Wales and the West Country, areas identified as Arthurian heartlands, with little interest in aligning themselves with a patriotism based on Saxon laws and liberties.

Because the Stuarts were a Scottish dynasty, they appear to have per-formed something of a volte-face in emphasizing the Arthurian story rather than the Irish-Graeco-Egyptian foundation myths of the Scottish royal line. James was aided in this balancing act by his emphasis on Welsh roots and links with the Tudors through Fleance son of Banquo, a genealogy happily dramatized for the King by Shakespeare in *Macbeth* (1605). Although he was, in his own words, a 'Monarch sprunge of Ferguse race', thus identifying 'Irish ancestors as the ones who first brought law and civilisation to Great Britain', James does not appear to have stressed this dimension in an Anglo-Welsh context.[44] Unlike the Tudors, the Stuart kings appear to have run with both the hare and the hounds in their different realms: the 1684–6 portraits of the Scottish royal line in Holyroodhouse emphasize the national, rather than British, foundation-myth. It was necessary to keep these dual identities in play, because of the potential embarrassment in the Brutus/Arthur story's implicit claim to English overlordship in Scotland. The divided account that the Stuart monarchy thus gave of its origins was nonetheless acceptable because, despite some Scottish claims to incorporation in the new polity of 'Great' Britain, contemporary ideas of Britishness still excluded Scotland from equal participation in Brutus's inheritance (as opposed to incorporation under it). Pro-Royalist ballads on the Bishops' Wars of 1638–41 state for example that 'The vaunting *Scot* shall know what valour / Doth in a *Britains* breast reside' and praise two Welshmen who as 'undaunted Troian worthies … Withstood full fifteene thousand *Scots*'.[45] The exclusion of the 'Scot' from the Trojan/Aeneas/ Brutus Pale suggests that Scotland's claim even to be part of Britain was viewed as doubtful in 1640, at least by the anonymous English composers of ballads in praise of their Welsh fellow-Britons.

After the Restoration of 1660, Charles II's royal ideology in England was forced to an extent to compromise with the Saxonists. Obadiah Walker's characterization of Charles as Alfred rendered the King the hero and protector of Saxon common law rather than its opponent, but at the cost of making him more definitively English, a mode of depiction which was to expand after the exile of the Stuarts in 1688. Although Charles used both Arthurianism (particularly via his characterization as Augustus/Aeneas in the poetry of his Laureate, John Dryden) and the Scottish foundation-myths to support his position, William of Orange's regime began to turn away from Tudor and Stuart British monarchical imagery. In the 1690s, Sir Richard Blackmore portrayed William as Arthur and the Saxons as Catholics: but this ingenious typology did not catch on.[46] The eighteenth century belonged to Saxon Gothicism: by the 1790s, even Scottish radicals were appealing to the legacy of King Alfred rather than the ideals of the French Revolution.[47] Arthurianism went into abeyance under the Hanoverians, not to be revived until the Victorian period, when, in the hands of Alfred Tennyson and the Pre-Raphaelites, it reappeared as a symbol of British royal unity, the nostalgic underpinnings of Empire.[48] Later, A. C. Swinburne revived the explicitly Celtic dimension of Arthurianism in his poetic romance *Tristram of Lyonesse* (1882). By this time, however, it is at least arguable that interest in Arthur had become merely a celebratory and nostalgic gesture, lacking the real political content it had had in developing the nature and influence of British monarchy before 1700. The 'Matter of Britain', the stories of Arthur and his descent, were the Celtic keystone in the architecture of British monarchical identity.

Yet if this aspect of Celticism was early incorporated into British culture and its representations, the identification of the Celtic as 'other' also had a long history. When Britain as a modern political entity was formed in the period 1688–1707 (an age which saw Union with Scotland, penal legislation in Ireland and consideration given to abolishing the Irish Parliament, together with the actual abolition of the Council of Wales and the Marches), an ambivalence emerged in attitudes towards the Celt. No longer could Scots or Irish be classed completely as outsiders: they were part of the state, integrated to a greater degree than ever before. Moreover, whereas Wales and Cornwall were already integrated by virtue of monarchical ideology, Scotland and Ireland were not. Yet more seriously, where Wales and Cornwall were under-urbanized and sparsely populated, Scotland and Ireland were geographically and demographically much more significant, with the second and third biggest cities in the British Isles (Dublin and Edinburgh). In 1700, the combined population of the 'Celtic countries' was closer to 80 per cent of England's than the 25 per cent it now is. How did all this affect the image of the Celt in Anglophone and Anglocentric eyes ? In the first part of Chapter 1, I shall explore both the historic representations of the Celt and Celtic as 'other', and how these appear to have altered under the pressure of a political settlement which incorporated large numbers of these aliens into the state itself. The Celtic citizen was, especially if unreconciled to the British polity, bound to be a source of uneasiness and resentment in the core cultural zones of those who were its mainstay and natural support. These in turn, unwilling to invest the marginal Celt with political significance, sought to distance him through an *ad hominem* ethnic caricature, often expressed through ridicule.[49]

Chapter 1

Self and other

To see ourselves as others see us

One of the most curious features of modern theories of nationalism is their tendency to argue that their subject is a new arrival in human history, and that it has little or no place in political consciousness until the era of the French Revolution. Differing accounts of nationalism have this premiss in common. Hans Kohn in 1943, Boyd Shafer in 1955, E. Kedourie in 1960, Kenneth Monogue in 1967 and many others broadly agree on this single era's status as a watershed. As Ernest Barker remarks, 'the self-consciousness of nations is a product of the nineteenth century'. On the eve of one of the greatest upsurges in the phenomenon in the last hundred years, Peter Alter wrote in 1989 that 'received opinion holds that nationalism in the modern sense does not date back further than the revolutionary political turmoil that troubled the second half of the eighteenth century. It was born in France.'[1] A great many of these assumptions root nationalism in the circumstances of early modern state formation. For Ernest Gellner, nationalism is 'the inseparable *ideological counterpart of modernization*, of the transition from agricultural to industrial society, in every country of the world';[2] for Benedict Anderson, the 'imagined community' of the nation is 'made possible by the rise of print capitalism and new genres such as the newspaper and the novel'.[3]

In discounting the presence of nationalism in the pre-modern state, such theoretical positions undermine any nationalist reading of medieval and early modern armed or cultural struggles within the British Isles (or elsewhere) and appear to refuse any specifically territorial identity to the 'Celt'. Are they right to do so? In the days of Queen Elizabeth 'Welsh peasants' gathered 'in mountain-top assemblies to intone their genealogies, and to hear the bards recount ancient victories over the Saxons'; the English saw intermarriage with the Irish as 'degeneracy',[4] and the Gaelic poets of Scotland voiced a cultural identity with Ireland, while non-Gaels such as Blin Hary (*c*.1440–93) shared a Celtic distrust of 'Saxon seed' on behalf of 'brave true ancient Scots' who do not wish to see 'the Saxon blood in

Scotland reign'.[5] Both Celt and non-Celt identified 'self' and 'other' in
terms calculated to claim national kinship or arouse national enmity. It is
possible to argue that the 'otherness' identified and resented by both sides
was not truly 'national' in the modern sense, but that is far from rendering it non-national in *any* sense.

What appears to at least sometimes occur in modern nationalist theory
is that too much emphasis is laid on 'contractual' nationalism with its
constitutional and documentary formats, and too little on collectivist
culturalist nationalism, which identifies its chosen people-nation as
unique, and possessed of unique qualities, qualities not simply tribal, but
national and territorial, 'true Scots' for example defending the nation of
'Scotland': these issues will be discussed further in Chapters 3 and 4.
(Gellner of course suggests that cultural integration is itself 'sociologi-
cally rooted in modernity', and this view can also be held to be implicit in
Anderson's work).[6]

Together with institutional assumptions of the nation, grounded
largely on its modern condition, and read back into the nineteenth century in a teleological manner, there is also the apparent semantic fact that
the term 'nationalism' itself is first found only in 1836, according to the
OED, though it is cited then as if it were an already established term.
Indeed, its constitutive terms are far older: 'nationalist' is cited from 1715,
'nationality' from 1691, while two early medieval references reveal yet
more significant contexts: 'Of Ingland the nacion Es Inglis man thar in
commun' (1300) and 'Be cause I am a natyff Scottis man' from Blin Hary's
explicitly nationalist *Wallace* (1470) – the first recorded instance.[7] There
seems therefore ample evidence to suggest that 'nationalism' is a concept
much older than 1789. As Susan Reynolds wisely wrote some years ago:

> It seems normally to be taken for granted that the nation-states of today are
> the true nations of history and that only they can ever have inspired loyal-
> ties which deserve to be called nationalist. Allowance may be made for units
> like Scotland or Brittany ... None the less, any past unit of government ...
> evidently did not enjoy the manifest destiny of solidarity ... The trouble
> abut all this for the medieval historian is not that the idea of the ... real
> nation is foreign to the middle ages, as so many historians of nationalism
> assume, but that it closely resembles the medieval idea of the kingdom as ...
> a people with a similarly permanent and objective reality.[8]

Quite. Modestly stated, Reynolds's position undercuts much of the enterprise of theorists of nationalism, whose teleological assumptions are
often strong and frequently staggering. To demonstrate this, one only has

to read essays written on nationalism before the collapse of the Soviet Union: for example, James Mayall's 1990 *Nationalism and International Society*, which stated that 'there are no more empires to collapse' and likened the USA and the Soviet Union as similarly constituted 'informal systems of economic and political influence'.[9] The belief that the Soviet Union was not a territorial empire was widespread in the early to mid-1980s, but is now conveniently forgotten. As Cairns Craig has pointed out, there is something of disappointed Marxism in much contemporary nationality theory.[10] Eric Hobsbawm's view that 'linguistic and cultural community … was a nineteenth-century innovation' naturally excuses Marx from his neglect of nationalism, but it is questionable whether it addresses the ascertainable detail of the medieval and early modern periods. While it may be true that commonality and fixity of language only became possible under print capitalism, the essentially national movements towards the vernacular date back to the dawn of this period and before it: to the late fourteenth and early fifteenth centuries in the cases of both Scotland and England, where the approach to a linguistic standard was clear by 1470. If imagining the nation did not require the homogeneity of a modernist state, far less did it display the totally disparate and portable identities postulated by postmodernism. Homi Bhabha may be right to call the 'continuous narrative of national progress' a 'narcissism of self-generation' in modern times, but this is far less clear in preceding centuries: it is a late twentieth-century view of how nationality exists, is 'produced' or 'constructed'. As Philip Schlesinger rightly points out, such 'acute perception of new forms of affiliation has degenerated into seeing old collectivities as choosable life-styles or sub-cultures'. The past, as ever, must be re-entered on its own terms.[11]

When this is done it becomes apparent that far from nationalism being an elite ideology 'foisted on a credulous population by a self-serving political elite' (a patronizing formulation in any case),[12] it has deep roots in the consciousness of groups and societies. In 1511, the authorities in Aberdeen ordered the townsfolk 'to liberate Richard Scheirly Englishman, from Prison, in regard he had only come to Town to perform his pilgrimage to St. Ninian'.[13] Popular anti-Englishness was widespread: if Continental chronicles say little else about Scotland, they often mention its Anglophobia, as do travellers. In 1435, Aeneas Sylvius Piccolomini, the future Pius II, 'noted that the Scots liked nothing better than to hear abuse of the English', while Andrew Borde, an English student at Glasgow University in the 1530s, stated that 'it is naturally geuen, or els it is of a deuyllysche dyspocion of a Scotysh man, not to loue nor fauour an

Englyshe man. And I ... dwellynge amonge them, was hated'. Such examples bespeak popular outlook, not elite manipulation: in 1661, John Ray remarked on a visit to Scotland that Scots 'could not endure to hear their country or countrymen spoken against'.[14]

Chauvinist attitudes of this kind were gradually forced underground in Scotland (indeed, their unpleasant if occasional resurfacing has only recently begun to be noted), since it was the fate of the Celtic countries (the justification for this term is to be found in the arguments both of the Introduction and Chapter 2) to be marginalized into mere ethno-cultural tribalism by the alternative contractually formed superstructure of the British state, leaving chauvinism with no territoriality to defend, and (in Scotland especially) nursing its own perceived divided ethnicity, a matter which will be discussed later in this chapter. The only bipartite contractual relationship required in the early development of Britain was with Scotland (the Treaty of Union): elsewhere, legislation was often simply imposed in a one-sided contractualism. Indeed it may be noted that contemporary theories of nationalism can be argued to favour the large-scale imperial states of the nineteenth and twentieth centuries, and to work against small or submerged nations like Scotland, the Ukraine and the nationality problems bequeathed by the Austro-Hungarian Empire.

Most contemporary nations are, as Brian Singer observes, formed of a 'loose, incoherent complicity' between ethno-cultural and contractual/ legal and politico-territorial forms of nationalism.[15] It is arguably difficult for their nationality to function if deprived of the interchange between internal cohesion and external visibility manifest in the conjunction of all these elements. Where there are strongly particularist identities, the contractualist superstructure frequently requires renegotiation, as in the case of Canada and Quebec, Spain's autonomous provinces, Austria-Hungary in the 1867 settlement, and the UK in the case of Ireland, and to a lesser extent Scotland and Wales. It has been both the strength and the weakness of British state formation that its contractualist element has been largely both unwritten and non-negotiable, based on the absolute sovereignty of Parliament and the centralization of State functions. Complacency regarding these has led to an inability to respond contractually to subordinate national demands. Refusal to concede Irish Home Rule despite the return of a majority of Irish nationalist MPs from the island for over a generation arguably led to catastrophically violent pressure for change which has left the legacy of an intractable problem, and a belief in the gun as its only solution. Even in Scotland, hard-line Unionist predictions of disaster, collapse and even violent conflict ensuing on devolution were

regularly voiced in the years before and in the lead-up to the 1997 referendum: 'the most dangerous proposition ever put to the British people'
has hardly justified this inflammatory rhetoric, which subsequently
switched to over-emphasizing the significance of Scottish Anglophobia.[16]

For most of British history, though, a continuing but usually contain-
able tension has existed between the Celtic 'other' residing within the contractual state, and those 'Britons', from all origins who identified
themselves with that state. There was long a general willingness to participate in British endeavour in Scotland, Wales and (to an extent which is
now often unappreciated) Ireland. Protest was, if at times frequent, often
low-level and symbolic, even though it was needlessly exacerbated by the
unconditional political and religious claims of British nationalism, which
was intolerant of any but local peculiarities, and a mocker of those.
British identity did not 'bed in' with a series of compromises on the road
to a negotiated constitution; with the sole (and partial) exception of Scotland, it rested (and rests) on an imposed assumption of homogeneity
with the central concerns of the core English state which preceded it:
hence Newbolt's *Island Race* is absolutely and unproblematically an 'English' one, while even in 1999, Radio 4's programmes on the history of England can be termed *This Sceptred Isle*. Arthur had returned, but Welsh
nostalgia for lost greatness was now incorporated into the heart of English dominance. Nor is this merely historic, for it is the past which has
made our present, and this is particularly noteworthy in the means our
present uses to record and represent itself. Even today, the BBC licence fee
underspend on programmes made outwith London is noteworthy (e.g.
2.5 per cent of budget in Scotland):[17] for British public broadcasting rests
on precisely these assumptions of a homogeneous public taste, where
cricket (the most televised sport) is regarded as equally the game of Shetland, Derry and Gloucestershire, and where an escaped tiger in London is
a lead story, but one in Belfast a comedy turn. The political tensions
underlying the decision to reject a Scottish six o'clock news programme
in 1998 clearly brought these features to the surface. As Seamus Heaney
recalls of his childhood, even the voice that read the weather seemed to
speak the language of British centralism, part of that 'government of the
tongue' which he has sought to confront by exploring the obscured redo-
lence of Irish place-names.[18]

British government, from its 1688–1707 foundations, was always a
'government of the tongue', putting sociolinguistic and cultural pressure
to bear on alternative languages, consciousness and practices within the
British Isles. Indeed, the Celtic countries fared worse than they had done

before in some important respects. Support for the exiled Stuart dynasty tended to be strong in Ireland and Scotland in particular: this was no coincidence in that the Stuarts were more dependent on and had shown more favour to centres of power outwith London than their successor regime was to do. But this support, particularly when explosively combined with Catholicism, placed the 'otherness' of the Celt at a considerable disadvantage. What might in other circumstances have been regarded as harmless if humorous eccentricity, was now combined with suspicion of political disaffection so profound as to generate a much more damaging and extreme set of caricatures. It is arguable that in the eighteenth century more xenophobia was directed internally in the British Isles than externally towards France and other rivals. Only when Jacobitism subsided into defeat could the marks of Scottish patriotic difference (plaid, pipes and so on) become picturesque and indeed fictionalized synecdoches for national peculiarities, rather than marks of horror at alien intrusion (see Figure 1). In Ireland, Jacobitism was succeeded by radical nationalism: and thus the portrayal of Irish 'otherness' never diluted into such amusing local particularism.

The presentation of the Irishman as ape has a long history, dating back far beyond Perry Curtis's citation of Darwinian cartoons in the nineteenth century,[19] into the age of Swift's Yahoos in *Gulliver's Travels* (1726) (themselves an ironic depiction of how the English view the Irish) and the 'wild Irish' of an even earlier generation.[20] In the days before the nineteenth-century discovery of the gorilla and the codification of the great apes, which allowed Charles Kingsley to term the Irish 'white chimpanzees ... if they were black, one wouldn't feel it so much',[21] simian qualities were usually those already identified in the supposedly half-human 'savages' of the New World. In both *A Modest Proposal* (1729) and *Gulliver's Travels*, Swift ironized the reputed savagery of the Irish Yahoo by implicitly contrasting it with the cold genocidal violence of the Houhnhnyms and their allies, the rational educated English planner, planter and projector: but such visions nonetheless retained a powerful currency. Similar characterizations were often applied to Highlanders: 'Iroquois, a Negre, a Laplander', 'as desperately courageous as Sioux or Pawnees', 'as alien ... as a war party of Iroquois', 'hill tribesmen' with an 'immemorial zest for plunder' as various authors describe them (the latest of these quotations dates from 1973!). In early colonial times, commentators could diagnose the Highlander's ability to get on with Native Americans as a sign of their common savagery.[22] When James Fenimore Cooper wrote *The Last of the Mohicans* (1826), Sir Walter Scott's charac-

THE HIGHLAND VISITORS.

Figure 1 *The Highland Visitors.* Published by J. Dubois, 1746. 10″ × 8″. Scots, portrayed as Highlanders, are depicted killing, stealing, looting and raping in a quiet English village: the rural idyll (pub, church and countryside) set at risk by a mob. Fortunately, help is at hand in the shape of the dim ranks of the British Army, just visible in the distance. All Scots, whether bent on economic or political intrusion, tended to be portrayed in this tartanized fashion as alien invaders until the last quarter of the eighteenth century, then tartan began to subside into a referent for amusing local colour.

terization of the Highlander was his model. By this stage defeated 'savages' could be portrayed with an air of nobility (see Figure 2).

Nonetheless, the inheritance of such negative terminology is striking: citizens of the core state of a growing worldwide Empire were being repeatedly described in terms normally reserved for the inhabitants of the most far-flung and 'savage' of its possessions. It was small wonder in such circumstances that those thus labelled should have been regarded as expendable troops in imperial wars: savages used to fight savages, and as disposable as the enemy they faced. In 1651, the Scots Army at Worcester was described as made up of 'barbarians', and for subsequent Cromwellians they were 'cattle', 'an inexhaustible Magazeen of Auxiliaries' to be expended in war.[23] This was itself ironic given the Scottish Covenanters' own brutal attitude towards Highland and Irish troops, but no consistent distinction was made in English minds between types of Scot: hence the characterization of the 1745 Jacobite Rising as 'Highland', though thousands of Lowland troops were levied for Prince Charles, and the simulta-

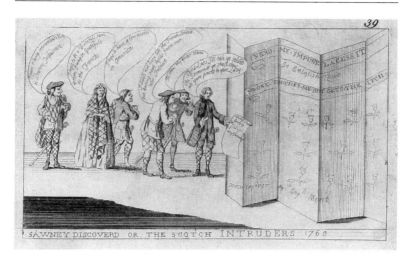

Figure 2 *Sawney Discoverd or the Scotch Intruders*, 1760. 10″ × 8″. An image of Scottish reputation in transition. Greedy tartan-clad Scots queue to extract favours from George III's new administration. Though still armed, flea-ridden ('No One Touches Me But Gets The Itch') and sexually voracious ('Come Lads Ill tak ye behind the Screen & ye shall shew all yere parts to yere Lady'), the Scots have substituted opposition to the British state with a lust for its perquisites ('I hope to have a Commission in America'). Nonetheless, there is a veiled threat of return to violence if these 'subsidy junkies' (as they would now be termed) are not satisfied: 'I wood not have left the French service but having such hopes from our new Intrest', says one. Continuing treachery is hinted at: they 'may be Gratefull to the French' even if their British ambitions are realized.

neous characterization of *all* Scotland as potentially disloyal. Disloyal Scots were usually portrayed by government propaganda as lice-ridden cannibals with insatiable and disorderly sexual appetites (see Figure 3). As such, the Frasers were slaughtered on the field of Culloden; less than twenty years later, they were being slaughtered again in Canada, where in the Seven Years War the Scots casualty rate was almost four times as high as that of the English or American troops involved.[24] Like Indian colonials in later years, Highlanders were often characterized as childish, with the charming, angry, volatile and ultimately immature and unreliable natures of both toddlers and adolescents. Where in the eighteenth century pro-government propaganda had shown them thus, in the nineteenth this view was more comfortably and influentially emplaced in fiction (cf. Scott's *Waverley* (1815)), where Flora's adolescent enthusiasm,

On Broomstick, by old Moggy's Aid,
  Full royally they rode:
And on the Wings of Northern Winds
Came flying all abroad.—
                    Hopkins Jun.r

The Garden of Eden is before them,
  and behind them a desolate Wilderness.
                    Joel Chap. 2. Ver. 3.

The Flying MACHINE from EDINBURGH in one Day,
    performd by Moggy MACKENSIE at the THISTLE and CROWN:

Publish'd according to Act of Parliam.t

Figure 3 *The Flying MACHINE from EDINBURGH in one Day*. Published according to Act of Parliament. Price 6d. No date (mid-eighteenth century). 8″ × 6″. A version of the Scots arms emphasizing Scottish noise and violence crowns an image of poverty-stricken Scots riding to London on a witch's broomstick, itself phallically suggestive. This print probably exists in an intertextual relationship to more explicit depictions such as *The Scotch Broomstick & the Female Besom*, which shows flying Scots ravishing English women with their 'broomsticks'. Greedy, noisy, violent and sexually disordered, the Scots are also agents of the Devil.

Fergus's volatility and Bradwardine's childishness (itself reflected in his similarity to his own boyish portrait) underline this view[25]. Like the Irish, they needed to be taken care of; but unlike the Irish, they were no longer to be feared, except as imperial shock troops by Britain's external enemies.

The Irish, unlike Scots, even Highland Scots, were also depicted as stupid. Eighteenth-century Irish jokes from the chapbooks of the day still have a modern ring to them:

> A gentleman who had been shooting brought home a small bird with him, and having an Irish servant, he asked him if he had shot that little bird? Yes, he told him. Arrah, by my shoul, honey, replied the Irishman, it was not worth the powder and shot, for this little thing would have died in the fall.[26]

And so on. The Welsh too were regarded as humorously stupid, though little to be feared save in their capacity as larcenists ('Taffy was a Welshman, Taffy was a thief'). Contempt was more usual:

> There was a large market in England almost till the end of the eighteenth century for engravings of comic cartoons of 'Poor Taffy' (and his wife), a Welsh man and woman who could not afford a horse, shown riding a goat, leeks poking out of their hatbands, round cheeses bulging from their panniers, and patchments of ancient pedigrees sticking out of their pockets.[27]

On St David's Day, they were baited 'by the Rabbles hanging out of a Bundle of Rags in a representation of a Welshman mounted on a red Herring with a Leek in His Hat'.[28] In chapbooks such as 'The Pleasant History of TAFFY's Progress to London', Welshmen were revealed as poor, illiterate and disaffected: inhabitants of 'Goatlandshire'.[29] Patronizingly domesticating as 'Goatlandshire' might be as a term implying the incorporation of Wales into the English county system, travellers were often struck by the country's separateness from England: Elizabeth Baker remarking in 1772 that 'the people in general are so different from the English one is amazed to think they are subjects to the same monarchy'.[30] Such recognition of Welsh identity was by no means always complimentary: Ned Ward famously thought the Principality 'the fag-end of creation': the margin of the margins.[31]

During the Jacobite period, James 'III''s title of 'Prince of Wales' was, by a neat semantic trick, sometimes used by pro-government propagandists to suggest the alien qualities of the Stuart dynasty, through the suggestion that the 'Prince of Wales' was Welsh: 'Perkin ap Dada', a pretender (Perkin Warbeck, a pretender against Henry VII, was the subject of a famous play by the English dramatist John Ford) bearing a Welsh name ('ap') and the son of a foreign Catholic ('Dada', the Papal Nuncio under James II and VII). The affection borne by the Welsh for their language, which 'distorts the truth, favours fraud and abets perjury', was a means of deepening the dislike on which such prejudices rested:[32] how often does one still hear the complaint that the Welsh speak Welsh when they could perfectly well speak English, an attitude sometimes extended to France and other foreign countries. This prejudice was made manifest in the eighteenth century by the large-scale imposition of monoglot Anglophone clergy by the Anglican Church in Wales on its parishes, which in the end helped to drive many of the Welsh 'into the arms of Methodism'.[33] In retaliation, the Welsh developed a patriotic publishing industry, while the Honourable Society of Cymmrodorion, founded in 1751, worked (within its boundaries of respectability) to protect the language even as the gentry was intensifying British linguistic conformity in abandoning Welsh names for their children.[34] Although attempts were also made in Ireland to make language the badge of nationality, only in Wales did they meet with a success which irritated many. In 1866, *The Times* could still declare the tongue 'the curse of Wales', while Matthew Arnold, replying *in its defence*, commented that 'the sooner the Welsh language disappears as an instrument of the practical, political, social life of Wales, the better'.[35] Since Arnold was among the most enlightened inspectors of schools, it was unsurprising that the 1870 Education Act enshrined an implicit hostility in its apparent neutrality in making 'the English language compulsory in all Welsh schools'.[36]

As was often the case with Gaelic speakers, mockery and caricature attended Welsh attempts to speak English: 'if an English dramatist wanted to raise a good-humoured laugh, he had only to conjure up a Welsh "shentleman"'. Like Scots, particularly Highland Scots, Welshmen were often mocked for their devotion to their pedigrees and claims to highborn descent entertained no matter how deep their current poverty. The Welshman was 'ready to rattle off his pedigree to the ninth generation or even back to Brutus and Adam'.[37]. Scots, particularly Highland Scots, were accused of the same behaviour. Such blending of poverty and dignity was regarded as ridiculous in wider British society, which in the eighteenth century increasingly manifested values of commodity and 'show', open exhibitions of wealth aimed at securing access to good marriages or social and political power, frequently put on by an upper-middle-class itself richer than many Scottish or Welsh gentry (one Scottish Jacobite colonel's estate, for example, produced less income than the headmastership of

Shrewsbury School). Moreover, England had relatively few noble families in terms of the Continental norm: closer to 0.1 per cent than the 1 per cent of France and 2 per cent of Scotland in 1707. Part of the mockery of pedigree thus rested on the unique status of the English 'norm', and its misunderstanding of the more truly normative Scottish situation as poverty-stricken pretentiousness.[38]

Such proverbial indigence gave rise to stories about the greed, opportunism and careerism of the proud but penniless Celt, which themselves were linked to darker caricatures of his cannibalism and disorderly appetites. The story of Sawney Bean ('Sawney' was the generic term for a Scot), who had reputedly formed his whole family into a cannibal gang to dine off travellers,[39] was only the most famous in a widespread pattern of narratives which nibbled at the margins (a similar tale was told about an alleged Devonshire cannibal!), and 'darkest Africa' was to furnish its store of similar terrible tales in the nineteenth century.[40] Bean's horrific hunger was a suitable metaphor for the rapacity attributed to his fellow-countrymen, whom mid-eighteenth-century cartoons showed rising from vermin to vainglory at English expense. The widely reproduced print, *Sawney on the Boghouse*, purported to show how unfit these greedy primitives were for British civilization: it shows a filthy hairy Scot in a plaid with both his legs crammed down two lavatory pans, while urine and excrement dribble between his legs onto the ground (see Figure 4). The message is clear: so far are these Children of the Mist from being housetrained that they cannot even use the facilities of civilization when offered.

'Sawney' is frequently, if not always, presented in the dress of a Jacobite Highlander, or at least as an aggressive and contumacious external threat to British social order. 'A fig then for Sawney, his malice is vain', sang the exponents of 'English Liberty', supporters of John Wilkes (1727–97), professional English patriot and Scotophobe. They represented a broad strand of opinion:

> Scots, so the Wilkite argument went, were inherently, unchangeably alien, never ever to be confused or integrated with the English. In Wilkite prints they were invariably … portrayed as wearing tartan kilts … Highlanders and Lowlanders, cultivated patricians, like the Earl of Bute, and the poorest, most illiterate clansmen were also conflated in a common sartorial foreignness.[41] (See Figure 5)

In this, Wilkes and his fellow-travellers were building on the legacy of anti-Jacobite propaganda. In the Wilkite reading, the Jacobite Scots were

Figure 4 Hogarth, *Sawney on the Boghouse*, 1745. Price 3d. 10″ × 8″. A much-reproduced classic image of the violent barbarian's failure to understand even the simplest conveniences of civilized life. 'Sawney' is an undifferentiated term for a Scot: it is not simply Highlanders who are being referred to.

Figure 5 *The Caledonians Arrival, in Money-Land*, 1762. 10″ × 8″. An anti-ministry print which portrays the incoming Prime Minister, the Earl of Bute, in the guise of a clan chief with eagle's feather handing out favours to an endless stream of his Scottish cronies.

winning by ingratiating ambition what they had lost in bold assault: a point made clearly by prints such as *The Caledonians Arrival, in Money-land* (1762), which shows a horde of greedy Jacobitical Scots plunging over the Border to raid England's flesh-pots. As one English view put it: 'Into our places, states, and beds they creep; / They've sense to get what we want sense to keep'.[42] The inflammatory racism of Wilkes's supporters uncannily foreshadows its postcolonial counterpart in the 1960s and 1970s: *They* are taking our jobs; *They* are unclean, with un-British personal habits; *They* are poor, greedy criminals; *They* are a threat to our women; *They* will not adopt our culture, and so on (Figures 6 and 7). Indeed, the description of Welsh-speakers in Wales as 'an ethnic minority' by Welsh organizations in recent times reveals an underlying similarity of attitude with this historic scorn. But the incoming Scots *did* adopt British culture, and the antipathy faded as the resented 'otherness' of the incomer became concealed and lost. Caricatures of Scots in England are harder to find by the end of the century; but those who remained in Scotland, especially if they in any way manifested persisting differences (i.e. not tokens, such as Burns Night) of habit, custom or politics, were still liable to be drawn by a bitter pen. The 'parcel of Paddies' was still liable to be joined by the 'Scotch pack' in the alienizing language of the day should

Figure 6 *The Scrubbing Post*, early 1760s. 10″ × 8″. Scots, infested with fleas and other parasites, rub themselves gladly against the post of the title. The legend ('To scrubb oneself wher'ere it itches / is better far then Clothes, & Riches') suggests that this poverty is a natural state of affairs, and preferable to the airs and ambitions Scots are now putting on in Britain.

either prove troublesome. Ironically, one of the processes by which Scots were collectively alienized was through the suggestion that they acted collectively as a 'mafia' in their own interest (cf. Figure 5).[43]

By 1800, however, other factors were at work. As early as the 1730s, the Patriot Whigs had sought to develop a new discourse of British patriotism, 'Patriot Gothic', cast in a Saxon mould as had been the ideology of the Cromwellians of a century before.[44] As the challenge posed by the Jacobite Risings and their implicit threat of Celtic irridentism diminished, this strain of Gothic patriotism was broadened to include elements of an heroic Celticism softened by nostalgia, as in Thomas Gray's poem 'The Bard', which depended on information supplied by Ieuan Fardd, 'one of the original members of the Cymmrodorion Society'.[45] That this was possible was to some extent due both to the Patriots' emphasis on druids as an ancient British priestly caste (fitted into a Gothic picture, but Welsh/Celtic in origin) and also to the adoption of Gothic values and

The Whipping Post.

*Mac with a Thistle turned Jack Ketch
Makes poor Britania shew her Breech.*

Figure 7 *The Whipping Post,* early 1760s. 10″ × 8″. This is an image which returns us to Figure 1 (*The Highland Visitors*). Britannia is being flogged with a thistle as her clothes fall from her, suggestive of forthcoming rape. Her (English) husband looks on helplessly, while the British Lion sleeps and the Union Flag lies on the ground.

racial identity beginning to gain ground in Lowland Scotland (of which more in the last section of this chapter). So fashionable had the Druids become by mid-century that John Wood's (1704–54) design for Bath Circus may well have been based on Stonehenge, while the bards of that era were beginning to be seen as 'noble and inspired apostles of freedom', and thus entirely compatible with British Gothicist ideology, which stressed the natural disposition to freedom among Germanic peoples.[46]

A renewed attempt to give priority to Celticism proper without unduly threatening this growing British consensus was made by James Macpherson, whose Ossian poetry (chiefly *Fingal* (1761) and *Temora* (1763)) presented the heroic deeds of the Fianna, suitably accommodated within the garb of classical epic and that of the contemporary cult of sentiment which raised agreeable sensations in his British and wider European audience. The demands of politeness ensure that deaths on the battlefield are dealt with by Macpherson with an obliquity unknown to Homer, and foreign too to the savage triumphalism of Iain Lom or Alasdair MacMhaigh-stir Alasdair and other Gaelic poets.[47] At the same time, the nostalgic sense of a cause already lost which pervades Macpherson's work portrays the heroic Celticism he purports to iconize as a designer accessory of the culture which has superseded it. In the choice of his subject-matter, Macpherson celebrated the prime Celtic political myth, which as I suggested in the Introduction had never been adopted into Britishness as Arthurianism was. Yet, in rendering his epic alive only in the reminiscences of the aged Ossian, the Last of his Race, Macpherson conferred on his subject-matter the passivity of heritage: thus there was only a contestation of the premises of British Gothicism, not its conclusions.

For this reason among others (such as the implicit anti-Irishness in Macpherson's presentation of what by origin were Irish stories) Irish critics responded negatively to Ossian, while in England the *canard* grew up that Macpherson 'stole' the Fenian legends from Ireland, rather than drawing (as he did) on Scotland and Ireland's common cultural heritage. What Macpherson did do was to declare the importance and centrality of the Celtic contribution to British society in a manner which rendered it devoid of all threat. In much the same way, the 1760s and 1770s saw an antiquarian colonization of the British periphery through the collection and codification of a once-despised but now appreciated cultural heritage, bowdlerized by the collectors in such a manner as to challenge neither the ruling sentiments nor politics of Britain: 'the Bard became the icon of the age', preparing the way for the isolated and vatic Romantic poet of the next generation.[48] This was a major part of the phenomenon known as Primitivism.

In essence, Primitivism was a high cultural codification of orally based folk culture, which was beginning to suffer large-scale attrition through improved communications, migration to cities, enclosure, clearances and war. Primitivism provided a cultural counterweight to the modernization and rationalization of society encompassed by the Enlightenment through its display of commitment to the preservation and transmission of the past, particularly the past of Scotland, Wales, Ireland and the outlying regions of England. Just as Macpherson's Ossianic endeavour began with *Fragments of Ancient Poetry Collected in the Highlands of Scotland* (1760), so Evan Evans published *Specimens of the Poetry of the Ancient Welsh Bards* (1764) and Charlotte Brooke her *Reliques of Irish Poetry* in 1769, its title a tribute to Bishop Percy's English *Reliques* of four years earlier.[49] Celticism was in the main stream of a Primitivism which became fashionable throughout Europe, and which led Napoleon to found an

Academie Celtique in 1806, while the bards themselves, for so long despised, persecuted and almost extinct, were swept up by sentimental Romanticism as the avatars of its lyric ideal.

Primitivism's commitment to the past was thus both profound and vacuous, for the past it praised was dehistoricized. Celts were no longer unwanted aliens, with manners, mores and language barely reconcilable to British civic society; they were now permitted to be the picturesque representations of both the heroic bedrock and finer feelings of that society. Primitivist politics, concerned with the exploration of emotion and feeling as synecdoches for nation and culture, sought in the Celtic mood music with which to romanticize the stolidity of John Bull. This process reached its apogee in George IV's 1822 visit to Edinburgh, when Sir Walter Scott presented the whole nation to the King as Celtic, in contradistinction to his novels where he had repeatedly emphasized the Gothic/Saxon heritage of the Lowlander (see Figure 8).[50]

Romantic backwardness was to mark the portrayal of the Celt from then on up to the present. Travel was becoming easier; the countryside was altering under Improvement, and the *mentalités* of Europe were shifting. Modernity, with its rapid advances and deep-seated insecurities, was emerging. As Matthew Arnold, that crucial influence in the history of Celticism, put it in 'The Scholar Gypsy': 'this strange disease of modern life, / With its sick hurry, its divided aims' looked back nostalgically to a primitive world.[51] In Arnold's poem, this was to be found in the unspoilt traditions of the gypsy community; elsewhere, for 'gypsy' one could write 'Celt': such an interchangeability is implicit in the romances of George Borrow for example.[52] Because the 'Celt' now became something to look back on, to memorialize under the drifting gaze of social change, the depiction of Celtic society did not greatly alter between the eighteenth and twentieth centuries: its purpose was to stimulate the onlooker's memory and imagination, and its change would defeat that object: as John Glendening puts it, 'tourism and romanticism were intertwined from the first'.[53] Hence the *Brigadoon* phenomenon, where media portrayal of (say) the Scottish Highlands emphasizes their primitive qualities, qualities in another dimension described as 'unspoilt'. In the 1980s, the Scottish *Sunday Mail* newspaper advertised itself in London through the dominant single image of an isolated bothy in a green, rainswept land, underneath which was the legend 'More Scottish than Grannie's Hielan Hame'. Similarly, both Irish and Scottish tourist and other advertising images (e.g. for alcohol) stress the emptiness and primarily agricultural habits of their respective countries: Murphy's Stout conjures up images of

The FIRST LAIRD in AW SCOTIA — or A VIEW at EDINBURGH in August, 1822.
"O'my Bonny Bonny Highland Laddie; my Handsome, Charming, Highland Laddie."
Published Sept. 3, 1822, by JOHN FAIRBURN, Broadway, Ludgate Hill.

Figure 8 *The First Laird in Aw Scotia.* Published by John Fairburn, Ludgate Hill, 1822. 8″ × 6″. George IV as Jacobite Highlander, attended by Sir Walter Scott. The song 'O my Bonny Bonny Highland Laddie', quoted under the title of the print, belongs to a cycle of the 1720s and 1730s of which there were many Jacobite variants. Here the mockery of Celtic garb is promarily directed at the King and the novelist who is his complacent, craven sidekick. The ordinary citizens of Edinburgh are dressed in the standard British fashions of the time.

isolated pubs in a sodden, undeveloped landscape. Even ironizing such images can reinforce them: Sir Compton Mackenzie's *Whisky Galore!* (1949), which pits the wily rural peasantry against the urbanized incomer, exalts even in its wit the time-honoured theme of ancient community value, and its hidden ways of solidarity.[54]

Such depictions and expectations contribute to tensions in modern Scotland between 'white settlers' and locals: the incomers expect a united and rather primitive community, and they patronize it and overlook its divisions accordingly. For them it is often an 'imagined community', but one only to be imagined by themselves: the Highlands are cleared for the imagination as once they were cleared of people. Developing trails and tourist facilities to show off the uniquely local 'product' to other outsiders is in incoming eyes often a positive development: if this meets with hostility, and disenchantment sets in, the initial praise of authentic and aboriginal folkways gives way to the obverse of Primitivism, which stresses the laziness and intractability of the 'savage' (since, after all, he has declined to 'advance' into modernity). In response, incomers can often experience exclusion and hostility accentuated by the fact that they have lumped in a paradigm individual and social relationships of as great complexity as one might find anywhere. A community is a place where people live diversely, not a recreational space into which to project an imaginary totality: for example, the misunderstanding of crofting economics leads incomers in late twentieth-century Scotland to term those who work crofts but also work part-time not to be 'real' crofters, under the illusion that full-time crofting is a 'true' activity, an illusion welcome because of its Primitivist allure. The image of antique peasant poverty is spoilt by a crofter who drives a taxi, so to the incoming gaze he is not 'authentic', not picturesque, poor or primitive enough to be 'traditional'. It is small wonder that those who smart under this paradigm do not welcome its proponents when they come to live next door.[55]

Thus the antiquarian tourism which searched for the unsophisticated culture of declining rural localities (whose decline was often linked to enclosure and clearance) in the pre-railway age can be seen as directly linked to the tourist industry and counter-stream migration of today.[56] From the beginning, 'Celtic' tourism was cheaper and more middlebrow than its aristocratic predecessors: 'Superseding the aristocratic Grand Tour of the early eighteenth century, and far cheaper and more convenient, travel in Wales, Scotland and Ireland provided a stock of experiences which could be recounted for a life-time'.[57] These countries were ideal for the traveller not only because of the 'authentic' quality of their people, but also because they (like Native Americans) were renowned for the virtues of hospitality. Despite the fact that real Scots were often undernourished and undersized, images of strength and vitality, linked to food and outdoor exercise, portrayed them as a hardy and huge race. Even today, the claymore-wielding Highlander of the 'Crisp of the Clans' (Highlander Crisps) and the rippling muscles of his equally potent counterpart on Scott's Porage Oats, alike testify to the manner in which images of cannibalistic savagery were transmuted into those of appetite, loyalty, strength and bravery.

The development of these portrayals was by no means always unwelcome to those thus portrayed. Clan chiefs such as MacDonell of Glengarry became themselves exponents of the Primitivist picturesque: it set them apart, giving them an air of importance which masked their comparative poverty (though many were taking action to alter this state by clearing their tenants off the land in pursuit of more money).[58] In Aberdeen, Francis Peacock (1723–1807), the burgh dancing master and 'Teacher of Manners and good breeding' designed (at least on one view) modern Scottish Country Dancing from a blend of French and Highland antecedents, thus adding a 'civilized' air to the primitive and 'authentic'.[59] By the 1780s, London society was entertaining Highland dancing competitions, while Welsh harpers were becoming fashionable.[60] Antiquarian societies devoted to the exaltation of traditional cultural distinctiveness as a mode of social enhancement and group identity within a broader British upper and middle class multiplied. Being primitive was a new hobby for the sophisticated, at least in Wales and Scotland. In Ireland, the 1798 Rising and the strength of the United Irishmen showed a considerable unwillingness to become a similar kind of Celtic theme park, while northern Protestants were much less amenable than many urban Scots to a surrender of themselves into the Celtic mode. And a kind of surrender was involved: the 'lack of specific place information' in Macpherson which gave 'free range for the imagination' was an emptying of Scottish territory's history and territorality of their significance.[61] As Clare O'Halloran remarks: 'In the Irish case, however, Ossian could not be used to validate that imagined past, in part because their fantasy did not conform to the primitivist paradigm which the poems represented.'[62] In other words, Irish difference was still too deeply politicized to accept its own portrayal as elegy.

This was not the case in Wales, where the reabsorption of Druidism from British Gothic ideology, and the strongly unifying presence of the Welsh language within the now-popular image of an ancient bardic people did much to reinforce local identity, and to provide a dignified if limited framework for the renewal of a traditional high culture which had faced steep decline from 1720. The patriotic qualities of the Welsh language, defended by small presses and with a limited voice in the early eighteenth century, were confirmed as the property of all Wales, though a social stigma remained regarding the *continuing* use of Welsh, with its implications of a *persisting*, not merely a nobly antique, divagation from British norms. Welshmen with wider ambitions used the very name of 'Welsh' as 'a synonym … for drunken, ignorant, and superstitious',[63] and if William Richards's 1686 prophecy of 'the imminent death of the Welsh language', which he thought would be 'Englished out of Wales', proved exaggerated, it nonetheless remained true that societies such as that of the

Ancient Britons (1715) and Cymmrodorion (1751), were essentially apolitical and reactive. The culture of 'the princely past of ancient Wales' was 'revived for a literate middle class of yeomen and merchants'. Alehouse bardic coteries were open to the public from 1789, and *eisteddfoddau* began as a display of cultural particularism which marked Wales out as a place of unthreatening antiquity. Primitivism and Romanticism, in restoring a bardic past, also restored some of its heroes such as Owain Glyn Dŵr, whose presence in Welsh culture was revivified in this period.[64]

Such renewals and revitalizations however gained at least some of their strength and popularity from their role as tourist commodities, pieces of local charisma which could be explored, experienced or bought. Such charisma was next door to kitsch, and kitsch was unsurprisingly the end-product of Celtic tourism. As Thomas Richards points out:

> Kitsch may be defined as elaborately aestheticized commodities produced in the name of large institutions (church, state, empire, monarchy) for middle-class home use. Kitsch is in short charisma – charisma which has been recently manufactured.[65]

Kitsch expresses itself politically through the reduction of complex identity to simple commodity. Markets were formed (and of course they still exist) for the purchase and exchange of Celtic materials, crafts, 'reliques' and tourist experiences, often subversively portrayed as 'fantastic and ... eccentric'.[66] At first these reinforced an identity of colourful locality, bound into the progressive enframing power of imperial British identity discussed above; later their market divided into popular tourism, rejection (in Scotland at any rate) by the intelligentsia, and continuing use as localist markers of 'Britishness' at upper- and middle-class social functions. Over time kitsch multiplied from individuated commodity charisma to a commodified environment of signification, the 'tartanry' later despised by Scottish intellectuals being one example (the process was weaker in Wales, and was hijacked by the forces of political opposition in Ireland, as I intend to show). This environment emplaced an acceptance of history as heritage, where 'the past solidifies around us' into commodity, becoming object rather than process: this was naturally suited to the continuing discourse of Primitivism, since it objectified an idealized past detached from the processes of social change.[67]

Kitsch became of key importance in marrying Primitivism to the displays of the British Empire, such as the great variegated shows of the Great Exhibition (1851), the Diamond Jubilee (1897) and the Empire Exhibition of 1924–5.[68] Commodities were a central 'expression of the diversity of empire and its inheritance' in these shows: a portrayal of marginal histories through material representations.[69] The Primitivist rehabilitation of the Celtic was one of the first stages in this process of 'domestication and reconciliation' of the alien 'other' which was a 'persistent element' in Britain's empire exhibitions.[70] Colourful diversity which bore no deeper implication was a key component of the Primitivist aesthetic: it ethnicized the political Celt, just as later it presented a paradigm of many peoples but one Empire. In other words, the ideology which developed the notion of a unitary Britain was that subsequently used to endorse a unitary imperial purpose. Thus the dissolution of the illusion of imperial solidarity has a symbiotic relationship with tensions over the notion of unitary Britishness itself.

It is certainly arguable that the decisive development in the alignment of Primitivism to the wider concerns of the British Empire is to be found in the royal adoption of its motifs and values. In this process, Scotland occupies a central place, beginning with the sea of tartanry which greeted George IV's arrival in Edinburgh in 1822: 'Messrs Wilson of Bannockburn had forty extra looms at work to meet the demand' (see Figure 8). The King's inclination for nostalgic representations of Celtic valour (given a whiff of enticing danger by Sir Walter Scott's preposterous suggestion that Jacobitism was still alive in the hearts of the people), was taken up by Queen Victoria, who as a baby of six months 'was painted wearing a "Scotch bonnet"', and thereafter became an advocate of the garb.[71] On her first visit to Scotland in 1842, the Queen specifically asked for 'Oh ! wae's me for Prince Charlie' to be sung, in a 'graceful act' of solidarity with the traditions of the Highland past. Scotland became the Queen's 'dear Paradise', where 'she learnt to stalk, eat bannock and dry the Prince of Wales' socks by her tenants' peat fires', a realm of escape where she and her husband could enjoy the 'ancient way of hunting' on the cleared land,[72] re-enacting a legendary past in a country possessed of the distinctive but passive qualities of the picturesque: the number of 'Queen's Views' in Scotland testify to this metaphor of sight as possession. Land without people, landscape without community, makes for the best views.

The royal image became decisively tied to Highlandism through the occupation of Balmoral Castle in the 1840s and its decoration in tartan,[73] which confirmed Celtic authenticity as inherent in at least the Scottish iconography of the royal family. Queen Victoria herself contrasted her 'romantic little kingdom' with '*un*-poetical England', in a comparison which exalted the fey and backward in Scotland in true Primitivist style, just as Albert was portrayed stooping over a pool to spear salmon with a leister.[74] At the same time, the Scottish nobility was itself toying with Jacobite adventurers in the shape of the Sobieski Stuarts, for whom Lord Lovat built a Celtic fantasy palace on Eilean Aigas, 'decorated in a manner which exceeded the kitsch of Balmoral itself'.[75]

The Primitivist message of nostalgic Celticism had always had an imperial subtext: that the bravery of the 'wild Highlander', once undisciplined in its noble savagery, could now be formed and tamed into a formidable fighting machine in the cause of Empire. The controlled use of the Celt's primitive ferocity in these conditions was a necessary part of his improvement and serviceability. This view, which still has its adherents, is not significantly contested by those who romanticize the Celtic soldier, since they usually share the same essential premiss, expressed by James Michael Hill as 'the attack against all reason, against all odds', which he holds to be the denominating feature of Celtic warfare.[76] The Victorian period emphasized both the native qualities of the Celtic Scottish soldier (e.g. his mountaineering skills) and his new-found virtue as a Briton: the 'pluck' which, allied to his native talents, gives them a scope hitherto inconceivable.[77] The Highlander is like the Indian or Zulu, but they and other native peoples do not (yet) have the 'British' qualities to allow their native courage and ferocity to prevail, until they, like Kipling's 'Gunga Din', adopt the dutifulness and *sangfroid* of ascendant Britishness:

> In front where dusky forms appear
> Down went the steel 'gainst levelled spear;
> Behind the Ashantees were left,
> As forest trees by lightning cleft.
> The ripping sound of Sniders rung,
> The deep Artillery gun gave tongue,
> But 'twas the Highland spirit gave
> The lead audacious, calm and brave …
> One bravely reckless Celt went on
> Bounding with eager steps alone
> A target for a hundred guns,
> Keen as a hound on scent he runs
> Forward ! the lads of the plumed array
> There Britain's hope, there Britain's stay.
> Up and at them, there's work to be done;
> Up and at them, the victory won!
> As in days of old with broadsword and targe,
> Hurrah ! the wild shock of a Highland charge!
> 'Freiceadan duibh, an gualain a cheile!'[78]

A. C. Macdonell's 'Rush on Coomassis' (1896) displays in its very title the 'audacious … bravely reckless' quality of the Highlander as British soldier it celebrates. The Celtic spirit is valorized, but only in the context of Anglo-Saxon discipline and military technology: the 'Sniders' and 'Artillery gun' give to the Celt a dimension beyond the 'days of old with broadsword and targe' in which peoples like the 'Ashantees' still dwell. Yet the heroicism of the charging Highlander(s) enables the conflict with the Ashanti to be presented as a daring and difficult task, rather than a clean sweep with Western guns. Though the technological supremacy of the British Army is clearly crucial, it merits only a line or two among the many devoted to portraying the audacity of a Highland charge as bringing victory over the colonial opposition. This victory confirms Celtic Britishness, while implicitly hinting that by using a 'Highland charge' rather than (say) machine-guns, the British are fighting fair against their much weaker opponents. There is much late Victorian verse of this kind.

Such imaging of the Celtic Scot in the contexts of popular culture, royal iconography and military achievement continued into the twentieth century. Just as the monarchy had once used Welsh Arthurianism to engender pan-British solidarity, so after 1820 it used the tartan pageantry of a Celtic Scotland romanticized in Highland and military terms, which in turn were subsequently represented as an evolution from the raw vigour, boldness and loyalty discerned by the British Empire in its colonial native subjects. Given the strength of the Jacobite Risings, and their aftermath in the culture clashes of the 1760s, it was understandable that the integration of Scotland into the British polity had priority in the contemporary politico-cultural agenda, though Primitivism was not without its influence on Welsh and (to a lesser degree) Irish culture. If it was, however, particularly important to incorporate Scotland into British consciousness, the failure to accomplish this in the case of Ireland, while in the short term appearing less relevant, was eventually to prove disastrous. This was a situation foreseen by Edmund Burke, arguably the greatest politician Ireland produced in the crucial eighteenth century, when he exasperatedly wrote that 'Ireland, after almost a century of persecution, is at this time full of penalties and full of Papists': oppression as a form of integration does not work well.[79] The identification and characterization of the Irish Celt, extended and eventually contested as it was, was to have the profoundest impact on the manner in which Celtic identity was expressed in the British Isles.

Popery and wooden shoes

The identification of the Irish Celt as a dangerous and unfamiliar 'other' had a long history. One of its roots was in the fear of 'going native', which held heavier sway among colonists in Ireland than in Wales, also heavily populated by incomers. Indeed,

> As early as 1368 the English were worried by the problem of colonists who had gone native. Whole families of Norman overlords were speaking Gaelic, wearing Irish dress, patronising native music and becoming indistinguishable from the race they had been instructed to colonise.[80]

It would require a study in itself to account for the particularly marked quality of such fears in Ireland, but two possibilities present themselves. First, the Irish interior took much longer to colonize than was the case in Wales; secondly, as Britain was eventually to learn to its cost, Irish political and cultural difference was intractable. To these two reasons for English fears, a third was added in the relative failure in Ireland of the Reformation. Following the marked savagery of the late Elizabethan campaign, the 1641 Rising confirmed many in England (and indeed in the Presbyterian Scottish Lowlands) in their terror of an alien unknown, the 'wild Irish' (a term which first appeared in the preceding century[81]), whose ethnic savagery was held to be compounded by their cruel and duplicitous religion.[82] In the end this double suspicion was counter-productive: for whereas Episcopalian (and Catholic, as long as such did not dominate) Highlanders enlisted under their chieftains could provide an edge of 'native barbarism' to the British Army, doubts remained concerning the wisdom of giving Catholics, Irish Catholics not least, significant command. Thus the alien was further alienized.

Just as Welsh bardic poetry in the fifteenth century had anticipated the coming of a messianic national deliverer, so Irish bards looked for similar manifestations. However, these frequently centred round the Fenian or associated cycles, and were thus (unlike Arthur) inaccessible to the iconography of the British monarchy. Even the Stuarts, who claimed Irish descent, were seldom regarded as eligible for such imagery until their dynasty was both openly Catholic and tottering, when James II and VII briefly became 'regarded as the final avatar of the prophesied Liberator of the Gaels', with Tyrconnell his viceroy as his heroic swordsman.[83] More usually, only 'a cautious sympathy' was evinced: an unknown poet who praised the Stuart viceroy, the Duke of Ormond, as exalted above 'Conn [the Hundred Fighter], Niall, Goll [MacMorna], Brian [Boru] and Fionn MaCumhal', came in for criticism,[84] although similar kinds of praise poetry based on the Fenian cycle were still addressed to nobles in Scotland. Indeed, the Scottish identification of the Gaeltachd as a cultural unit spanning both Scotland and Ireland was not now perfectly reciprocated by Irish writers, who scorned the Scots Gaelic 'dialect': 'Nothing but merest mumbling can the best of those attain who are striving how to fashion poems in the speech of the Scot', as Daibhi Ó Bruadar put it.[85] Such growing divisions were not helped by the use of Irish troops in Scotland by the Royalists in the 1640s, where they were loathed and feared by the Covenanters, whose Campbell allies were already describing themselves as 'North British', a new identity detached from traditional Gaeltachd sympathies.[86] John Buchan may have offered a warning to Presbyterian anti-Irishness in the 1920s by recalling the excesses of their predecessors after Philiphaugh in 1645:

> Our General Leslie is no ane to weaken in the guid cause, for there's word that his musketeers hae shot the Irish in rows on the Yarrow haughs, ilk ane aside his howkit grave, and there's orders that their women and bairns ... are to be seized ... as daughters of Heth and spawn of Babylon, and be delivered up to instant judgement.[87]

After 1689, however, Irish messianic verse turned increasingly to the Stuarts as agents of deliverance, and its language of idealized nationality began to wear a surprisingly modern form, which 'could equally well have been taken from the pages of later nationalists like Pearse, Corkery or De Blacam'. It is more than arguable that modern Irish republican nationalism has its origins in the Jacobite cause: some of the evidence for this is given below. Even in the twentieth century, Jacobites like Patrick Sarsfield retain a place in the nationalist pantheon alongside republicans such as Wolfe Tone. In the late eighteenth century, Maire Bhui Ni Laoghaire's poetry continues to call on royal and Catholic Spain for help in fomenting Jacobin revolution, so thoroughly melded are the two traditions; while not long afterwards, the hope that 'Young Bony and O'Connell will free old Ireland' bespeaks a similar outlook.[88]

The *aisling* tradition which articulated many of these sentiments was one in which Ireland, portrayed as a deserted woman, appears to the poet in a vision to tell of her abandonment, her ill-treatment by her current master (England) and her hope for the triumphant return of her lover-deliverer from overseas (the Stuarts, Napoleon, O'Connell). Such typology, echoed also in Scottish poetry in Gaelic and Scots, was instrumental in defining the imagery of later nationalism: indeed, the *aisling* proper survived until the mid-nineteenth century.[89] The young woman of the hopeful *aisling* becomes the 'Dark Rosaleen' of political tradition, the 'colleen with three flowers, / And she more young than I' (the 'flowers' are Robert Emmet, Wolfe Tone and Michael Dwyer) who spurs her menfolk on to violence and vengeance against the stranger. On the other hand, the ageing or old woman of the occasional *aisling* of failing hope can be aligned with the image of the Sean Bhean Bhocht, the 'Poor Old Woman',[90] who memorializes the violent sacrifice of the dead generations in order to give hope to the nationalism of the living: she is the central figure in songs such as 'Glory O, Glory O, to the bold Fenian Men' and 'Four Green Fields':

> 'I had four green fields [Ulster, Munster, Leinster and Connaught]
> Each one was my jewel,
> But strangers came,
> And tried to take them from me;
> But my fine strong sons,
> They tried to save my jewels,
> They fought and they died,
> And that is my grief', said she.[91]

At moments of crisis and hope, the vision of one can transmute into the other: Yeats's *Cathleen Ni Houlihan* (1902) provides perhaps the first formulation (at least in English) of this powerful image of renewal, where at the critical moment the Poor Old Woman sloughs her age and becomes 'a young girl', when she receives the assurance of Michael's willingness to give his life for Irish freedom as the French fleet moors in Killala Bay. The messianic deliverance of Ireland (by France, Spain or her own young men) was linked in the eighteenth century to ideas of the Second Coming and the claims of Catholic triumphalism, as in Aoghan Ó Rathaille's 'The Assembly of Munstermen':

> The Pope with the true clergy comes to where the destruction was wrought;
> In his right hand he held a seal (wax) and a candle;
> The boughs burst forth into blossom, and a cloudless heaven welcomes
> The grace of the Son of God, which is come unto us;
> Comes the wanderer without a blemish – though he has been evil spoken of –
> To his rightful place in his full power and pure beauty;
> He will submerge the band who deposed and struck at him;
> And for that I will say nothing against him.[92]

Here the secular and sacred aspects of nationalist messianism are neatly balanced: 'the wanderer' is the Stuart Prince, but also surely with a hint of the Christ of Isaiah 53, rejected by man but yet an epitome of the purest beauty. In such royalist and religious poetic smithies was the sacrificial nationalism of Padraig Pearse forged, although by the time of O'Connell there is perhaps an increasing tendency to see the messianic deliverance as occurring from within Ireland, not by the help of the Catholic powers. Nonetheless the imagery endures. As late as 1914

> [Roger] Casement had suggested that a Jacobite marching song, 'Searlus Og' ('Young Charles'), be adapted for the Volunteers. Pearse's version was called 'An Dord Feinne' ('The Fenian Chant') and it promised that foreigners would be routed by Gaelic force.[93]

Similarly, when Sean O'Casey (1880–1964) came to write his political war ballads in 1916–18, he explicitly referred them to the 'hoped for return of the young Stuart', calling them *Songs of the Wren* (the 'wren' was a code-bird for the Stuart prince).[94] Likewise, James Larkin, the nationalist Irish trade union leader of the 1913 Dublin strike, spoke of lighting 'a fiery cross in England, Scotland, and Wales':[95] the 'fiery cross' had last rallied the Highlands to war in the Jacobite period, and had most recently appeared as the cover emblem of Theodore Napier's neo-Jacobite Scottish nationalist magazine, *The Fiery Cross*, published in Scotland in the decade before the Easter Rising.[96]

Although these images were to achieve a widespread currency in Irish cultural and political nationalism, it is important to recall that the *aisling* tradition itself was that of Irish speakers, mainly the native Irish, as opposed to the Old English (colonists who had remained Catholic), Church of Ireland or northern (more often Presbyterian) Protestants. However, the Old English patronized some of the *aisling*'s composers, for after 1688 the distinction between them and the native/'wild' Irish was increasingly fading. The 'Glorious' Revolution was only the latest in a series of processes which had begun through English suspicions of settlers 'going native' and had been accentuated by the Reformation and the Rising of 1641. Edmund Spenser argued in the 1590s that the Old English were 'degenerate ... Papists';[97] by 1690, the conflation of ethnicity and religion remarked on by Sir Richard Cox in *Hibernia Anglicana* was yet more complete: 'if the most ancient Natural Irish-man be a Protestant, no man takes him for other than an English-Man; and if a Cockney be a Papist, he is reckoned in Ireland as much an Irish-Man as if he was born on Slevelogher.[98]

As a result of these kinds of sentiments, the distinction between 'Celtic' and 'Catholic' in writing about Ireland was often slurred over in a view which presented 'all Irish as Catholics, and all Catholics as Irish'.[99] As time went on, not only did the distinction between different kinds of Irish Catholics become less visible; the distinction between 'Irish' ('Old', 'Wild' and even Protestant) and 'Celtic' was itself often lost to outsiders, to the enragement in particular of Northern Protestants, students from whose community in Scotland protested bitterly when they were disparaged as 'Irishmen' in the 1720s. But distrust for Irish nonconformist Protestants was already familiar among members of the regime who, according to Orange folklore, had liberated them from Popery. As early as 1695, Lord Chancellor Porter had suggested arming Irish Catholics to 'subdue the Scots of Ulster', while the term 'West Britons', though in use since the 1630s to describe the 'British Irish', was not universally accepted. Despite the stringent sectarianism of the Penal Laws within Ireland, this process continued, aided no doubt by the shared revolutionary politics of both Catholic Defenderism and the United Irishmen in the 1790s, illusory as this rapprochement may have been.[100] By the end of the eighteenth century, 'the lumping of Irish Protestants along with Catholics into a single Hibernian stereotype reflected a new perception of them [the Irish] as separate and even foreign'. Implicit analogies between the Irish and Native Americans paralleled similar eighteenth-century views of Scots. Fourteenth-century concerns about 'going native' continued and were compounded: in 1663, Henry Bennet likened English settlers in Ireland to Creoles.[101] As Jonathan Swift, Anglican cleric as he was, himself put it:

> Our *Neighbours, whose Understandings are just upon a Level with Ours* (which perhaps are none of the *Brightest*) have a strong contempt for most Nations, but especially for *Ireland*: They look upon us as a sort of *Savage Irish*, whom our Ancestors conquered several hundred years ago.

In other words, Swift, as a member of the Ascendancy, does not see himself as 'wild Irish', but is aware that that is how England sees 'us'.[102]

Almost certainly, a good deal of the reason for this persisting and increasing alienization of the Irish lay in the political threat they represented, the very territorialism of which was to undermine British identity's determinedly ethnic characterization of the Celt. In the 1690s, Ireland's Protestant MPs were talking of 'freeing themselves from the yoke of England', and a century later in Grattan's Parliament they appeared (in traditional accounts at least) to be on the verge of doing so.[103] Such Protestant behaviour was inconsistent with 'Britishness': the key reason, perhaps, why Linda Colley excludes the counter-example of Ireland from the 'Protestant = British' thesis of her immensely influential *Britons* (1992).

Since the Irish could not be (as had to an extent been the case in the seventeenth century) divided into 'good' Saxon Protestants and 'bad' Celtic Irish, the whole population was ethnicized as un-British. Northern Protestants who returned to Scotland for work in the nineteenth century found the Orangeism they helped to establish there stigmatized and 'shunned' as 'a mere Irish faction, a foreign import brought to disturb the peace of the country'. The 'Celtic fervour' of the 'Orangeman' was remarked on, and even overtly Protestant organs such as the *Glasgow News* wrote disapprovingly of Orangeism as an alien implant, despite the protestations of Orangemen that they were upholding Scottish Reformed values:

> We seem never able to escape from the possibility of the turmoil which occurred at the Boyne being resuscitated and sounding in our ears. There is seldom any healing element in the wings of the sun which dawns over the North of Ireland on the 12th. On the contrary it is a dispute and confusion of the most disgraceful kind. To the Saxon or the Scot who is a lover of social concord and has a taste for upholding the law, these rows are perfectly unintelligible.[104]

Such an editorial could have appeared in the Scottish press in 1974 rather than 1874, when Orange attempts to make Northern Ireland Scotland's quarrel on an ethno-religious basis foundered on the same territorialism visible above, which contrasts the two kinds of Briton ('Saxon' and 'Scot') with the 'wild' Irish of the Orangemen, who nonetheless consider themselves 'true' Scots. The *Glasgow News*'s stress in this editorial on 'social concord and ... the law' is succeeded by a self-congratulatory allusion to the 'freedom of opinion' of 'Great Britain' being above these 'wretched quarrels': the emphasis is on the civic state of Britain as against Irish ethno-religious war. This distinction is as emplaced in the British press today as it was 125 years ago.[105] Attempts (such as that of Hugh Ferguson in 1923) to transplant an 'Orange and Protestant Party' to Scotland rapidly foundered. Such success as Orangeism had come in the west of the country where there were large numbers of Irish Protestant migrants; by contrast, Dundee, where one in six were Irish-born in the late nineteenth century, had no Orange Lodge of note, for the Irish who settled there were overwhelmingly Catholic. Thus, despite occasional Scottish ethnic and sectarian convulsions, such as the 1923 General Assembly report on 'The Menace of the Irish Race to our Scottish Nationality', Scotland by and large accepted Irish immigration *where there was no religious divide among the migrants themselves.*[106]

Sectarian and ethnic hatreds within Ireland itself were a different matter, however, becoming increasingly potent as the nineteenth century progressed, and becoming crystallized by the Gaelicization of Irish nationalism after Parnell's fall in 1891 and the pressure for Partition evident in the last-ditch efforts of Unionism. James Craig, Prime Minister of Northern Ireland from 1921 to 1940, famously remarked that he was 'an Orangemen first', presiding over 'a Protestant parliament and a Protestant state',[107] a statement which indicated the degree of distancing which Northern Protestants sought within Ireland from the idea of being Irish. Much distance had indeed been traversed since the insurgents in the 1641 Rising had declared their intention to spare Scottish Presbyterians because of their 'Gaelic' origins. Indeed, since 1970 writers such as Ian Adamson have offered an alternative ethnicity for the northern Protestant community, that of the Cruithin:[108] a restorative account which coincided with the Loyalist adoption of Cuchulain as a heroic icon of resistance, a representative of 'the struggle of Ulster against the invading Gael'.[109] As a piece by 'Sam Sloan' in the UDA magazine *Ulster* put it in 1978: 'You are the children of the Cruithin, the sons and daughters of the Picts. This is OUR land, YOUR culture, YOUR heritage – you are indeed the people. You are older than the Gaels, older the Welsh, older even than the English.[110] Such ethnic posturing is suggestive of a determined, even a last-ditch attempt, both to alienize the other inhabitants of Ireland, and to provide an ethnic justification for a brand of Britishness falling into desuetude throughout the rest of these islands. It is also the case that, beginning with the Red Hand of the O'Neills, Ulster Loyalism has long defined its Britishness at least in part through Irish nationalist imagery, an important dimension to the struggle between identities in Northern Ireland which will be further examined in Chapter 4.[111]

Although Irishmen such as the Duke of Wellington (who, however, remarked of his country of origin that 'not everything born in a stable is a horse'), Sir Garnett Wolseley and Lords Roberts and Kitchener rose to the top of the British Army and Establishment, as so often elsewhere it was the exhibition of difference that proved to be at the root of British alienization of Ireland.[112] Just as Jonathan Swift had turned from English satirist to Irish madman after he had returned to Ireland and taken up Irish causes,[113] so 'the British need to ridicule the Irish grew more pressing as the demands of Irish nationalism became more assertive'.[114] Stock buffoons, and even the uneasy caricatures of O'Connell and Young Ireland,[115] gave way to simianization and the categorization of the Irish as 'Hottentots' in a bid to stem an increasingly apparent Nationalist tide.[116]

The genteel Irishmen of an earlier era, when Irish poverty and political disaffection seemed, if disgusting, remote, took a back seat to stronger views of the country as 'a backwater spawned over by obscene reptiles', full of 'naughty children', rather like the verdict of *The Times* on Governor Eyre's conduct in the infamous 1865 Rebellion that Jamaica's 'inhabitants are our spoiled children'. Tellingly, Denis Judd argues that Irish nationalism' stank ... in the nostrils ... it was an offence to many of those who cherished the vision of a world increasingly subject to Anglo-Saxon domination and control'.[117] The 'white negroes' were on the march. The identification of the gorilla and classification of the other great apes in the 1840s, provided, as Perry Curtis has argued, a fresh impetus in the context of rising nationalism to re-emphasize the ethnic gulf between Irish Celt and Anglo-Saxon. As *Punch* put it in 'The Missing Link' on 18 October 1862:

> A gulf, certainly, does appear to yawn between the Gorilla and the Negro. The woods and wilds of Africa do not exhibit an example of any intermediate animal ... A creature manifestly between the Gorilla and the Negro is to be met with in some of the lowest districts of London and Liverpool by adventurous explorers. It comes from Ireland ... The somewhat superior ability of the Irish Yahoo to utter articulate sounds, may suffice to prove that it is a development, and not, as some may imagine, a degeneration of the Gorilla.[118]

Passages such as this transform Swift's attacks on England's Irish policy from satire to reality. Although Curtis's arguments have been criticized, for example by R. F. Foster in *Paddy and Mr Punch* (1993), it remains the case that where political difference was at stake, there were, as had been the case with Scottish Jacobites in the eighteenth century, few caricatures to which British political cartoons would not stoop (see Figure 9). The *aisling* tradition itself was inverted and mocked by cartoons such as the 1860 *Fenian-Pest*, which showed Hibernia in the arms, not of the grisly Anglo-German foreigners of Aogan Ó Rathaille's (1671–1729) poetry, but equally unprepossessing Irish-Americans.[119] Apparent sops such as the 'revised Union Flag of 1900', which 'restored the cross of St Patrick to equivalent proportions with St George and St Andrew', were embarrassingly inappropriate: the St Patrick's cross being itself 'an 1800 English invention for a saint who was not a martyr and for a people who had never used it'.[120]

Events such as this showed that British nationalism was not competent to understand and deal with Ireland. British progressive alienization of all

Figure 9 *The Chevaliers Market, Or Highland Fair*, 1745. 10″ × 8″. Here anti-Scottishness is combined with virulent anti-Catholicism and more general xenophobia. Stalls sell relics, frogs and wooden shoes (both attacking France and the French), while 'Poison Gaggs and Spanish Padlocks' are available from the pedlar priest standing under the 'French Yoke'. Magna Charts, the Bible, the 'Scotch Directory for Worship' and the Book of Common Prayer are being swept away together with the currency and government stock: an interesting conjunction. Thistles grow out of stone, mocking Scottish poverty and Catholic claims on the miraculous alike. A donkey carries on its back the immediate results of a Stuart restoration, including a 'Petition to Dissolve the Union'. Thus at the core of this fine print's message is the threat to Britain and Britishness itself, not only from the major European powers outwith its borders, but also internally, with the restoration of an independent Scotland.

Irish who displayed difference prevented comprehension of the Irish situation, and led to successive crises at the end of the eighteenth and throughout the nineteenth century. Nationalist territorialism in Ireland was aided by the simple fact that the country was a discrete unit, a separate island: and not just any island, but *insula sacra*, the sacred place. While this was a sacramental, ultimately Catholic appellation, eighteenth-century antiquarians such as O'Halloran (the author of *Insula*

Sacra (1770)) 'proposed to demonstrate to the inhabitants of Ireland that they constituted one common stock' and to 'banish all unnatural divisions'. While there is controversy as to how far the Defenders and the United Irishmen managed this feat in the 1790s, a decade which also saw the birth of modern Orangeism, it remains true that Protestant nationalism was a thorn in the side of attempts to stigmatize the ethno-cultural Celt as unfit for territorial identity. Given that Protestants were themselves often categorized as 'Irish' in Britain, it is not surprising that O'Halloran's view of essential Irish unity remained popular among many. Irish rebel ballads were translated into English,[121] while the tricolour itself, with its orange, green and reconciling white and the ideology of Thomas Davis's (1818–48) Young Ireland bore witness to internal efforts to reduce mutual alienization and recognize instead a common enemy, as Swift had arguably done a hundred years before:

> IRELAND ! rejoice, and England ! deplore –
>   Faction and feud are passing away;
> 'Twas a low voice, but 'tis a loud roar,
>   'Orange and Green will carry the day'.

Wishful thinking or not, it was not, and did not prove to be in the interests of the British state that such sentiments developed. Davis's adaptation of the air of 'The Protestant Boys' ('The Protestant Boys will carry the day' – itself the air of 'Lilliburlero') for his song substituted national for community identity: a possibility which, if imperfectly realized, always existed in Ireland.[122]

Mighty northern Englishmen

The case in Scotland was very different. In the 1750s and 1760s, Scottish Enlightenment figures disassociated themselves from the 'Highland rabble' of the Jacobites, whom only twenty years before many Lowlanders had supported, and who had often been characterized as undifferentiatedly 'Scottish' south of the Border.[123] Their aim was almost certainly to smooth the passage of their own integration into Britain; yet at the same time they displayed a growing delight in the nostalgic (as opposed to contemporary) renditions of Gaelic Scotland. Despite Wilkeite opposition therefore, Anglophone Scots were increasingly adapting themselves to life and opportunities in England (see Figure 10). The Highland/Lowland divide in Scotland, evident from the late fourteenth century and exacerbated through the Reformation, widened further as Enlightenment Scot-

Figure 10 *Scotch Collops an Antidote for an English Stomach*, early 1760s. 10″ ×
8″. Scots in tartan (one with a drawn sword) accompany their fellow-countrymen who are now camouflaged in British clothing, but whose sentiments of
treacherous aggrandizement are unchanged.

land increasingly subscribed to a historiography and cultural theory
which sought to align Lowland Scotland with a Germanic and Teutonic
version of English identity, which posited a 'predisposition of the Germanic peoples to liberty' (and hence opposition to tyrannical Catholicism).[124] This version of Englishness, which largely substituted Alfred for
Arthur, can be dated back at least to Lutheran appeals to German nationalism in the sixteenth century, and was much evident in the development
of Whig thought in the seventeenth and eighteenth centuries: a 'historical investigation of Anglo-Saxon England … that had arisen in the sixteenth century in response to a *religious* need was found in the
seventeenth century to serve the highest *political* purposes'. Teutonism in
England was 'pioneered by the works of Richard Rowlands, also known as
Richard Verstegan (fl. 1565–1620)', who applied it both to 'English society' and King James VI and I, who was nonetheless also commended as
also descended from Fergusian and Arthurian Celts. The advent of the
German Hanoverians on the throne naturally further consolidated the
power of this ideology, especially with reference to the royal family: the
Bishop of Lincoln's dedication to George I of his version 'of Camden's
Britannia glows with pride in the common Saxon origin which linked the
Hanoverian king with his English subjects'.[125]

In response to this, and in an effort to make respectable a Scotland tinged with memories of Jacobite disloyalty, Enlightenment historians constructed 'a Scottish version of English whig identity, based on a commitment to English constitutional history' which involved jettisoning Scotland's 'past as a repository of political and institutional value', a process whose legacy can still be felt today. The patriot version of Scotland's history as a struggle for liberty was turned on its head: Scottish love of liberty was 'Gothic ... love of freedom' and hence entirely compatible with Britain.[126] Celtic Scotland was ethnicized to the margin, and presented as occupying only that space in which the retreating Gaelic tongue was spoken: hence Scottish writers denied Scottish national territorialism by relegating the 'Celt' to an ethno-cultural edge and making of themselves Germanic Englishmen. Antiquarians such as John Pinkerton (1758–1826) presented an image of ascendant Goths and slavish Celts ('what a lion is to an ass, a Goth is to a Celt'[127]), while identifying in James Macpherson's *Ossian* poetry 'the last effort of Celticism to injure the history of Britain', a judgement which proved somewhat premature.[128] Pinkerton's verdict that 'Scotland was held back by its degenerate Celtic population' was, if an extreme statement, one which proved compatible with the racialist enthusiasms of nineteenth-century science. Robert Knox (1791–1862), the Scottish doctor, 'tried to earn a living by lecturing on the superiority of the Anglo-Saxon race after his dealings with the Irish body stealers and murderers, William Burke and William Hare, had ruined his medical career'. Indeed, scientific or quasi-scientific trends strongly reinforced Scottish Gothicism: as Colin Kidd observes, George Combe (1788–1858), 'intellectual leader' of phrenology, was a Teutonist, and thought that 'the Scotch Lowland population ... has done everything by which Scotland is distinguished'.[129]

This was an extreme position, and it was a more refined variant of Teutonism which gained the greatest currency. Sir Walter Scott, as well as subscribing (in novels such as *Waverley* and *The Antiquary*) to the Teuton/Celt distinction in Scotland, suggested through his pageantry and presentation of Scotland *to England* a more subtle reading: that Celticism was the emotional side of the Scot, and Teutonism its intellectual corrective. In doing so of course, he endorsed a valedictory sentimentalism which offered little critique of the business-like lairds in extravagantly traditional dress who were destroying Highland life through eviction and improvement: 'by applying a sentimental Jacobite gloss to a basic Whig constitutionalism, Scott turned the Scottish past into an ideologically neutral pageant'.[130] Scottish history itself was relegated to 'the nightmare of … feudal oppression and backwardness' from which Union had delivered it:[131] king-killing and civil war in England were regarded as temporary aberrations on the path of progress, but in Scotland as typical manifestations of ungovernable brutality and a Celtic–Teuton split. Except among specialists, this view of Scottish history survives: there has long been an unwillingness to compare English magnate unrest on the margins (e.g. in 1402–3, 1536 and 1569–70) with its Scottish equivalent, for example. Uneasiness developed concerning even the trappings of Scotland's separate past: when it was proposed to found a Society of Antiquaries in Scotland in 1780, it was objected that 'it was not … consistent with political wisdom, to draw the attention of the Scots to the ancient honours and constitution of their independent monarchy'.[132]

Both Scotland benorth Tay in general and the Highlands in particular suffered from this change of emphasis. Highlanders were (despite the fact that many were Episcopalian or Presbyterian, and that apart from remote islands, indigenous Catholicism was strongest in the north-east Lowland/Highland border) frequently categorized as 'Catholic' by way of oppositional complementarity, thus marginalizing them further (cf. Figure 9). The Scottish Wars of Independence were integrated into British history: Bruce became 'an English baron' who 'would have scorned the savage kernes [note the Irish term] of the Highlands, who were never admitted to be Scots'.[133] The 'Lowland Teutons' who fought with Wallace (note that for the more (at least nostalgically) patriotic James Hogg (1770–1835), Wallace was by contrast 'chief' of 'the tartaned clans') and Bruce thus became Germanic lovers of liberty whose opposition to their English brethren was fundamentally misdirected: 'mighty northern Englishmen' who 'saved old Scotland from her friends', as the poet John Davidson put it.[134] The Jacobite Risings became 'Celtic intrusions into the Germanic Lowlands', and the substantial Lowland contribution to them forgotten. Even Lowland radicals began to talk in terms of the grandeur of the constitution under King Alfred (of England, 871–900),[135] while the Highlands were 'colonised by an empire of signs', as a remote and romantic world peopled by 'the indispensable atavistic natives'.[136] A seventeenth-century Highlander could say that 'my Race has bene tenne hundreth yeris kyndlie Scottis men under the Kingis of Scotland':[137] by the eighteenth century, such political territorialism, already under pressure, was becoming forgotten, to be replaced by the steady growth of a pan-Anglo-Saxonism which reached its apogee around 1900.[138]

Dissenting voices remained. Although many Scottish radicals in the French revolutionary period accepted an Anglo-Germanic reading of their rights and liberties, the strong presence of Irish radicalism in Scotland, both in the shape of United Irishmen and the Catholic Defenders, suggested that traditional links had not altogether disappeared, a suggestion reinforced by the use of Jacobite rhetoric by radicals in the Scottish militia and in the Rising of 1820, as well as support for Daniel O'Connell's repeal of the Union in the 1830s.[139] Sometimes 'Sawney' and 'Teague' are still linked in street ballads in eighteenth-century fashion,[140] but more typical of the breaking of Celtic links is the extraordinary distance between the Scot and Irishman evident in the writings of Thomas Carlyle (1795–1881), himself unsurprisingly an avid Teutonist, as were most nineteenth-century historians:

> We English pay, even now, the bitter smart of long centuries of injustice to our neighbour Island ... Crowds of miserable Irish darken all our towns ... the sorest evil this country has to strive with. In his rags and laughing savagery ... he lodges to his mind in any pighutch or doghutch ... The Saxon man ... may be ignorant, but he has not sunk from decent manhood to squalid apehood ... The time has come when the Irish population must either be improved a little, or else exterminated.[141]

It was only a century since the Scot, too, had been seen in these terms, before sheltering under the umbrella of 'Saxon' identity (see Figure 11).

There were, of course, still exceptions to the trend towards Scottish Teutonism. William Burns (1809–76) in *The Scottish War of Independence* (1874) attacked the view that the English were 'kindred offshoots from the great Teutonic stem, separated for a time by an unfortunate war', arguing that this would render 'the history of our country' devoid of meaning.[142] More importantly, W. F. Skene's *Celtic Scotland* (1880), if not so politically explicit, was to provide considerable literary ammunition not only for the ameliorative Highland policy of the Napier Commission in the 1880s, but also for the whole Celtic Twilight movement, including its Irish nationalist manifestations.

The idea of a Scotland ethnically divided between Celt and Teuton, or more complicatedly, Celt, Pict (or Picto-German) and Teuton, still has an afterlife in internal and external perceptions of the country: it has been very influential in demarcations of Scottish identity in the last two hundred years. As a representation of Scottish ethnicity it has limited accuracy, being a half-truth at best: but that was not its purpose. Rather it sought to confirm, indeed demand, equality of treatment in Britain for Scots prepared to accommodate themselves to the manner and even the title of Englishmen, while marginalizing (and arguably exploiting and

Figure 11 *This is the Butcher beware of your Sheep*, late 1740s. 8″ × 6″. A relatively rare anti-Cumberland print depicts a Scot in a pose of crucifixion being skinned alive, presumably for eating – (an axe (for jointing?)) lies near. Swift's *Modest Proposal* of twenty years earlier, with its 'recommendation' for the English consumption of Irish children, shows how little separated certain aspects of the Scottish and Irish experience at this stage.

tyrannizing) those of their fellow-countrymen who spoke a different language, had some distinct cultural trappings (though the extent to which
'Highland' and 'Scottish' culture are symbiotic is underestimated) and
who professed, or could be held to profess, a different religion. At the
same time, the 'wild Highlander' thus constructed was held not only to be
a different race from the Lowland Scot, but also simultaneously the
romantic side of that same Lowlander's psychology: hence Scott could
portray the whole of Scotland as 'Highland' (because Romantic) for
George IV. In other words, Scotland was geographically split between
Celt and Teuton, while every Scot, at least every Germanic Scot, was also
psychologically split between douce responsibility and romantic wild-
ness: a convenient internal division between conformity and escapism
which has left a profound legacy in the literature and culture of Scotland,
in notions such as the Caledonian Antisyzygy, or novels such as J. M.
Barrie's *Farewell, Miss Julie Logan* (1932), where entering the Jacobite glen
enables the newly appointed minister to release his Celtic, emotional side
in the shape of the Jungian anima of Julie Logan, a Catholic Jacobite hero-
ine. Thus the legacy of Scott has its hidden inheritance in twentieth-century Scottish literature. Scott himself of course, in *The Highland Widow*,
portrayed a man torn between the continuing emotional demands of the
Celtic feminized land, personified as his mother, and the rule-governed,
disciplined life of the British Army. His death indicates (like Adam
Yestreen's madness in *Julie Logan*) that the Scot thrives best by keeping his
emotional Celticism suppressed.[143]

The personification of the land and national identity as a woman, present in the literary typologies of Ireland, Scotland and Wales, allowed not
only the imaginative depiction of a Scotland out of touch with its history
to inform books like *Julie Logan* and Neil Gunn's *Butcher's Broom* (1934),
but also provided a route for the diminution of the Celt by those who
wished to associate Celticism with emotionalism and feminine weakness.
This process, and the importance of the opposition to it mounted by the
cultural revival in Ireland, will be key topics in the next chapter.[144]

Chapter 2

Gendering the Celt

They always fell

If the eighteenth century saw the Celt's transformation from feared to noble savage, the nineteenth witnessed a significant further softening of the Celtic image. Some of the signs of this change were already visible in the Primitivist/Romantic period, when the association of the sentimental with emotionalism gave the Ossianic Noble Savage a feminine dimension, one intensified by a nineteenth century which also identified such emotions with women's 'hysterical' qualities.[1] At the same time, the Ossianic hero's capabilities as a man of action were undercut by the elegiac mode of commemoration which was all that either Primitivism or Romanticism offered to the Celt. Just as Scottish history (for example) was detached from its British present and reformulated as harmless pageant, so the Celtic hero existed only to be 'sad but lovely' and to stimulate 'the joy of grief'. 'The cry of the hunter is over. The voice of war is ceased', observes Macpherson: hence the potential for heroic action, the male sphere, is destroyed. If Ossian was 'the last of the race', Welsh iconography was similarly depicting *The Last Bard* (1774) as a survivor's farewell to heroic culture. This image is presented with especial sophistication by Scott in Chapter 22 of *Waverley* (1816), where Flora McIvor sings to the novel's English hero and surrogate tourist a lay of the last bard in suitably Sublime surroundings. The eighteenth-century bard is now absent, and a woman sings his song: Celticism is in transition from the last phase of heroic recollection to the first of Romantic charm.[2] Following Scott, femininity became an increasingly crucial component in defining the characteristics of the Celt.

Despite invoking the Celtic past and Scotland's links with Ireland,[3] Macpherson was in fact creating an epic which drew a line under that past, commemorating it in Jacobitical form as a series of victories ending only in overwhelming defeat. This was the Ossianic metaphor which enthralled a European audience alive to sentiment and pathos, and newly aware of its own historicity: a Celtic *Götterdämmerung*, evident in

Macpherson's own work from his 1758 elegy 'On the death of Marshal Keith' onwards:

> See! the proud halls they once possess'd decay'd,
> The spiral tow'rs depend the lofty head;
> Wild ivy creeps along the mould'ring walls,
> And with each gust of wind a fragment falls.[4]

In Ireland, as we have seen, cultural commentators unwilling to sacrifice their past to the elegy of 'the primitivist paradigm' resisted such claims of Celtic entropy,[5] which in Britain provided an articulation both of a pathetic beauty and, in their ruins, of a Gothic Sublime. Certain practices which survived into the Romantic period endorsed this view of a picturesque but dying and outdated culture in the Celtic 'fringe'. Hereditary guardians of holy wells survived in remoter Wales until the end of the 1820s, Lammas celebrations in Tyrone into the twentieth century, while Clootie wells with reputed healing powers remain in Scotland to this day: that of St Boniface at Munlochy is reputed to be adorned with more than 50,000 votive rags. As Nigel Pennick has observed, while there are 91 sites associated with Celtic sacralism in England, 52 of these are in the West Country (of which 40 in Cornwall), and a further 12 in the West Midlands (i.e. bordering on Wales). Overwhelmingly, the remembered and elegized Celtic sacred landscape belongs to the identified Celtic lands.[6]

By the end of the eighteenth century, this elegiac mode had intensified under the new-found pressures of tourism, which rapidly expanded in the period after the French Revolution. As Katherine Haldane points out: 'the Napoleonic Wars ... made Scotland virtually the only (even partly) foreign place to which English tourists could safely travel at the turn of the century, aside from Ireland.'[7] These tourists and their successors responded overwhelmingly to the 'fixed image' of Scotland as a faded Celtic heartland, transmuted from the 'savages' of Wilkeite propaganda to a fey *Kulturvolk*, elusive in their mists, which, like the mists of time, conceal their savage past. As early as 1800, visitors were carving their names in Fingal's Cave in Staffa in celebration of the country's prime role as a locus for heroic nostalgia: tourists were (and are) thrilled with images of a heroic and unruly past, saturated with 'stories of ... lawlessness and ferocity'. Such 'ferocity' was often on picturesque display: in 1842, Victoria and Albert were met in Lochaber by 100 tenants in tartan, some armed 'with Lochaber axes'; at Dunkeld, Highlanders 'complete with claymores and battleaxes' were on show, 'many ... of gigantic stature'. In this manner, stereotypes of the huge savage Highlander were reinforced in controlled environments for the pleasure of the onlooker: even 'women and children ... were described as "strong", "hardy", "sturdy", and "robust"', imaged as possessing antique qualities of vigour. It pleased the tourist, too, to imagine that their visit to Scotland was a form of privileged travelling into the past: in the 1830s, one guidebook opined 'that a 1693 description of the people of Orkney was probably still adequate'. Such views can still be found, and not just in Scotland: a South Carolina tourist guidebook of 1989 suggests that 'Charleston is a way of life preserved', while the tourist urge to visit the past without a time machine is still present, and in this sense among others we continue to know ourselves to be in the Romantic era.[8]

Antiquarian and Celtic societies multiplied in the Romantic period. 'The first Highland Society Gathering was at the Falkirk Tryst in 1781', and it was shortly followed by The Highland Society of Scotland (1784) and that of London (1788), not to mention developments such as the 'Birmingham Celtic Club'.[9] In general, these societies were politically null, and indeed often only accepted their culture if it was stated in the restricted terms of current political and social acceptability: hence the Highland Society of London reacted with disapproval to James Hogg's collection of *Jacobite Relics* (1819–21), which it itself had commissioned. Hogg may have bowdlerized some of the songs, but they remained too close to the bone.[10]

Only in Ireland did such societies carry more purposive overtones, where nationalists such as Isaac Butt and Daniel O'Connell could be found among the officials of the Celtic Society (founded 1843),[11] and where cultural revivalism rather than elegy attended the figures of Cuchulain, Oisin and Fionn. Figures such as George Petrie (1790–1866) sought out the virtues of the Celt 'in remote rural communities' such as the Aran islands (where J. M. Synge was later to find his inspiration) seeking rather to endorse than elegize them. Equally significantly, Unionists like Sir Samuel Ferguson (1810–86) sought to link the 'Celtic revival' to an Ascendancy commitment to be 'leaders of the Irish nation'. Even in the language of Unionist Ireland, a territorialism of Irish nationality (aided of course by the fact that the Irish, British though they might wish to be, could not semantically belong to 'the island race' without pluralizing it) lent significant strength to an elsewhere supine ethno-cultural Celticism. Thus it was in Ireland that the Celtic and Ossianic societies which proved mere cultural recreations in Scotland and Wales passed almost seamlessly into increasingly potent forms such as the Society for the Preservation of the Irish Language (1876), the Gaelic Athletic Association (1884), the

Irish Literary Society (1891) and the Gaelic League (1893).[12] George Petrie's words in the *Irish Penny Journal* of 1840 look back to the *aisling* as well as forward to the sacrificial nationalism of twentieth-century Ireland, when he states that 'in the figure of the prostrate female we recognise at once the attributes of our country', a 'country … personified by a beautiful female figure'.[13]

In Britain, the retreat of the Celt from territoriality to mere psychology offers a telling contrast. The quintessential and defining text here is Matthew Arnold's (1822–88) *On the Study of Celtic Literature* (1867), which ironically was written in defence of Celtic Wales from an attack in *The Times* on Welsh as 'the curse of Wales' (see Introduction). Arnold wisely remarked that 'the strain of the *Times* … is the characteristic strain of the Englishman in commenting on whatsoever is not himself', but went on to compromise this perception through the resolutely Ossianic basis of his interpretation of the Celt. Wales is the place 'where the past still lives, where every place has its tradition … this poetry, and lives with it, and clings to it'. The Welshmen of the 1860s, however, are presented in Macphersonian terms as degenerate from their ancestors, who have only 'obscure descendants – bathing people, vegetable sellers, and donkey boys' (in similar fashion, J. P. Mahaffy, 'Unionist Provost of Trinity College, Dublin', suggested that 'the aborigines of this island' were 'the corner-boys who spit in the Liffey', among whom he numbered James Joyce). Class and racial scorn are mixed, and amidst such images it is little wonder that Arnold suggests that 'the fusion of all the inhabitants of these islands into one homogenous, English-speaking whole … the swallowing up of provincial nationalities, is a consummation … a necessity of what is called modern civilisation … the sooner the Welsh language disappears … the better'. He goes on to celebrate the fact that 'traders and tourists do excellent service by pushing the English wedge further and further into the heart of the principality; Ministers of Education, by hammering it harder and harder into the elementary schools'. Such sentiments presaged the framing of a policy hostile to the Welsh language in the 1870 Education Act, which was passed shortly after the publication of *On the Study of Celtic Literature*. In fact, Arnold's defence of the Celtic largely resides only in the safely antiquarian qualities of respect for some of its old literature: he does not recommend it for those still writing (when not kept from their art by their donkeys or street trading), remarking that 'anything of real importance … anything the world will the least care to hear … must speak English'.[14]

In contrast to the 'Germanic' qualities of 'the main current of the blood' of Britons, Arnold offers an intensely feminized reading of the Celt as a kind of decorative accessory to British identity, simultaneously womanish and childish. The Celts love 'bright colours', are 'full of fanfaronade' and lack 'balance, measure, and patience' in 'chafing against the despotism of fact' and 'perpetual straining after mere emotion'. The elegiac quality of Ossian has been resolved into a lack of realism characteristic of an emotional race wanting mature judgement: '"They went forth to the war", Ossian says most truly, *"but they always fell"'* (a phrase which Arnold revisited in his *Irish Essays*, to much the same effect). This 'falling' is one of moral as well as physical defeat, encompassing a feminine as well as a masculine fall:

> Some people have found in the Celtic nature and sensibility the main root out of which chivalry and romance and the glorification of a feminine ideal spring … no doubt the sensibility of the Celtic nature, its nervous exaltation, have something feminine in them, and the Celt is thus peculiarly disposed to feel the spell of the feminine idiosyncrasy … his sensibility gives him a peculiarly near and intimate feeling of nature and the life of nature.[15]

The Noble Savage's feeling for 'nature' is compounded with his romantic defeat, a 'feminine ideal' which in its turn is seen as deeply internalized in the Celtic nature, vulnerable (being immature and irrational) to 'the spell of the feminine idiosyncrasy'. The feminine qualities of the Celt are strongly endorsed, and there is a tinge both of possessiveness and carnal 'knowing' in one of Arnold's summations:

> all, with one insignificant exception, belongs to the English empire; only Brittany is not ours; we have Ireland, the Scottish Highlands, Wales, the Isle of Man, Cornwall. They are a part of ourselves, we are deeply interested in knowing them, they are deeply interested in being known by us.[16]

'They' are a part of 'us', like and yet unlike. Arnold's 'we' (masculine England) owns 'them' (feminine Celts) and wants to 'know' them, presuming that this desire is returned. Seamus Heaney's 'Act of Union' is an appropriate modern response to the implicit rapine of Arnold's sentiments, which denominated the Celt (as seen by Anglo-centric eyes) for generations to come. Owning was more important than knowing except where the two were synonymous:

> And I am still imperially
> Male, leaving you with the pain,
> The rending process in the colony,
> The battering ram, the boom burst from within.[17]

As Marjorie Howes remarks, 'femininity marked the Celt's difference from the Saxon, but also placed her in a relationship of natural complementarity to him'. This 'complementarity' would enable the Celt 'to become the angel in the British house of empire, sweetening and completing it', while sharing with her sex 'material ineffectiveness and incapacity for self-government' (see Figures 12 and 13). This was the outlook of a masculinized empire, with its increasingly exported emphasis on bravery, pluck and militarism, an emphasis which intensified and deepened the characterization of the Celt as the nineteenth century came to a close:

> the intermediate position the Irish occupied in the British hierarchy of races … helped make a particular version of nineteenth-century femininity a useful category for his [Arnold's] construction of the Celt: a cultured, sensitive, middle-class femininity associated with hysteria … By the late nineteenth century … the cultural equation of femininity with pathology … was even more firmly established.

Sophie Bryant, in an 1897 article in the *Contemporary Review*, argued that 'The Celtic Mind' had 'physical differences in nervous structure … making them liable to explode on very slight stimulus'. It differs from 'the Teuton' in its 'very quality'. One can only wonder if events like the 1895 trial of Oscar Wilde (seen as an effeminate Irishman posing as an English gentleman?), and the attack on Celtic Twilight and other 'decadent' artists in pathological terms by Max Nordau in his well-timed book on *Degeneration* in the same year, reinforced these comforting stereotypes. In an era of Irish Home Rule agitation, they were needed: Newbolt, for example, portrays Ireland as a woman driven hysterical by the history of her disenchantment with *The Island Race*, even though they now 'love that wronged thee': 'Down thy valleys, Ireland, Ireland … Still thy spirit wanders wailing, / Wanderes wailing, wanders mad.' The efficacy of such marginalizing imagery was blunted through its adoption by Irish patriots. In 1911, for example, Sir Horace Plunkett wrote defiantly :

> That Ireland … is spoken of as a woman is probably due to the appearance in our national affairs of qualities which men call womanly. And this impression is not merely the cheap attribution of racial inferiority by the alien critic which is familiar, it is our feeling about ourselves.

As L. P. Curtis observes, the 'sorrowful and irresistible paragon of Irish womanhood … was the one symbol on which the cartoonists of London, Dublin, and New York were wholly agreed'.[18]

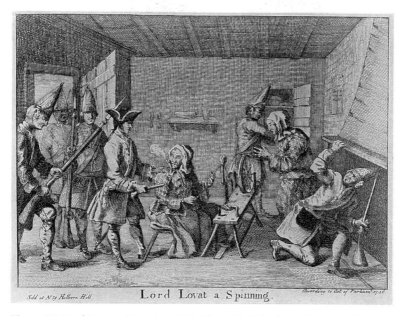

Sold at Nº 3 Holborn Hill.   Lord Lovat a Spinning.   According to Act of Parliam.ᵗ 1746

Figure 12 *Lord Lovat a Spinning*, 1746. 8″ × 6″. A feminized image of the Scot from the eighteenth century, indicative of duplicity and, ultimately, of weakness.

The Celt formed an important dimension of Arnold's cultural mission. In demonstrating that Britain 'owned' its 'feminine' Celts, Arnold wished to emphasize 'the greater delicacy and spirituality of the Celtic peoples who are blended with us', with a view to drawing attention to the need for their softer cultural qualities to water down the 'Barbarian' Gothic English aristocracy and the 'Philistine' middle class whom he attacks in *Culture and Anarchy* (1869). Such a mission does not lend any significance to the Irish, Welsh or Scots in themselves, however: Arnold is rather intent on identifying and praising the 'Celtic' spirit in its 'blended' form, present or fancied to be present in English literature. England's 'island race' is possessed of a conditional hybridity of blood and spirit on this reading, an internalized marriage of gendered qualities which imprison the Celt in the British domestic body, which both vampirizes it and gives it life. Where it is found separately from this conjunction, Celticism is often weak, exhausted and effeminate, rather like the women portrayed in the late nineteenth-century art analysed in Bram Dijkstra's suggestive and provocative *Idols of Perversity* (1986).[19] The Celtic lands themselves are

Rouled, o'er Hills the young · Adventurer flies ·
And in a Cottage sinks to this · Disguise ·
Fled his gay Hopes defeated his fond Scheme ·
His Throne is vanish'd like a golden Dream ·
By manly Thoughts He'd charm His Woes to rest ·
In vain! Culloden still distracts His Breast ·

J. Williams fecit

Figure 13 J. Williams, print of Prince Charles as Betty Burke, late 1740s. 8″ × 6″. Charles Edward's womanliness indicates his weakness: his 'manly Thoughts' are 'In vain', a golden Dream'. Now, like a woman, he is sorrowful: 'Culloden still distracts His Breast'.

associated with an exhausted variant of the Celtic qualities which have enriched a broader British literature and society: they have now only 'the eternal softness and mild light of the west … fading away', an Arnoldian view in keeping with earlier Romantic and post-Romantic evocations.[20] In David Lloyd's words, Arnold 'subordinates a colonized people's culture and literature to the major canon by stereotyping the essential identity of the race concerned'.[21] In this, his endeavour can be linked to those of the Scottish Teutonists, who saw the merits of the Celt as being present in the provision of a softer imaginative side to the Germanic vigour of imperialist industrialism; in similar vein, George Borrow, who at Birmingham thought himself 'a modern Englishman, enthusiastically proud of modern England's science and energy', gave way on his approach to 'the land of the bard' to a 'glow' of 'Welsh enthusiasm'.[22] Rigorous thought gives way to Celtic emotion.

Ernest Renan provided much of the basis of Arnold's portrait of Celticism in *Poesie des Races Celtiques* (1860), in particular the Arnoldian concept of a 'Celtic melancholy' growing from 'the characteristics of fatalism, unprogressiveness, and a fondness for defending lost causes',[23] and the notion that 'the Celtic race … is an essentially feminine race'.[24] Renan emphasized the declining, marginal qualities of the Celtic lands, 'confined by conquest within forgotten islands and peninsulas', full of 'delicious sadness', also stressing their vision of the feminine, 'woman such as chivalry conceived her, an ideal of sweetness and loveliness'. A Breton in 'an exhausted land, in an age when hope is dead', Renan states his 'only delight' is to be the way in which through him his ancestors, 'ancient fathers … attain life and utterance'.[25] While his elegy was less purposive than Arnold's, Renan nevertheless provided an image of a land of ancient masculine heroes now inhabited by diminutive feminized pygmies, removed from the idea of a contemporary Noble Savage of the Napoleonic period and Bonaparte's own *Academie Celtique*. It was, as so often, the Irish writer W. B. Yeats (1865–1939) who elegantly echoed while rebutting such images, in setting up a dialogue with heroic ancestors, not simply a passive voicing of their imagined and now in any case outdated concerns:

> *Pardon, old fathers, if you still remain*
> *Somewhere in ear-shot for the story's end …*
> *Pardon that for a barren passion's sake,*
> *Although I have come close on forty-nine,*
> *I have no child, I have nothing but a book,*
> *Nothing but that to prove your blood and mine.*

This mere 'book' was to become Yeats's version of 'the book of the people', and he the bard who would call descendants of Ireland's 'ancient fathers' to celebrate 'the wasteful virtues' once again.[26] In his copy of *Poesie des Races Celtique*, Yeats wrote three marginal comments next to Renan's description of the Celt's femininity: 'Delicacy', 'a feminine race', and 'The Ideal of Woman'. By 1897, in 'The Celtic Element in Literature', he was combating Arnold's emphasis on the feminine, and although he drew heavily on the defensive nationalist qualities of the Sean Bhean Bhocht and Cathleen Ni Houlihan, he on the whole retained an ambivalence towards a feminized Ireland, whether personified in Maud Gonne or, more generally, as 'an eroticized goddess figure who was both the embodiment of a transcendent national unity and a potentially devouring mother'.[27]

In the later nineteenth century, however, Arnold's and Renan's readings of the Celts as 'a shy, sensitive and imaginative race' remained dominant,[28] and the status of Celticism and the Celtic became recognizably aligned to other colonial perspectives, such as the 'Orientalism' identified by Edward Said. In Ireland, the Anglo-Irish were seen by some as 'resident Teutons', but the colonial ideology implicit in this was challenged by Unionist cultural nationalism, Standish O'Grady for example, envisioning their class as rather taking over the (heroic) function of now-expelled Celtic aristocrats, though he despaired of the reality of the Ascendancy 'rotting from the land in the most dismal farce-tragedy ever seen, without one brave deed, one brave word'.[29] Nonetheless, the inclusion of Protestant Ireland in a single typology compromised the British view of the Celt, despite the fact that, as Swift had observed (see Chapter 1), Irishness had also long been attributed to English immigrants by those at home. A cultural vision was being established, in which figures such as Charles Parnell provided a challenge to the image of the etiolated feminine Celt taken up elsewhere, for example in Wales, where the 1880s saw increasing national agitation. In this context, Parnell's fall in 1891, which fortuitously underlined the message of Celtic failure, may have had significant knock-on effects outside Ireland.[30]

If the cultural and political situation in Ireland continued to be hard going for reductivist Victorian Celticism, it gained much from other sources. The growth of Darwinism and the development of cognate ideas such as that of social Darwinism, provided a 'scientific' justification for the decline of the Celt as an 'unfit' race in the process of 'social evolution'. Naturally, the Celts who proved most of a problem to this view would receive its heaviest attentions: hence the increasing intensity of presentations of the discontented Irish as racial inferiors. 'Black-lead them and put them over with the niggers', suggested the ever-charitable Thomas Carlyle, a sentiment paraphrased with typically hypnotic eloquence by D. H. Lawrence (1885–1930):

> He was a young Irishman … he had the silent enduring beauty of a carved ivory negro mask, with his rather full eyes, and the strong queerly-arched brows, the immobile, compressed mouth; that momentary but revealed immobility, an immobility, a timelessness which the Buddha aims at, and which negroes sometimes express without ever aiming at it; something old, old and acquiescent in the race. Aeons of acquiescence in race destiny, instead of our individual resistance. And thus a swimming through, like rats in a dark river.[31]

Outside Ireland, the 'acquiescence in race destiny' was more gently treated than through such similetic smears, though the idea of the Celts as a race in decline remained. 'Celtic Darwinism' proved a key reinforcement to the idea that the Celts, though unfitted to territorial identity, had left a kind of hereditary cultural imprint on British society which helped give it a gentler, more sympathetic and feminine dimension. Figures such as the Scottish writer William Sharp (1855–1905) took this to its logical conclusion by living a double life as the woman writer 'Fiona MacLeod' for the last 12 years of his life, even giving her a separate entry in *Who's Who* and answering enquiries directed to her in altered handwriting. 'Fiona MacLeod' wrote a series of fey romances based in the Scottish Gaeltachd, which portray an exhausted society in decline: her name, the feminine of 'Fionn', indicates the feminized qualities of the Celtic heroic which Sharp strove to express. In *Pharais* (1893) for example, 'her' first novel, Lora and Alasdair, who suffers from hereditary madness, the 'mind-dark' of the Celtic peoples, attempt to commit suicide in the Cave of the Sea-Woman (return to Celtic womb/tomb). This proves unsuccessful, and Lora bears a blind child which dies, while her husband wanders along the seashore naked and crowned with moonflowers (symbolizing night/oblivion/the feminine, as in the traditional sun–moon dichotomy). The people of this Celtic world are presented as instinctual, intuitive, Catholic, sentimental, weak, passive and grossly superstitious. Unbearably slushy and lugubrious as the reading of this material now is, 'Fiona MacLeod''s fiction was one of the powerful influences in shaping twentieth-century elegizing of the Celt, and Sharp was, unlikely as it may seem, one of the propagandists-in-chief of a Celtic revival. In *Lyra Celtica* (1896), Sharp emphasizes Celtic cultural renewal,

while taking care to place it in an Arnoldian landscape of Britishness:
Celticism, claims Sharp, is just as easily discovered in 'Sussex and Hamp-
shire' as in 'Connemara or Argyll', and the Celt is 'spreading innumerable
fibres of life towards a richer and fuller, if a less national and distinctive
existence'. This cultural renewal, which is seen in a kind of *fin de siècle*
cocktail of 'tragic gloom' and 'old romance', is one of *mentalité*, not
nationality.[32] Predictably, there was Irish opposition to Sharp's ideas as
expressed by both his personae: George Russell ('AE': 1867–1935), Yeats's
friend and associate, attacked 'Fiona MacLeod' in the *New Ireland Review*
'for unsound ideas and derivative pseudo-Celticism'.[33]

Many were attracted, however, by just these ideas: the nostalgic fantasy
world of a beautiful faded West, full of 'The plaided ghosts of buried centuries' who 'Mix in phantasmal sword-play, or … wander o'er / Loved
scenes where human footstep comes no more', as Sir Noel Paton put it in
'Shadowlands'.[34] Pittendrigh Macgillivray reinforced the point in a speech
given at the Caledonian Hotel in Edinburgh on 21 November 1911: 'The
Gael … had gone forth in the quest of a dream … spoilt children of the
mist … Were they not Romance personified! … born with the fairies' gift
of second sight, and a little handful of gladness wherewith to outweigh
the evil of things.[35]

Journals such as *The Celtic Magazine* (founded 1876) reiterated essentially nostalgic and emotive definitions of their subject under the cloak of
an embracing enthusiasm: pieces such as 'The Celtic Side of Burns' by
James Cunningham are all too typical in this fixation on the 'Celtic' as an
ethno-cultural mindset.[36] Even Patrick Geddes's Celtic revivalist *Evergreen*
of 1895–6, which proclaimed 'a time of Renascence', largely remained
a vehicle for images of 'the majesty of Celtic sorrow, the eerie song of
northern winds … the chant of Ossian … amid the underlying moan of
Merlin for a passing world', indulging Celticism only in the context of 'the
larger responsibilities of united [British] nationality and race'.[37]

Celtic revivalism gained ground towards the end of the nineteenth century not only in Britain but abroad, where Henri d'Arbois de Jubainville
and Anatole Le Braz were producing works such as *Le cycle mythologique
Irlandais et la mythologie celtique* and *Le Theatre Celtique*. 'By the end of
the century', as Ann Saddlemyer informs us, 'innumerable scholars,
organisations and periodicals were devoted to the recovery of the Celt'. In
1899, a 'Pan-Celtic Society' was founded,[38] and by the turn of the century,
pan-Celtic congresses had begun.[39] The spirit of the Celtic revival even
seeped into the works of apparently unlikely writers, such as Edward
Thomas and A. E. Housman, whose western gaze echoed the association

of the Celtic lands (here the Welsh borderland) with marginality, mortality and decline: the 'ancient wrong ... ancient ill' of the Celt abused by the Saxon being a type for the general experience of mankind.[40] Likewise, Arthur Conan Doyle dwelt on the mystic depths of Celtic vengefulness in the Sherlock Holmes story 'The Devil's Foot'.[41]

An additional dimension was given to such approaches by the fresh enthusiasm for the Stuart dynasty (and, by extension, its Celtic adherents) which sprang up in concert with the centenary of Bonnie Prince Charlie's death in 1888 and the Exhibition of the Royal House of Stuart in London the following year. Well over a thousand artefacts and pieces of memorabilia were on show in this display of sentimental Jacobitism which, although patronized by Queen Victoria, entered the names of post-Stuart monarchs in parentheses where they were listed, thus implying a lack of legitimacy in the ruling dynasty.[42] Almost incredibly, a neo-Jacobite movement sprang up, which attracted many of the artists and men of letters of the time with its preference for Stuart romance over Victorian industry and Celtic nostalgia over Saxon business sense. In an age of *épater les bourgeois*, a display of preference for Celtic marginalia over stolid metropolitan respectability was an attractive badge for the artistic *poseur*, and some others who, remarkably, appear to been serious in their desire to restore the Stuarts.[43] A. C. Macdonell dedicated his *Lays of the Heather* (1896) to Prince Rupert of Bavaria, the Stuart heir: the poems it contains are a cocktail of British militarism and nostalgia where 'In realms of art the Celtic fairies play'.[44]

The Royalist, the first of the journals of these Jacobite societies, was launched in 1890. It carried articles which, among other things, stressed the distinction between Cornish and English identity, Irish Jacobite songs and code and Welsh Jacobitism.[45] There was also an association between Charles as the 'white king' and the 'whiteness' of the Celtic lands. *The Royalist*'s Celticist sentiments were of a piece with the somewhat nostalgic legitimism it professed, by contrast with *The Legitimist Ensign*, the journal of the Legitimist League, which actually sought to restore the Stuarts and ran a poster campaign in London on the eve of Edward VII's coronation in June 1902.[46] Yet even such politics of charade could support serious developments: in Scotland, the Nationalist and neo-Jacobite *Fiery Cross* journal, edited by Theodore Napier, blended both impossibilist Stuart nostalgia and the beginnings of modern Nationalist aims and means of agitation. Eccentric extremist as in many respects he was, Napier's journal attacked imperialism ('Scotland in 1746 = Transvaal in 1901') and militarism and commented on the cultural structures of Scot-

tish society in a manner which would be familiar to the nationalist theorists who followed him.[47] As well as apparently instituting the Culloden
anniversary commemoration which still takes place, Napier organized 'a
diamond jubilee petition to Queen Victoria protesting against the misuse
of national names' (i.e. 'England' and 'English' for Britain as a whole) that
may have attracted more than 100,000 signatures.[48] His journal ran for
eleven years, a good record in this era of the transient 'little magazine', and
among its aims were the restoration of the Stuarts, the Scottish Parliament, the clan system and 'the Restoration and Preservation of the Celtic
language and national garb'. *The Fiery Cross* also called for the 'Union of
the Celtic Races' (and for repeal of England's Union with both Scotland
and Ireland). Despite its romanticist tone (Napier dressed 'in the Scottish
Celtic garb of pre-Revolution times'), this Jacobite enterprise had a practical side, calling for the foundation of a 'A Scottish National Party'
(apparently the first-ever use of the title) and the politicization of a pan-
Celtic League, which would terrify John Bull:

> There is one thing that doth me affright,
>> If these three curs [the Celtic lands] should only agree,
> They'd viciously turn then and bite,
>> And biting would set themselves free.
>
> 'John Bull and his Vassals'[49]

Napier's journal tried to resuscitate the idea of Scottish history as a struggle for liberty, and called for the teaching of Scottish history in Scottish
schools. Amidst all its impractical extravagances it offered the beginnings
of a recognizably modern critique of certain aspects of Scottish society
and the Anglo-Scottish Union relationship. Napier's work was evidence
that hard politics could grow out of absurd romance.[50]

That amorous, violent man, renowned Cuchulain

> Is this country destined to resume its ancient position as the Hellas of the
> North some day? Is the Celtic mind ... destined to enrich the civil con-
> science with new discoveries and new insights in the future? Or must the
> Celtic world, the five Celtic nations, driven by stronger nations to the edge
> of the continent, to the outermost islands of Europe, finally be cast in the
> ocean ... Only our supermen know how to write the history of the future.
>
> James Joyce[51]

> Since the English occupation we have had no national art in Ireland at all,
> and there is not the slightest chance of our ever having it until we get that
> right of legislative independence so unjustly robbed from us ... The poetry

and music of Ireland have been ... the very bulwark of patriotism.

Oscar Wilde[52]

Despite the activities of such as Theodore Napier, the real threat to the Victorian image of the Celt came from a quarter other than that of Jacobitical nostalgia. Land reform, and the development of Land League politics in both Scotland and Ireland fed on an image of the Celt which, while nostalgic, had powerful implications for contemporary politics. It has been argued that one of the key texts here was W. F. Skene's (1809–92) *Celtic Scotland* (1880), which put forward a vision of Celtic agrarian society as a kind of golden age on which Anglo-Saxon ideas of private ownership and landlord rights had been imposed. Such a view had its forerunners – the idea of such traditional land rights can be found in Sir Walter Scott – but Skene stated it with unusual and idealistic power. Arguing that 'private property in land did not exist at first, but emerged from a right of common property vested in the community', Skene to some extent laid the foundations for what the twentieth century was to know as 'Celtic Communism', and in doing so provided a vision of Celtic society not as savage or disorganized, but rather collectivist and ideal:

> Yet though the conscious socialist movement be but a century old, the labouring folk all down the ages have clung to communist practices and customs, partly the inheritance and instinct from the group and clan life of our forefathers and partly because these customs ... without them social life was impossible.

As James Young argues, Peter Kropotkin endorsed Skene's views in 1912, when he claimed in *Mutual Aid* that the 'communist aspect of social life' was still to be seen in Lowland Scotland itself.[53]

Celtic revivalists 'seized on Skene's reconstruction as a social system ... in many ways preferable to contemporary lowland society': the Scottish patriot John Stuart Blackie contrasting the 'gentle, hospitable, hardy, loyal' Highlander with the demoralized rabble of the towns, going on to state that the clan system was 'the best possible system of government that has ever been or ever will be devised', destroyed by 'the virus of a systematic selfishness'. This was strong meat indeed: the idea that Celtic society provided good *government* being both new and remarkable.[54]

Throughout the 1880s members of the Celtic societies were active in the Land League pressing for the land reform which arrived via the Napier Commission of 1885 and the Crofters' Act of 1886. Pressure from such revivalists helped to stem the 'utilitarian premises' of landlordism and Clearance. The rehabilitation of the 'peasant proprietor' in some mainstream political economy was reinforced by the revivalist stress on the 'immemorial' qualities of Celtic community land use. On the Napier Commission itself, 'Celtic scholars demanded nothing less than the restoration of the highland township, as a surrogate for the clan-a community to which the individual property rights of existing landlords could be transferred'.[55] It is worth noting that more than a hundred years later land reform policies being put forward by the Labour Party in Scotland in 1999 still appear to rest on these concepts of community vs. landlordism. This emphasis on renewing for the twentieth century features of a society which the eighteenth had thought quaint was a major shift: it was thus no coincidence that it provided (albeit limited) political gains. Moreover, it was, or could be held to be, masculine: the stress was on the clan, the community of (male) tacksmen and tenants whose common purpose had once formed the chief's 'fighting tail', and who now needed an opportunity to rediscover their own heroic dimension. This idealism was of course not without its chauvinistic side, and the afterlife of Skene and Blackie's vision of the Celt in Scotland has led in the twentieth century not only to hazy idealization of the civilization of the 'Lords of the Isles', but also to the downright chauvinism of portrayals of the Gael in the media, series such as Channel 4's *The Blood is Strong* (1988) being a particularly marked example of this.

The consequences of these points of view were yet more dramatic in Ireland. The historicizing of Skene in Scotland and of Irish writers such as Eoin MacNeill (1867–1945), who portrayed 'the Irish as descended from a pagan warrior civilization ... who, when converted to Christianity, transformed Ireland into a unique island of sanctity and learning', played an important role in positively redefining the Celt and Celtic society. W. F. Skene's view of an idealized Celtic society at odds with mechanism and materialism can be detected in the writings of James Connolly (1868–1916) (who may have brought it with him from Scotland) and Michael Collins (1890–1922). Connolly viewed 'pre-Norman' Ireland as 'a kind of primitive socialist utopia',[56] while Collins likewise voiced precepts recognizably present in Skene when he wrote that 'Gaelic civilisation ... never exalted a central authority ... The land belonged to the people ... held for the people by the Chief of the Clan.'[57] Collins's terms would have been recognizable to many Scottish Celtic revivalists, as would Aodh de Blacam's (1890–1951) similar stress on 'the communal Gaelic State' with its 'communal ownership of the land'.[58]

The political cataclysm which transformed Ireland between 1916 and 1922 has helped to obscure these close links between the Irish and

Scottish Celtic Revivals. The masculinized, revivified Celt was centrally an Irish creation, but one influenced by and in turn exerting its influence on Scotland. By most measures of nationality, James Connolly was a Scot: described as 'Scotto-Hibernian' even in Dublin (where he came from Edinburgh at the age of 28), he spoke with a Scots accent and named his daughter, born in 1907, 'Fiona' after William Sharp's alter ego. Described by a contemporary as 'the most able propagandist ... that Scotland has turned out', Connolly was aware of the 'rural collectivism' of Land League politics and the Skenian view in Scotland, which he married successfully to its corresponding clannic 'primitive communism' in Ireland.[59] Claiming that before the time of the Normans, 'the Irish people knew nothing of absolute property in land', Connolly saw in 'the sagacity of ... Celtic forefathers ... the more perfect organization of the free society of the future'.[60] Yet when he wrote these words in *Erin's Hope* (1896), Connolly's major exposure to such ideas had come from Scotland, not Ireland. Connolly's Scots-Irishness is under-researched, as is the influence of Scottish ideas at pan-Celtic events in the 1890s following the foundation of the Pan-Celtic Society in 1888.[61] Padraig Pearse was present at some of these, such as the Eisteddfod and the Highland Mod in Edinburgh.[62] Douglas Hyde and Standish O'Grady wrote for Patrick Geddes's *Evergreen*,[63] while the Gaelic Athletic Association was founded in Scotland in 1897, thirteen years after its Irish parent: in 1899, Pearse visited the Glasgow GAA.[64] In 1894 Maud Gonne (1866–1953) was encouraging Irish nationalist links in Scotland (to the 'shadowy "Highlander" organizations' of Samuel MacGregor Mathers (1854–1918), who enjoyed the Jacobite title of 'Count Glenstrae'), while in 1896 Yeats was appealing to William Sharp on 'the need to further "the political understanding and sympathy of the Scotch Welsh and Irish Celts"'.[65] By the early years of the twentieth century there were eleven Sinn Fein branches in Scotland, mostly, it is true, dominated by expatriate Irishmen.[66] Ironically, Michael Collins once reconnoitred a plan to take Scotland's Stone of Destiny from Westminster before deciding on it as impractical:[67] the feat was of course accomplished by a group of Scottish students in 1950, the most prominent of whom, Ian Hamilton QC, was an approved candidate for the Scottish Parliament elections almost half a century later. So does the whirligig of time bring in its revenges.

In Ireland, Standish O'Grady, although a Unionist, provided a profoundly nationalist agenda in his presentation of the Ulster and Fenian cycles of Irish myth in *History of Ireland, Heroic Period* (1878), *Finn and his Companions* (1893) and *The Coming of Cuchulain* (1895). Conceived in terms which owed a significant debt to the heroicizations of Macpherson's *Ossian*,[68] O'Grady's mythic representations provided a 'warrior' discourse to compete with Arnoldian 'emotionalism'. O'Grady's observation that 'the legends ... represent the imagination of the country; they are that kind of history which a nation desires to possess', was to prove prophetic, more so than his hope that the Ascendancy would take over the function of the former warrior Celtic aristocrats.[69] Celticist interpretations by political reformers were simply too strong to be resisted: the Land Leaguer Michael Davitt (1846–1906), for example, argued that 'Ireland and its race have a mission in the world ... greatly differing from Anglo-Saxonism'. Attempts to ethnicize the Celt as alien and separate him from territorial ambitions were overturned by such views: the 'race' was also the nation, 'Ireland' (although ethnicity was largely defined by political sympathy rather than in racial terms).[70]

It has been argued that O'Grady had begun to rid Irish Celticism of any tinges of a 'disabling femininity', though on the other hand his images of 'the proud amazon' of Irish heroic literature are converted into Victorian 'fainting heroines' in the cause of this masculinization.[71] Whatever the triumphs or limitations of O'Grady's approach, it was W. B. Yeats who provided the fullest articulation of the attack on Arnold (and indeed Macpherson), and the recrudescence of a heroic male Celticism: in fact he encouraged O'Grady to continue to 'market' his vision of Cuchulain.[72] In Yeats's early writings 'he still apparently subscribed to the Arnoldian view of the Celt as dreamy, sensitive and doom-laden', but references are already creeping in to ideas of 'Fatherland' and 'heroic deeds'. Some of Yeats's earliest poems and articles were printed by *The Gael*, weekly newspaper of the Gaelic Athletic Association. Critical of the 'stage-Irish buffoon created for an English audience', Yeats castigated 'the convivial Ireland of the tear and the smile, a manageable, Unionist Ireland that need not be taken seriously'. Such sentiments were bound to clash with the sentimentalism of the feminized Celt, and as early as 1886 Yeats began, in an article on the Unionist poet Sir Samuel Ferguson, to reconstruct that image with a new emphasis on the 'persistence, implacable hate, implacable love' of the Celt, which began to articulate the language of twentieth-century Irish Republicanism.[73] In 1887, Yeats anticipated Arthur Griffith (the founder of Sinn Fein) by comparing Hungarian and Irish nationalism, while in 1893 it was Yeats's collection of stories called *The Celtic Twilight* which gave its name to the entire movement. In *The Wanderings of Oisin* (1889), his first long poem, Yeats deliberately translated Fionn's companions not as 'Fena' or 'Fianna', but 'Fenians', thus providing 'an intentionally political echo' of the Irish nationalists of 1848 and 1867.[74] Throughout the poem, Oisin's reviewing of his own past lacks the self-involved nostalgia of Macpherson's Ossian: rather, there are implicit hints of a coming 'final defiance'.[75] One image, that of the falcon and the falconer in Book III, was revisited in Yeats's evocation of revolutionary apocalypse, 'The Second Coming', thirty years later.[76] Although here as elsewhere in Yeats's early poetry, there is still much imagery devoted to the fading, twilit and feminine qualities of *fin de siècle* Celtic nostalgia, Oisin's concluding speech to Patrick is of a different order, with its passionate embrace of the martial destiny of the Fianna, at war against the demons of hell.[77] Whether or not these 'demons' represent a traditional view of alien influence (Yeats stressed the importance of the *aisling* tradition elsewhere[78]) matters little: the barely suppressed call for renewed and liberating violence is one by which Yeats (in this mood – sometimes he called it more cautiously a 'delirium of the brave') is re-masculinizing the Celt and banishing the shadows of the Romantic Ossian. Just as the Burkean sublime inhabited the obscurities of Macpherson's Fianna, so 'a terrible beauty is born' out of the clarity of Yeats's Fenians.[79]

Yeats drove home the point. By the early 1890s he was publicly noting that 'Moses was little good to his people until he had killed an Egyptian … we wish to grow peaceful crops, but we must dig our furrows with the sword'.[80] In *The Countess Cathleen* (1892) he presented a play set during the Famine, where sacramental fidelity conquers the money-grubbing utilitarianism of the demonic (and by implication English) merchants. Yeats's allusion to Catholic theology in the play, that 'A learned theologian has laid down / That starving men may take what's necessary / And yet be sinless',[81] was itself neatly paralleled in contemporary agricultural agitation, when James Connolly and Maud Gonne circulated a leaflet in Mayo to the same effect, 'Rights to life and the Rights of Property', which quoted several Church authorities.[82] If Cathleen in this early play is 'an image of the nation', *Cathleen Ni Houlihan* (1902) expressed Yeats's nationalism at its most explicit, with the Sean Bhean Bhocht's appearance to call the hero (and by extension the audience) to sacrifice themselves utterly for Ireland: 'they that have red cheeks shall have pale cheeks for my sake, and for all that, they shall think they are well paid'.[83] As in *The Countess Cathleen*, the characters who will not listen to this appeal are materialist and money-grubbing: the moral is that 'to strive for mere material prosperity was to become English; to compensate for material penury with imaginative wealth was to become Irish'.

Although the play has a woman as a central figure, it is (and this Yeats's

play has in common with the picture of Cathleen Ni Houlihan given by
Maud Gonne to Pearse's school[84]) in essence a call to male violence,
memorialized and sacralized, seeking the bloodshed of the 'devoted' male
victim for his female nation: it was no coincidence that Yeats's later plays
such as *A Full Moon in March* (1935) dealt with men killing themselves in
symbolic devotion to a woman. As he informed Lady Gregory in 1903,
'My work has got far more masculine': the nation remained feminized,
but in a new active relationship with the heroic Celts who were her faith-
ful servitors. It was in vain that the revivalist academic Eoin MacNeill
commented in 1916 that 'we have to remember that what we call our
country is not a poetical abstraction ... There is no such person as Caitlin
Ni Uallachain [Cathleen Ni Houlihan] or Roisin Dubh [Dark Rosaleen]
... who is calling us to serve her'.[85] The die had already been cast. Stephen
Gwynn observed that 'I went home asking myself if such plays should be
produced unless one was prepared for people to go out to shoot and be
shot' (later characterized by Yeats as 'Did that play of mine send out / Certain men the English shot?').[86] Yet more significantly, Arthur Griffith, the
founder of Sinn Fein, commented on 12 April in the *United Irishman* that
'nothing save victory on the battlefield could so strengthen the national
spirit as the creation of an Irish theatre'.[87] *Cathleen Ni Houlihan* was but
the political counterpart of 'the vivifying spirit' of excess which Yeats
found at the heart of 'The Celtic Element in Literature', 'a new intoxica-
tion for the imagination of the World'.[88] This twentieth-century Irish
nationalism certainly proved itself to be: 'I dreamt of enlarging Irish hate,
till we had come to hate with a passion of patriotism', Yeats stated in 1907;
in 1903 he said that a nation, 'like a great tree', should lift its 'boughs
towards the cold moon of noble hate no less than the sun of love'. Sharp's
feminine moon was now more 'Blood and the Moon' than moonflowers,
for Yeats had a plan for 'a national ideal' 'more enduring than those of
Brunnhilde, Siegfried, Parsifal: the spiritual destiny of the Celt'.[89]

Yeats's writing gave vitality to the heroic Celtic past on a new scale. He
earnestly praised his co-workers in this task, such as Lady Gregory
(1852–1932), whose *Cuchulain of Muirthemne* (1902) and *Gods and
Fighting Men* (1904) (she also contributed to *Cathleen Ni Houlihan*)
appeared in the first years of the new century. Much as Yeats lionized
O'Grady and Lady Gregory for their representations of Cuchulain, it was
his own envisioning of the heroic Irish past which was political dynamite.
Yeats's and Maud Gonne's plan for a 'Castle of the Heroes', a kind of acad-
emy of heroic Celticism with Rosicrucian overtones, was never realized
by its original proponents (though it remained a matter of nostalgia for

Yeats as late as 1938),[90] but was manifested in a close relation, Padraig Pearse's experimental schools at St Enda's and St Ita's, for boys and girls respectively.[91] Countess Markievicz did something of the same extramurally, when she founded Fianna na hEireann, a deeply nationalistic 'boy-scout militia': 'Even the Irish equivalent of the boy scout movement, the Fianna, was based on the Cuchulain idea of youth enlisted in the service of the nation, and trained to die, if need be, for the nation.'[92] The heroic figures of mythology were beginning to make their political presence felt.

At St Enda's, opened in 1908, Pearse emphasized the 'Boy-Deeds of Cuchulain' and other important (fighting) qualities of the Gael. Pearse's educational purpose in what was quite a modern school, with extensive self-government for pupils,[93] was by contrast ancient: 'to recreate and perpetuate in Eire the knightly tradition ... the high tradition of Cuchulainn ... the noble tradition of the Fianna ... the Christlike tradition of Colm Cille'. In 'the main hall' of the school there was 'a large mural of the young Cu Chulainn taking arms'. This was the ancestor of the Oliver Sheppard statue of Cuchulain in the Post Office, where Pearse was to live out his 'myth of redemptive self-sacrifice'.[94] Later, not only Pearse, but Cathal Brugha and Michael Collins were to be identified with the hero: Cuchulain loomed over the typology of the period.[95] As Desmond Ryan, sometime teacher at St Enda's, was to put it, 'Cuchulain was an invisible but important member of the staff'.[96]

Pearse's Cuchulain shows some notable similarities to Yeats's, although the influence on Pearse of O'Grady and 'the German thinker, J. G. Herder' has been thought to be greater.[97] For Yeats, Cuchulain was a Blakean Orc-figure, 'creative joy separated from fear', in a genesis which transposed the Celtic hero from the sentimental nostalgic dimension of Romantic Primitivism to the revolutionary-visionary dimension of Romantic radicalism. Blake's Orc is a figure of international revolution in America and France and also (in contrast to the feminized Celt) of emergent and virile masculinity. Cuchulain's 'heroic manhood' was important to O'Grady, his 'spiritual beauty' to George Russell, but it was Yeats's image of the creative, rejuvenating Cuchulain, 'the man of passions and ungovernable will'[98] which is most closely echoed in Pearse's stress on Cuchulain's links with youth, rebirth and political violence, combined with the terrifying potency of Catholic sacramentalism, itself expressed in frequently blasphemous terms, as when Pearse said that 'we may have to devote ourselves to our own destruction so that Ireland can be free'.[99] Pearse's Skene-like idealization of the Gaelic polity was combined with his Catholicism to suggest a combination of 'the pagan ideals of strength and truth ... the

Christian ideals of love and humility'. 'There seems little doubt', F. S. L. Lyons observes, that 'for him [Pearse] both the crucifixion and the legend of Cu Chulain pointed the way to the sacrifice of one man for the benefit of the people.' Yeats obligingly memorialized Pearse in his own terms within, of course, the context of 'A General Introduction for my [i.e. Yeats's] Work' (1937): 'in the imagination of Pearse and his fellow soldiers, the sacrifice of the mass had found the Red Branch in the tapestry; they went out to die, calling upon Cuchulain.'[100]

As Thomas MacDonagh, one of the leading figures in the Rising, said in 1916, 'I am going to live things that I have before imagined'. It was such sentiments that paid oblique tribute to Pearse and Yeats and helped to ensure that the Easter Rising was 'almost as much a monument to the Irish Literary Renaissance as to the Irish Volunteers'.[101] This was symbolized in the very conduct of the Rising itself: Sean Connolly, an actor at Yeats's National Theatre, 'was to have appeared in a revival' of *Cathleen Ni Houlihan* on Easter Monday 1916: instead, 'the player Connolly' 'led his men on Dublin Castle and was shot dead in the first day's fighting' on the 'painted scene'.[102] As Yeats stresses in *The Death of Cuchulain*, one of his last plays:

No matter what's the odds, no matter though
Your death may come of it, ride out and fight,
The scene is set and you must out and fight.[103]

Pearse could not have wanted it better put: though Yeats's artistic ambivalence ensures that these words are spoken by Eithne, who betrays Cuchulain.

In attempting to create terminological distancing from the more feminized aspects of the Celtic Twilight, Pearse and his allies emphasized the 'Gael', rather than the 'Celt', as the motor for masculinized and militant confrontation with Saxon materialism.[104] It was the Gael who was to be 'the saviour of idealism in modern intellectual and social life'.[105] Douglas Hyde pointed this up in the stress he laid on the 'racial' quality of what was 'most Gaelic, most Irish'. This side of the Celtic revival led to a rapid expansion in the Gaelic League (founded in 1893),[106] from a matter of only 43 branches in the mid-1890s to 'nearly 600 branches' in 1904. Suddenly, everyone wanted to be a Gael, and almost everyone could be one. Despite the apparently ethnic rhetoric of the Gaelic League and those Home Rulers who appealed to an image of 'Celt and Saxon, locked in mortal combat', the fact was that many of the leaders of the Celtic revival and subsequently of the 1916 Rising had clearly English or English settler ancestry: indeed, it has been noted that in the Treaty debates of 1921, those of 'English' ancestry were more likely to be Die-hards (Pearse's own father had been born in Bloomsbury).[107] While it is true that the Gaeliciz- ers made much of the language issue, their ethnic rhetoric was essentially territorial, concerned with the renewal of the Irish nation. Even James Joyce, sometimes held up as a strongly anti-nationalist writer, wrote pos- itively of 'a new Celtic stock' compounded of the different peoples of Ire- land.[108] As with the Cuchulain cult, engagement with Irish mythology as the symbolic expression of nationhood and national qualities revitalized the image of the Celt, but at the cost of a ferocious devotion to abstracts and absolutes. In 1921, the pragmatists toned down their Cuchulain and Fionn (the Gaelic League sunk from 819 to 139 branches between 1922 and 1924), but others did not. The new IRA 'became ... the personifica- tion of the Fianna', addressed by an anti-Treaty Eamonn de Valera as 'worthy descendants of Claremen who fought under Brian Boru'.[109] Cuchulain, Queen Maeve and the Sean Bhean Bhocht continued to adorn Republican areas in Northern Ireland in the age of the Provisional IRA.[110] In a new phase of conflict, the myths found different uses. Both Standish O'Grady and Yeats would have been amazed to see Cuchulain bearing a Red Hand and a Union Flag on a 'UDA mural in East Belfast'.[111]

In Scotland, Theodore Napier's contribution was continued by Revivalists such as Ruaridh Erskine (1869–1952), whose political mix of Marxism and Celticism both foreshadowed the politics of Hugh MacDi- armid and echoed those of Countess Markievicz: like their Irish equiva- lents, figures like Erskine or Wendy Wood (1892–1981) were often born in England or had English ancestry.[112] Erskine 'was to do more than any other individual to implant Gaelic national ideals in Scotland in the first quarter of the twentieth century', and helped to lay the foundations for the Scottish Renaissance. In 1901, he 'was the Scottish delegate at the Pan- Celtic Congress held in Dublin' and was influenced by Irish nationalism, which he believed (ethnically and territorially) 'would be reciprocated ... in Scotland because of ... the underlying "racial cohesiveness" of the two nations'. Erskine planned for a future when a re-Celticized Scotland would join a 'Celtic federation' of nations. Both he and the revolutionary John Maclean (1879–1923) were supporters of 'Celtic communism', and welcomed the 1917 Bolshevik Revolution:[113] their radical mantle was later to pass to the leader of the Scottish Renaissance, Hugh MacDiarmid (Christopher Grieve 1892–1978). MacDiarmid, like many Celtic radicals who based their values in nostalgia for a vanished and imaginary polity, exhibited strong elements of other ideas, such as Jacobitism, not normally associated with Communist sympathies: in this too the Irish and Scots were often at one (see Introduction).[114] MacDiarmid's own adoption of the personae of eighteenth-century Jacobite poets echoed Yeats's use of the personae of Eoghan Rua Ó Suilleabhain and William Dall O'Heffernan in his creation of Red Hanrahan.[115] Like O'Grady and Yeats, MacDiarmid sought to re-masculinize Celtic culture, and indeed succeeded so well that he has often been blamed for his macho vision of Scottish culture and society by critics less radical than himself.

The Scots National League, founded in 1920 (a significant year in Irish history) owed its beginnings to such Celtic revivalism. Its principal leaders were Liam MacGille Losa (William Gillies) and Ruaridh Erskine. Many of the original members had a Land League background, and were thus the inheritors of Skene's vision of the Celt, now transferred to Irish politics with terrifying resonance. Despite this, and despite the sectarian issues inevitably raised by a predominantly Catholic Irish nationalism in Presbyterian Scotland, members of the League saw Irish Celtic culture as suffering oppression from the British state, and 'had a great affection and admiration for the Irish and their nationalist aspirations'. Gillies, in fact, 'impressed by the rise in Sinn Fein', launched Comunn nan Albanach in 1912 with the aim of securing 'a similar phenomenon ... in Scotland'. In 1916, 'he openly supported the Easter Rising', being 'dismayed by the lack of support it received from both Scottish socialists [despite this being Connolly's background] and Gaelic enthusiasts alike'. Gillies continued to argue for that 'Celtic communism, from which Wallace drew his inspirations ... to work out freedom for our beloved land' (the enduring and misleading presentation of Sir William Wallace as the guardian of the common man thus taking yet another form) and the National League agitated for 'an unadulterated Celtic state'. To this end MacDiarmid welcomed Irish immigration into Scotland, as sustaining 'the ancient Gaelic Commonwealth', while by 1930 the creation of Clann Albann, 'a paramilitary nationalist organization', suggested that the Scottish Celticists were bent on following the Irish example to a disturbing conclusion. It was thus not surprising that the new Scottish National Party rapidly distanced itself from Celtic Revivalism and chose rather to find its values in the douce petit bourgeois Presbyterianism of small-town provincial Scotland.[116]

If Celticism disappeared towards the political fringe in Scotland, it remained more central in the case of literature and the arts. Hugh MacDiarmid presented a strongly re-masculinized Scotland in the shape of *A Drunk Man Looks at the Thistle* (1926), while praise for the Irish example remained commonplace, MacDiarmid himself commenting that 'Scottish anti-Irishness is a profound mistake', while Somhairle MacGill-Eain's (1911–96) poem on the 'National Museum of Ireland' conjures up 'the hero / who is dearest to me of them all … Connolly / in the General Post Office of Ireland / while he was preparing the sacrifice'.[117] James Leslie Mitchell (Lewis Grassic Gibbon 1900–34) revived images of a feminized Scotland in the context of a Pictish folk culture in the North East,[118] while Neil Gunn (1891–1973) enthusiastically took up the ideas of the Irish nationalist Daniel Corkery's *Hidden Ireland* (1925) in articles such as 'The Hidden Heart' (1928) and novels like *Butcher's Broom* (1934), where the landlords of early nineteenth-century Scotland are portrayed in similar terms to those of Corkery's hostile Ascendancy. Gunn identified certain radical and folk values in Scottish society with Celticism, and argued like his Irish forebears in terms of the 'Celtic unconscious rebelling against the tyranny of the iron wheel', Celticism as anti-utilitarianism and anti-mechanism, personified as Dark Mairi of the shore in *Butcher's Broom,* or the transrational circular snake of Celtic mythology in *The Serpent* (1943).[119] Belief in the Celtic *geist* as the agent for renewal in Scotland was enduring. MacDiarmid, who had put it forward in 'Gairmscoile' in the 1920s, was still returning to it forty years later:

> Yet, beloved, as who upon the Cornish moors
> Breaks apart a piece of rock will find it
> Impregnated through and through with the smell of honey
> So lies the Gaelic tradition in the lives
> Of our dourest, most unconscious, and denying Scots.
> 'The Highlanders are Not a Sensitive People'[120]

Here, as in Arnoldian Britishness, the Celtic spirit was confined within the Scottish body, but the aim was to free it, not celebrate its incorporation.

Characteristic too of the Scottish Renaissance writers was a sympathy towards Catholicism and opposition to Presbyterian Unionism: such can be found in Edwin Muir's (1887–1959) *John Knox: Portrait of a Calvinist* (1930) or John Buchan's (1875–1940), *Witch Wood* (1927) . Novelists like Gunn remained sympathetic to the ideology of 'Celtic Communism', while the idea of a heroic renewing (male) Celt as an agent of deliverance for community or nation is likewise present in books such as Fionn MacColla's (1909–75) *The Albannach* (1932), which stresses Scotland's and Ireland's commonality of purpose symbolized in an Irish *aisling* (Aoghan Ó Rathaille's 'Gile Na Gile') which calls for the deliverance of Ireland by a

Stuart 'of Scottish blood'.[121] An even more explicit image of the heroic deliverer, subtly presented, can be found in the central character of Finn in Gunn's *Silver Darlings* (1942), who represents 'Finn MacCool come back to us'.[122] The struggle against Arnoldian Celticism at the end of the nineteenth century had a profound influence on Scottish literature in the twentieth, and in the end, though at a far slower pace than in Ireland, on the Scottish consciousness itself.

Celtic by image and design

If literature in both Ireland and Scotland reflected the tensions surrounding the term 'Celtic' at the turn of the twentieth century, the political significance of 'Celtic' design and artefact had a much longer history. In Scotland, the use of tartan to signify national antiquity and authenticity can be dated back at least to the marriage of James VI to Anne of Denmark in 1596, and by the end of the succeeding century tartan had become conflated with the symbols of Jacobite nationalist patriotism. Nor was this only the case in Scotland. English Tory squires used tartan to signify their 'honesty' which favoured a Stuart king and country, and the Jacobitically-inclined Sir John Hynde Cotton even had a bespoke set made for himself in Edinburgh in 1743–4. In the Rising of the next year, Charles Edward Stuart's army was dressed in tartan, where possible irrespective of origin or nationality: even the Manchester Regiment found itself wearing it.[123] Subsequently banned (until 1782) in civil society by the government because of its political associations,[124] tartan survived in the British army as a token of Celtic heroism and derring-do against all odds: thus it was useful when Scottish troops were chosen for especially risky duties, since it symbolized their suitability for them. Revived as a symbol of a militarized Celtic Scotland now loyal to the British Crown by Sir Walter Scott for the 1822 visit of George IV, tartan never looked back in a long diminuendo which has lasted to the present day. During the 1822 visit, guides were produced 'for Those Chieftains and Men of Unquestionable Family' as to 'the precise nature' of full Highland dress (with which they 'might not be wholly familiar'), so that they should appear as befitted the social class to which they belonged. Tartan was again legitimate as an object denoting Scottish identity, but only as the token of participation in a British caste system, to which the Scots' 'chivalrous barbarism' (Scott's words) had something to contribute.[125]

Tartan's role as a sign of British caste was of course boosted through its adoption by Queen Victoria at Balmoral in the 1850s, from which high point it steadily declined to the status of a designer accessory, with a host of different and largely factitious setts available to distinguish one as a member of a socially noble or ancient family: part of the heritized environment of kitsch, which gave a sense of belonging often bereft of the history its display was intended to celebrate. In keeping with this, tartan was much used for society weddings and evening dress, where the two major forms, the 'Montrose' and 'Prince Charlie', alike reeked of patriotic nostalgia and social caché (the 1960s began, in tartan as elsewhere, a more demotic and widespread usage). In society at large, by the mid-twentieth century the growth of a powerful new British popular culture had made matters worse. Tartan, once a symbol of Scottish identity and antiquity, almost became a total substitute, in the hands of the music hall giant Sir Harry Lauder and the comic Scot tradition, for the thing it had once symbolized (see Figure 14). The chief Celtic artefact of Scotland, which had once stood for nationalist pride and an ancient claim to fame, became ineluctably associated with comic buffoonery and the plaintive rendition of sentimental songs. Scots laughed at the American fondness for their icon, but in fact it was their own culture which was doing it most damage. Indeed, tartan's recently changing status has been best made plain by a decision taken on the other side of the Atlantic. When in 1998 the US Senate agreed Resolution 155, on the creation of a National Tartan Day on April 6, it was for the most un-Harry Lauder-like of reasons: the date in question was that of the Declaration of Arbroath, one of the earliest statements of anti-colonial nationalism in the world, and one which some in the United States felt was a herald of their own Declaration of Independence 450 years later:[126]

> For so long as there shall but one hundred of us remain alive, we will never consent to subject ourselves to the dominion of the English. For it is not glory, it is not riches, neither is it honour, but it is liberty alone that we fight and contend for, which no honest man will lose but with his life.[127]

Nationalism of this kind was tartan's original symbolic habitat. Yet in Scotland, many of the intelligentsia have felt that it could no longer be used for this purpose: indeed, a demythologizing school had arisen which denied that it ever had been, so dislocated had Scots become from their own history. Yet in the 1990s, and not just in the United States, the signs are that tartan is capable of enjoying a recrudescence, not just as Celtic chic rather than Celtic cliché, but as the means of marketing on a global scale a newly autonomous Scotland. It is also now to be found as a sign of

Figure 14 Henry Mayo Bateman, *Sir Harry Lauder*, painting, 1915. 8″ × 6″.
Tartan as mockery and entertainment.

Scotland and Ireland's common heritage: Irish tartan appears to be
increasingly on sale and available in Scotland, the shared experience of
the two nations now more unquestioned than has been the case for many
centuries. Tartan is not only the most widespread, most recognizable, and
most central of Celtic artefacts: it also stands, in Scotland's case, on the
brink of returning to serious use as a national symbol, not merely a
demeaning theme park frippery.

Scotland's Celtic artefacts have been symbolically the most volatile and
controversial (from the point of view of their 'genuineness' or otherwise),
partly because of the internal divisions visible in Scottish culture and historiography since at least the seventeenth century: in other words, Scotland has been the country which has been most adept at mocking and
belittling the artefacts which display its 'Celticism' because of its inherited
controversies over whether it is 'Celtic' or not. This need to demytholo-
gize perhaps betokened an unease with a comfortable state of affairs
where such artefacts made no statement of meaningful difference, acting
merely as a set of ethno-cultural markers within the British military and

to a lesser extent civil castes: hence tartan (for example) served as a most unproblematic image of Scottishness outside Scotland itself. No Welsh or Irish artefacts have been so clearly adopted as were the Scottish pipes and tartan: Irish regiments might put shamrocks on their notepaper and the Royal Welsh Fusiliers sing 'Men of Harlech' in a quaint recollection of victory over the Saxon belied by their uniform, but the cases were hardly comparable. Partly as a result, it was easier for artefacts to serve as signs of restorative political awareness in Ireland. In Scotland, what dwindled into acceptable kitsch became in Ireland the visible sign of renewed politico-territorial distinctiveness.

By the 1840s, the frontispiece of *The Spirit of the Nation* was already showing the aggressive qualities which would mark a good deal of nineteenth-century Celtic depiction in Ireland, with the design by Frederic Burton showing an interlacing harpist and a young girl watching the rising sun, original emblem of Fionn and hence here of the reborn spirit of Fionn: it was naturally taken up as the 'emblem of the Fenians'. The green of Irish (Catholic) nationalism became increasingly widespread, both as statement and chic: even the novelist George Moore (1852–1933), not usually associated with his Irish roots, 'painted his hall door green' as a contribution to the Renaissance 'badly' wanted by the Celt. Moore also became involved in the Gaelic League, which placed a renewed emphasis on Irish music, dancing and storytelling, which in its turn was reflected in design, the Irish Arts and Crafts Revival contributing to images such as those of the Dun Emer Guild banners, 'designed by Jack B. Yeats and his wife and embroidered in 1902–03 by Lily Yeats and her assistants' and 'the revival of Celtic jewellery'.[128]

Naturally, given the agenda of the Gaelic League and policies aimed at 'The De-Anglicizing of Ireland', Celtic design rapidly consolidated its political overtones, which increasingly began to accompany the newly masculinized image of the Celt. One of the interesting features of Irish patriotic 'design' , if one can call it that, in the nineteenth century was the revivification of the Irish wolfhound, long an established national symbol but in the 1830s and 1840s a dying breed. Associated both with Fionn and Oisin, its survival 'in its present form, may be said to be a product of the Celtic revival'. Remnants were crossed with Scottish deerhounds to produce a new dog, for which Captain Graham was able to found the Irish Wolfhound Club in 1885.[129] By 1903, when Queen Maeve and her wolfhound appeared on the notepaper of the new National Theatre, it was possible once again for patriotic Irishmen to own the canine symbol of their nation, itself possibly linked to the pursuit of physical force nationalism, as in Yeats's 'Hound Voice', which celebrates 'chants of victory amid the encircling hounds'. Like the Scottish Deerhound, beloved of Sir Walter Scott, the wolfhound was a noble dog bearing witness to the warrior pursuits of a Celtic society from a now-vanished era: the restoration of its Irish national pedigree thus served as a rebuttal of the picture of the Irish as mean, immobile and poverty-stricken presented in the British media.[130]

The use of Irish materials such as bog wood in furniture was also evident in the nineteenth century, and where such materials were used, 'motifs ... in ... carving were generally Irish'. 'Bracelets of bog oak were ... popular', while the set of Irish national symbols – (shamrock, harp, round tower and wolfhound (oak was presumably served by the widespread use of the wood itself)) – appeared 'on tea services, glass jewellery, book covers, work-boxes, on banners, in graveyards, and ... [for Catholics] in church'. Indeed, by the end of the nineteenth century, the inevitable progression towards kitsch brought about by the mass production of charisma had rendered such artefacts 'suspect by the Celtic Renaissance':

> all four emblems as a group, and the shamrock by itself, were thought to indicate a shallow, sentimental and ineffectual feeling for Ireland, or to symbolize the lip-service paid to an Irish identity by the royal family and by the Viceroy and Castle officials. Curiously enough, round tower or wolfhounds on their own were acceptable. So were archaeological symbols like high crosses, Celtic interlace and the 'Tara' Brooch, since they were reminders of Ireland's great cultural achievements of the past.[131]

Scotland on the whole lacked this nascent Irish suspicion of kitsch. The Celtic revivalism of figures such as Patrick Geddes (1854–1932) and publications such as *The Evergreen* appeared to lack clarity of purpose, balancing their patriotism very carefully against 'the larger responsibilities of united nationality and race' which Scotland owed to Britain. The journal's promise to present a 'revival of ancient Celtic design' was imperfectly kept, though *Evergreen* designs were pretty clearly influential on some modern Scottish figures such as Alasdair Gray.[132] Otherwise, despite scenes such as *The Awakening of Cuchulain* and *The Combat of Fionn* from John Duncan's (1866–1945) decorations for Ramsay Garden in Edinburgh, the overwhelming stress in Scotland appears to have remained on dim feminine figures, patterning and the dreamy, mystical atmosphere of a fading civilization amply compatible with *On the Study of Celtic Literature* (see Figure 15).[133] It was not until a much later phase in Scottish

Figure 15 John Duncan, *Saint Bride*, painting, 1913. 8″ × 6″. Feminized and dreamy figures flit across the sea.

national identity's twentieth-century development that more Irish features could be seen, and then only at the fringes, where a faint echo of the Irish Renaissance could be discerned at the turn of the 1980s, when the extreme nationalist group Siol Nan Gaidheal (Seed of the Gael) adopted a quasi-paramilitary appearance based round elements of Celtic design, which also appeared on their posters. As 'a sign of a renewed Scottish Renaissance, a golden symbol of the rising sun of a Gaelic Scotland was emblazoned on the white banners of the new Siol Nan Gaidheal.' White was the colour of the Stuarts, and the Rising Sun was the emblem of Fionn: like the Irish Volunteers, Siol Nan Gaidheal presented an 'aggressive combination of militant activism and Jacobite romanticism'. Unlike the Volunteers however, SNG's threat was mainly sartorial.[134]

The stimulating influence of the Glasgow School on Art Nouveau, with its blend of 'Japanese, Primitive and Celtic art', was to an extent rendered possible because of the politically unchallenging nature of Scottish Celtic design.[135] Herbert MacNair (1868–1955) and Charles Rennie Mackintosh

(1868–1928) developed a style linked to 'the Celtic symbolism' of their artistic contemporaries, including John Duncan and Phoebe Traquair (1852–1936), who was herself Irish-born.[136] Vague and unthreatening in its Celticism, it gained international recognition, while in Scotland the combination of Scottish Renaissance massiveness combined with 'flowing Art Nouveau detail' contributed to a mixed and heritage-conscious architecture.[137] Period settle designs set the tone for a 'Celtic' furniture, while the design for the 1896 poster for Glasgow Institute of Fine Arts showed a mixture of traces of Celticism and the influence of Aubrey Beardsley. Besides the Glasgow School, the Celtic Revival symbolized by *The Evergreen* also contributed to a great expansion in Celtic subject-matter and design features.[138] Jessie M. King's (1875–1949) designs indicated the continuing influence of the dreamy, feminized and sentimentalized Celt, while Marion Wilson's (1869–1956) Celtic *Triptych* (1905) in beaten tin emphasized the variety of design use in this area. 'Mysterious' Scottish themes became common in paintings such as Edward Hornel's *The Brownie of Blednoch* (1889) and Hornel and George Henry's *The Druids: Bringing in the Mistletoe* (1890), which combines Pre-Raphaelite coloration with an exotic and extravagantly realized Celticism that offers implicit opposition to the Utilitarian progressive norms of the advanced industrial state, though one commentator has described it as 'Wagnerian as much as it is Celtic'.[139] Areas of artistic endeavour such as painting and furniture were supported by other fields of design, such as William Marshall's 1885 ceremonial dirk with a scabbard adorned with Celtic decoration, or the continuing use of Celtic design in plaid brooches. Celticism was visible throughout the country: William Robb's turn-of-the-century Ballater snuffbox was a case in point, with its 'thistles and celtic-style interweaving bands' providing an admixture of Scottish national representation and pan-Celtic iconography.[140] Such developments by and large continued to fulfil nostalgic and fashionable roles: it is instructive to compare sculptures such as J. Pittendrigh Macgillivray's bronze head of *Thenew, Mother of St Kentigern* (1915) with its Irish equivalents such as *The Children of Lir*.[141] Pearse's St Columba (Colm Cille), with 'great love' for the Gael, was arguably of a different order of cultural meaning. Pittendrigh Macgillivray was himself, of course, well able to give voice to the idea of the 'Children of the Mist' (*vide supra*), a limiting self-definition from which the artefacts of Celtic revivalism in Scotland by and large offered no escape.

In Wales, the Romantic fashion for *The Beauties of Cambria* (1821) and the Welsh landscape was accompanied as the nineteenth century progressed not merely by the enduring icon of the Bard, which seemed most resilient in Wales, but by vatic alter egos such as the image of the Preacher, which portrayed Welshness as both spiritually pure and politically unthreatening, as Peter Lord argues:

> The image of the preacher certainly expressed national pride, but it was also a part of the wider structure that allowed Welshness and Britishness to coexist. It was an expression of a kind of introverted and self-congratulatory patriotism which might prosper within Wales, and within a particular stratum of society … without threatening a broader British loyalty. The image of the preacher fed the myth of the moral superiority of the nation, and set in the context of imperial imagery it succeeded in giving the vague impression of Wales as the moral conscience of the Empire.[142]

If one accepts this argument, then Welsh self-images were being used to answer local needs rather than engaging in a wider dialogue: needs moreover which responded to external demands rather than interrogating them. Such were the basic principles for establishing a market in kitsch, which should focus our attention still more on the early scepticism of designer Celticism in nineteenth-century Ireland and its relative absence elsewhere.

By 1900, Celtic design was deeply integrated into the artistic expression of the Celtic countries, Scotland and Ireland in particular. In these terms it was the equivalent in artifice of pan-Celticism in the political and cultural world. In Scotland, its longstanding symbolic integration into British political and class norms rendered it a niche product: in Ireland, it and its accompaniments, such as Gaelic League membership, increasingly appeared to form part of a political agenda which contained in its symbolic expression elements of a redefinition of the (partly colonial – see Chapter 3) relationship between England and Ireland. The Celtic chic in the decorative arts which in 1899 allowed Liberty's to develop 'two highly successful ranges inspired by Celtic art: "Cymric" silverware and "Tudric" pewter', was by contrast null of any intention beyond chic (cf. the implicit presence of 'Tudor' and its contemporary association with heritage Surrey stockbroker house design in the title of the latter product).[143] On the other hand, the Irish wolfhound was very much alive.

Chapter 3

Nationality, identity and language

The postcolonial Celt?

Postcolonialism is one of the key areas in literary and cultural studies since 1980, having also broken through into history by way of an increasing awareness of the limitations of Eurocentric themes and examples in world history. As the colonial era drew to a close, the icon of Hellenism was challenged through a renewed emphasis on an Africanized Egypt in Cheikh Anita Diop's *The African Origin of Civilization* (1955), as well as in *Black Athena*, and the books in the same school which followed them. Western attitudes to the East have been anatomized by writers such as Edward Said, in *Orientalism* (1978) and elsewhere (although Said's view has recently been challenged by Linda Colley with regard to the seventeenth and eighteenth centuries). Within Europe itself, historians are increasingly conscious of the way in which selective West European examples have synecdochally and inappropriately stood for the whole range of European experience, in a process where 'the geography is as suspect as the generalizing is grandiose'.[1] In *Europe: A History* (1996) for example, Norman Davies argues that there are several kinds of axe-grinding Western history (e.g. Protestant, American, Imperial), and that all alike have devalued 'the diversity and the shifting patterns of European history' by various means, of which anachronism is one:

> Anachronism is particularly insidious. By taking transient contemporary divisions, such as the Iron Curtain, as a standing definition of 'West' or 'East', one is bound to distort any description of Europe in earlier periods. Poland is neatly excised from the Renaissance, Hungary from the Reformation, Bohemia from industrialization, Greece from the Ottoman experience.[2]

In his determination to correct these errors, Professor Davies, like many writers conscious of the postcolonial shift, does his utmost to show fairness to 'outsider' traditions, such as the Islamic civilization of medieval Spain. His identification of anachronism as a key perversion of historicity is one which descends ultimately from Butterfield's 1931 analysis of the nature of Whig history ('Real historical understanding is not achieved by the subordination of the past to the present'): it is of central importance to the correct understanding of Celticism's place in the postcolonial spectrum, as we shall see.[3]

Britain and British history have responded to the postcolonial shift, but with much greater inequality and uncertainty than is the case on a wider stage, due in no small part to the persistence of anachronistic reconstructions of 'Britishness', an identity which may well have only ever been held, except at times of war and crisis, by a relatively restricted elite. As late as 1998, the sociology of Britain and Britishness remains prey to easy assumptions which regard 'Britain as a leading European example of the stable nation-state, one that has remained free from nationalism'.[4] To some extent, J. G. A. Pocock's historic calls in two 1970s articles for a new 'British' history which took into account the variegated status of the 'Atlantic archipelago' were answered in the years that followed by the 'four nations' history of Hugh Kearney or John Morrill or the 'three nations' version espoused by Linda Colley. In Ireland a revisionist history developed which adopted a much less nationalist approach than had its predecessors, and tended to give British intentions and caricatures the benefit of the doubt. Clearly, this kind of history was amenable to the 'four nations' approach, suggesting as it implicitly did that Irish Britishness had been underestimated. At the same time, tensions which remain largely unexplored are clearly visible between such assessments and Said's view in *Culture and Imperialism* (1993) of Ireland as a nation as clearly and unproblematically colonial as Burma, or Linda Colley's anachronistic dismissal of the country from her accounts of Britishness. For writers such as David Cairns and Shaun Richards, 'Edward Said's statement of the relations of power inscribed in the discourse of Orientalism are equally applicable to Celticism', and they cite the 'notion of the Irish as a race of covert blacks' (or worse apes) in the Victorian period in support.[5] The Provisional IRA itself assumes a similarly anti-colonial sentiment, with its advice to its supporters that interrogators will regard them as '"Paddy", "Muck-Savage" or "Bog-Wog"', inferior tribesmen for whom the British aim is 'the bloody-minded destruction of our culture, our language, music, art, drama, customs'.[6]

Yet would the Burmese have produced so many poets, playwrights, politicians and soldiers accepted within the British Establishment as Ireland did? And to the answer that these were overwhelmingly Anglicans, it could be returned that English Catholics had for long periods been almost equally debarred from the heights of office. In other words, the

religious question cuts across the national one: even despite it, conformity was easier for Irishmen. Edmund Burke (1729–97) might have been
depicted as a potato-eating Jesuit, but he was a man of great influence and
greatly respected, an espouser, as George III himself said, of 'the cause of
the gentlemen', despite his Catholic connections and 'accent which never
quitted the banks of the Shannon'.[7] Matthew Arnold, indeed, described
him (with regard to his views on Ireland) as 'the greatest of English [*sic*]
statesmen'; and indeed Burke himself uses the pronoun 'we' to describe
English attitudes to Ireland. No Nigerian could have passed as 'English',
and few Australians either.[8] In this as in everything else, Burke was no
Burmese: yet his sympathy for India and oppressed Indians lends support
to the postcolonial reading of Ireland which his successfully British career
elsewhere undermines:

> This multitude of men does not consist of an abject and barbarous populace
> … but a people for ages civilized and cultivated … There have been (and still
> the skeletons remain) princes once of great dignity, authority, and opulence.
> There, are to be found the chiefs of tribes and nations. There is to be found
> an antient and venerable priesthood, the depositary of their laws, earning
> and history … a nobility of antiquity and renown; a multitude of cities, not
> exceeded in population and trade by those of the first class in Europe.

Conor Cruise O'Brien's argument that Burke's displaced Irish sympathies
fuelled his radical outlook on the colonies is a powerful one. Notable too
is the manner in which he writes of Hinduism (and later French Catholicism), as if they were spiritual mainstays to societies of comparable value
in their proper national environment to the claims of the Church of
England. The manner in which Burke became an Anglo-British patriot
was one which made him an instinctive pluralist in social and religious
matters: hence the keynote of his political thought is 'circumstances',
the differing demands and needs of differing societies. This pluralism was
alien alike to British imperialism and the universalist strains of the
Rights of Man in revolutionary France and elsewhere. Edmund Burke
was one of the few major figures from the Celtic countries to attempt
dialogue with British political norms. In doing so, he both developed
British political theory (e.g. through the doctrine of representation rather
than delegation as regards the duties of Members of Parliament) and
remained himself frustrated of high office in the British polity.[9] For most
who sought that office, conformity was the key. James Boswell's
(1740–95) displaced Jacobite nationalism found its correlative in the
Corsican liberation struggle under Pasquale Paoli; but at home the Laird

of Auchinleck was an assiduous seeker after every British office on offer which he felt he had a claim on securing, eventually deserting the Scottish Bar for the English in the hope of state reward. This turned out in the end to be the Recordership of Carlisle, the legal equivalent of 'go out and govern New South Wales'. Conformist as he tried to be, Boswell was not conformist enough.

If the eighteenth century witnessed the kind of division and uncertainty about how and when to conform discussed in Ken Simpson's *The Protean Scot* (1988), the mid-nineteenth consolidated, as suggested in Chapter 1, a unitary British identity based on common overseas achievement and seriously challenged at home only by Irish unrest and Scottish claims for greater dialogic contribution to Union. These were manifested in the National Association for the Vindication of Scottish Rights (which typically collapsed with the onset of the consolidatingly British Crimean War), and the Wallace cult, which led to the fund-raising campaign for a monument on the Abbey Craig in Stirling, finally opened in 1869. Others followed. Small though these concessions to patriotic sentiment were, *The Times* was impervious to dialogue, arguing that 'Wallace' was 'the merest myth' and stating that 'Scotchmen ... seem to do nothing but masquerade in the garments of their grandfathers' in a development stigmatized as provincialism.[10] The pattern was predictable: Wallace was an icon, even for Scottish Unionists, of politico-territorial selfhood, and hence far more irritating than Highland dancing and tossing the caber. The capacity of Wallace to irritate continues, of course, to be manifest in certain attitudes displayed towards *Braveheart*.

A unitary attitude to Anglo-British imperial values (discussed in Chapter 1) depended on an internal organic unity to sustain them as components of a single external ideology. For this reason, even sentimental politico-territorial displays in Scotland and Wales (as opposed to localist ethno-culturalism) were disruptive, and in Ireland stigmatized and dangerous. Burke's view that differences in civilization and politico-social circumstances should be respected was not accepted in the cases of the American colonies and India (though with regard to the latter country it had continuing minority support). In the imperial age, Burke remained in advance of much British Irish opinion in his attitudes to colonialism. *The Dublin University Calendar* for 1887 proudly lists the names of 86 alumni, 'Gentlemen, who have obtained Writerships in the Civil Service of India': as Ian Campbell Ross has noted, 'a shared sense of English national culture' pervades much of the *Calendar* throughout the latter part of the nineteenth century.[11]

Such evidence from Scotland would be (and is) used as evidence of complicity in Empire, support for Britishness and so on. In Ireland, the change in the country's status has removed its Britishness from the consciousness of British historians. As D. George Boyce notes, very little space is allotted by British history to 'the event which destroyed the unity of the United Kingdom': Irish Britishness is simply airbrushed out.[12] And yet the still-surviving complexity of the two countries' relations was borne witness to by the display of Queen Victoria's statue at Cork in 1995 to mark the 150th anniversary of the University College there. A protester 'was arrested for interrupting the proceedings with shouts of "What about the Famine?"', but 'dismissed by some as a nationalist crank'. Both the display of the statue and the reaction to the (apparently solitary) protest against it tell a much more interwoven story of historic identities than a simple colonial model would show, although more sophisticated postcolonial commentators might simply suggest that Ireland had a longer independent history than many former colonies, so that 'the generation born after the departure of the colonizing forces' would be more open to 'hybridity and cultural mixing' than those who themselves fought for independence. Whatever the truth of this (and it offers theoretical support to the current flourishing of Irish historiographical revisionism), the Cork incident clearly reveals a complex picture.[13]

The disappearance of Irish Britishness from the view of the *Britons* (1992) offered by many eminent historians is indicative of what is perhaps the central underlying problem for 'four nations' and postcolonial British history, as once for their Whig predecessors: that anachronism which manifests itself in an almost unconscious subjection to the status quo (this is in addition (as argued in Chapter 1), a particular problem in theories of nationalism). British historicity of this kind is constructed with half an eye on what Britain is in the late twentieth century: in true Whig fashion, the problems of modern identities form a template for judging centuries where the evidence for a problematized British narrative is slight, or where evidence for it from Ireland is overlooked. Ireland's colonial status is easy to overestimate because the country is now independent; Wales and Scotland's colonial position is (or has been) downplayed for the opposite reason: they are British. 'Four nations' historians too often concentrate on what made Britain congeal as a state, the issues of state formation: even where their agenda departs from this, their arguments tend to be on the *qui vive* for a British angle or perspective.[14] As a result, they often seek evidence which stresses homogeneity and commonality, downplaying or ignoring expressions of tension, oppression and difference, especially where these persist beyond the time of Anglo-Scottish Union. Ireland (now independent) is often called 'England's oldest colony', but Wales (the better candidate) is not so termed, because to do so would be to acknowledge its current territorial potential as an un-British nation, and to pose an implicit challenge to the cultural and national integrity of 'Britain'. England can have no 'British' colonies, because Britain *is* England is very much the unspoken assumption. Reliant on England (rather than small Continental countries) as a model for the development of the rest of Britain, 'four nations' historians are liable to view Scotland in particular as a simple and subordinate parallel to this chosen model in the process of state formation. Adopting Michael Hechter's (1975) theory of internal colonialism from a British to a Scottish dimension, such historians posit a central belt or south-eastern 'core' in Scotland which gradually succeeds in subduing a Highland/Northern and Welsh (in England's case) 'periphery'. As John Morrill writes:

> Both England and Scotland for centuries consisted of an Anglo-Norman core with a bare and fluctuating control over the mountainous wholly Gaelic-speaking borderlands to the North and West, and the Norse speaking fastnesses beyond those borderlands.[15]

Both England and Scotland? There are several things wrong with this statement. First, it is anachronistic, assuming a demographic and political domination of Scotland by the 'core' central belt which was not clearly the case in the sixteenth and seventeenth centuries (the period under discussion): in 1750, half of Scotland's population lived north of the Tay. Secondly, in the manner of generations of British historians, it makes Scotland English: 'Anglo-Norman' makes a fine Scot-free substitute for the 'Teuton Lowlander' of a century ago, and Scotland is thus once again a site of ethnic conflict rather than territorial consolidation. Thirdly, the statement is linguistically anachronistic in suggesting the remoteness of Gaelic, spoken by the Kings of Scots until after 1500 and in central Scotland much later: Alexandra Gordon, last speaker of Perthshire Gaelic, died in 1990. Fourthly, the defeat of the Norse at Largs in 1263 was arguably 'core' rather than 'peripheral', as Largs is only 25 miles from Glasgow. Fifthly, the distinctive contribution of northern and north-eastern Scotland to the culture and polity of the Scottish state was entirely non-core (Aberdeen is almost as far from Edinburgh as York is from London, and further than Wales), but nevertheless integrated. To take only one cultural example, early higher education in England revolved around Oxford, Cambridge, the Inns of Court and Gresham's College, all 'core'; in Scotland, there were two universities in Aberdeen and one (briefly) in Fraserburgh, 165 miles from Edinburgh. It would be possible to continue, but the qualities of a history which seeks conformity and minimizes difference and nuance are evident enough in the above: as Davies puts it, 'Diversity schematized is diversity denied'.[16] Unfortunately, they are also evident in centuries of British historical perspective on the Celtic 'other', which makes 'four nations' history's camouflaged Anglo-centrism all the more disappointing, and also fundamentally incompatible with the postcolonialism which succours it. Postcolonial theory rebuts the colonizing gaze, and anatomizes it; 'four nations' history, all too frequently, sees through its eyes afresh. As William Ferguson more wisely remarks, 'recent research … freed from the incubus of Germanist fixations, has shown that … Gaelic Scotland has left a marked imprint on the [national] institutions and culture'.[17]

Postcolonial theory, in the shape of stereotyping, the colonizing gaze, and the 'other' as recipient of the colonizer's fear and loathing, certainly has attractions in accounting for the Celtic experience as it has been depicted in the foregoing chapters. The simianization of the Irish and their depiction as 'blacks', the Celt's role as a Noble Savage, his importance as a weaker life-form in the definition of Anglo-Teutonic experience and the dismissal of Scottish and Irish customs and lifestyles, all have echoes in the wider Empire. In 1799, a visitor to St Kilda remarked that 'Nothing [in] Captain Cook's voyages comes *half* so low'; in the 1980s, the editor of the *Express* newspaper was still remarking 'that he would rather go looking for worms in a dunghill than visit Ireland', while other sympathetic Britons opined that 'the easiest way to learn Gaelic is to murder someone for the IRA' and that Ireland is outside the modern world, 'based on the pig and potato and presided over by the priest'.[18] The Celts, like Indians, were 'children'; just as blacks could not have built Zimbabwe, so English and French craftsmen must have erected Scotland's castles and cathedrals (twenty years ago, pre-*Black Athena*, the author heard this argument applied to suggest that the Greeks had built the best bits of Persepolis!); just as Indians should learn English, so Welsh, Scots and Gaelic must be excised. Michael Chapman, who has been amongst those most sceptical of linguistic oppression, argues that the famous example of the Lewis child who had a skull hung around his neck by the teacher for speaking Gaelic is one reiterated by numerous secondary texts,[19] but proved to be typical by none. This may be so, but I recall the use of Scots being sharply rebuked in my own schooldays in Aberdeen in the 1970s: with the advantage of having grown up within the texture of the culture, I see no reason to doubt accounts of widespread assaults on the indigenous language by authority figures at an earlier period, whatever the truth of the Lewis story.[20]

Secondly, the manner in which the Celtic revival used folk culture and a nostalgic vision of a classless peasantry (as well as more sophisticated notions of demotic culture such as Joyce utilized in *Finnegan's Wake*[21]) to sustain its nationalism in an Irish and to a lesser extent Scottish context was of a piece with emergent nationalisms everywhere. Ernest Gellner notes the importance of a 'putative folk culture ... healthy, pristine, vigorous' to the life of nationalism,[22] while Emyr Humphreys draws attention to the importance of 'myth-making ... among defeated peoples' as 'a source of consolation' and 'a most potent weapon'.[23] Unconsciously exemplifying Ferdinand Tonnies' 1887 definition, the Celtic Revival strongly adopted the *Gemeinschaft* of the rural idyll in opposition to the urban, industrial and utilitarian world of British *Gesellschaft* – David McCrone has recently argued that this remains an important factor in the self-image of the Celt and Celticism.[24] It lies at the core of much of Yeats's and Lady Gregory's presentation of an idealized peasant nation. These features were combined explosively in Irish Celtic revivalism after 1890, which, whatever its factual limitations, emphasized the bankrupt quality of 'British' nationalism in dealing with its internal diversity.

John Bull, adorned as he is with the Union Flag, was in the seventeenth century (he was not entirely invented by Dr John Arbuthnot) originally (and of course remains) an essentially English symbol, an 'invented tradition' in Eric Hobsbawm's and Terence Ranger's terms.[25] Moreover, even modern sociologists have been complicit in the strong elision between the cultural semantics of 'English' and 'British' which marks the colonial attitude towards diversity found in such traditions. In 1975, in *The British, Their Identity and Their Religion*, Daniel Jenkins wrote that the key British characteristics were 'reserve, respect for privacy, the ideal of the "gentleman", modesty, fair play, and the social style that derives from them'.[26] Not only are all these primarily English, they are southern English and middle- and upper-middle-class southern English to boot. That they are the values of public school Englishmen as surely as they have been those of public school Indians, Africans and Scots is not in doubt: they are the values of external, imperial Britain. They dominate and form the recipient to their mould: as signs of identity, they are more usefully seen in the Oxonian from Kenya than the Tyneside docker or Northern Irish Orangeman (who claims to be more loyal to Britain than Ian Paisley, heir to none of the above marks of 'identity'?). Yet the idea that there are real

and persisting 'British' features of just this type is, if in decline, an enduring one, sustained from without by Hollywood's procession of well-
spoken villains. Efforts to overcome the palpable anachronism and
class-based quality of such views was visible in the 'Cool Britannia' theme
(originally a label on Ben and Jerry's ice-cream, so postmodern as well as
postcolonial) associated with the 1997 Labour Government, which
accepted and courted representations of Britishness through vibrancy
and variety rather than through doomed images of reserve and nostalgia:
but, within six months of its appearance, this phrase was as readily
mocked as the backward-looking suburbanism of John Major had been a
few years earlier. The evident increasing unsatisfactoriness of the idea of
pan-British values often remains unanalysed: but the reason for it may lie
in the colonial, externalizing, 'core' nature of those values in the first
place. Many Scots adopted and adopt them, though fewer than before, as
badges of British class and power. There are still Indians, and even Irish
who do the same. But if Britishness depended on the British Empire, it is
doomed; and moreover, if so it is by its nature in part colonial, a demand-
ing appropriation which denies variety.

Part of the manner in which homogenous identities succeed derives
from not only the suppression of diversity, but also the suspension of
belief in that diversity or its value among those who are its heirs. This is
part of the process of consolidating the 'imagined community', in Benedict Anderson's phrase, itself redolent of Enoch Powell's view that 'the life
of nations no less than that of men is lived in the imagination';[27] in postcolonial terms, the systematic downplaying or rubbishing of Celticism
and Celtic culture was part of the British imagination in which many of
the Celts themselves took part. When Hunsey Vivian, MP for Swansea,
addressed the Swansea Eisteddfod in 1863 with the caution that the par-
ticipants should 'Remember that you are all Englishmen, though you are
Welsh', he was exemplifying the process of imagining a 'common attachment' to national (i.e. Anglo-British) values. The display of national culture could only be approved if it consented to disown its nationality.[28]

Of course, the contrary case can also be made: that the 'Celts' and
'Celtic' are themselves synthetic constructs which conceal equal levels of
diversity. This case, implicit both in Anderson's and Gellner's theories of
nationalism, though rebutted by the later work of Anthony Smith and
Adrian Hastings,[29] has been argued from a number of quarters, more
forcefully in the late 1990s as it became more apparent that the constitutional form of Britain was changing. Just as the idea that nations and
nationalism cannot predate the French Revolution is increasingly on the

defensive, however, so Celtic commonality has its own long history to celebrate. Up to 1100, the term 'Scoti' meant either Scots or Irish; in the fourteenth century, Robert I of Scotland could still write to the Irish as members of the same people, '*nostra nacio*'. Edward Lhuyd (who, like many Welshmen, claimed to be not 'an Englishman, but an old Briton') demonstrated pan-Celtic affinities at an early date in his *Archaelogia Britannica* (1707), while the Breton Abbé Paul Yves Pezron (1639–1706), in his contemporary *Antiquité de la Nation, et de la Langue des Celtes, autrement appellez Gaullois* (1703) was strongly influential on later writers, though admittedly his pan-Celticism extended only to Welsh, Bretons and Cornish.[30] Lhuyd's plan to provide a 'survey of all the Celtic nations' (Wales, Ireland, Scotland, Cornwall and Brittany), examining history, natural history, geology and philology, was 'a stupendous task which has never yet been completed':[31] it is indicative at an early date of a perceived commonality in Celticism, one evident also (and crucially, as William Ferguson has argued) in the writing of the great Latinist George Buchanan (1506–82), who 'recognised the essential substance of the concept' of 'Celtic' and Celticity. More recently of course, writers such as Michael Hechter have emphasized the commonality of the 'Celtic experience' of relations with England.[32]

Among the critics, Malcolm Chapman, while agreeing with Lhuyd's achievement (he neglects Buchanan and earlier Scots-Irish links), implies that it in its turn was merely a construct, which is no doubt true of all human societies if one traces them back far enough. As it was, Lhuyd was drawing on a commonality evident at an early date, a date significantly in his case at the dawn of the print capitalism era which Anderson finds crucial to the process of the imagined community, and in the Scots-Irish cases even earlier. In other words, appreciation of Celtic commonality precedes the means of its distribution. Differences at different stages of its development are another matter, and are inevitable: to insist, as Chapman does, that Celtic culture should be recognizably homogenous over space and time if the adjective is to have any meaning is too high a demand for any nationality to meet. France in the age of Louis Quatorze is far removed from the France of Jacques Chirac, and intolerably distant from the culture of Clovis the Frank: yet the term 'France', and indeed English attitudes to the French, are used recognizably and similarly over centuries.[33]

In a later age the homogenization of the Celtic, the existence of pan-Celtic congresses, of common analyses of landownership, of nostalgic cultural and political ideals, was itself fed by the British gaze, which so often reduced diversity to a common level of mockery. Paradoxically, the 'caricature ... of national characteristics' may have helped to preserve the very 'discrete identity' it set out to undermine,[34] by revealing, in what may be called a typology of insecurity, the residual fears of Anglo-British identity about the true 'Britishness' of its periphery. Xerxes united Greece to a greater extent than the Greeks themselves ever could; and in a not dissimilar fashion, Irish nationalism became overtly 'Celtic' as the Anglo-Saxon Empire which overshadowed it climbed to its zenith. 'If you break a man's nationality', George Bernard Shaw remarked, he 'will think of nothing else but getting it set again': an organic metaphor from *John Bull's Other Island* which neatly balances the concept of the 'imagined community', a concept I will deal with in more detail in Chapter 4.[35]

Organicism was (and to a large extent is) one of the major postulates of a British identity: the indissolubility of Britain through common experiences, common struggles, intermarriage and shared interests. This rhetoric does however, systematically subvert itself by its interchangeable use of 'England' and 'Britain', which, more than a harmless slip of the tongue, is a deeply held semantic preference which has historically indicated the limits of real British integration. As Gwynfor Evans put it in 1981:

> What is Britishness? The first thing to realize is that it is another word for Englishness; it is a political word which arose from the existence of the British state and which extends Englishness over the lives of the Welsh, the Scots and the Irish. If one asks what the difference is between English culture and British culture one realises that there is no difference. They are the same. The British language is the English language. British education is English education. British television is English television. The British press is the English press. The British Crown is the English Crown, and the Queen of Britain is the Queen of England. The British Constitution is called by Dicey, the main authority on the subject, 'the English Constitution' ... Britishness is Englishness.[36]

An irritant to many outside England (evidently including Gwynfor Evans!), this interchangeability is usually held by others to be a harmless matter – except, revealingly, during times of crisis. In 1914, an advertisement appeared in *The Times* which asked 'Englishmen!' to 'please use "Britain", "British" and "Briton" when the United Kingdom or the Empire is in question – at least during the war'. *At least during the war*: the extent to which 'Britishness' was a concept only permitted to cohere under the threat of external aggression is reflected in this statement. In similar vein, in 1899 Robert Blatchford asked his daughter 'to play Rule Britannia

every night while the [Boer] war lasts'.[37] England's history of partial
absorption of its neighbours has of course a much longer history than
that of Britain, and no doubt lies at the roots of English ideas of 'Britishness': only between 1042 and 1066 has there been a 'kingdom similar in
territory to modern England' within the British Isles.[38]

The deep-seated quality of British organicism and the anachronistic
assumptions it so often conceals are particularly visible in Gwyn
Williams's 1979 BBC lecture, *When Was Wales?*, given in the aftermath of
that year's failed devolution referendum in the Principality. Williams's
arguments began with the idea of nations as imagined entities: 'nations
do not grow like a tree, they are manufactured' is his premiss, one which
interestingly anticipates Benedict Anderson's 1983 arguments. Williams
then went on to state that nationalists in Scotland and Wales were opposing the reality of Britain, 'erecting human will into an anti-historic force
and therefore into a myth … trying to shout down history to its face'. 'A
historic British nation', Williams proclaimed, 'is a central fact.' Did this
eminent commentator realize that his words could have been spoken by
an Irish Unionist a century earlier? One must doubt it, as collective amnesia about Irish Britishness has been necessary to sustain continuing
assumptions of British organicism. According to 1989–91 polling evidence, 55 per cent of mainland Britons wished to see Northern Ireland
leave the UK: evidence that remaining Irish Britishness is largely
unwanted outside post-1921 Ulster, where by contrast 75–80 per cent of
the population wished to remain in the UK. In other words, Unionism is
as popular among nationalist Northern Catholics as it is in Surbiton, so
radically has Irish Britishness been abandoned outwith Ireland.[39] As D. G.
Boyce remarks, 'when the Irish troops returned from the war in 1919 they
were welcomed back though streets festooned with Union flags': and this
was *after* Sinn Fein had won 73 of the country's 106 seats in the December 1918 General Election. Before the Easter Rising of two years earlier,
nearly 100,000 Irishmen had volunteered for the British Army's 'Saxon
shilling'.[40] In apparent amnesia of this past, Williams argued, in effect, that
other nations were 'imagined', but that *his*, Britain, was a 'fact', determined
by history, with a manifest destiny (what else can the extraordinary creeping Hegelianism of phrases like 'anti-historic force' imply?). 'Wales is an
artefact which the Welsh produce', states Williams; Britain by contrast is
real, a metaphysical truth-claim, not an 'imagined nation'. Time and
again, one encounters arguments such as Williams's: sophisticated examinations of nationality whose underlying assumptions are themselves so
clearly nationalist, assuming the 'central fact' of Britishness as the ulti-

mate deterrent to manufactured fantasy about being anything else. Williams described Welshness as 'a question of trivialities', in doing so trivializing it; in similar vein, on 19 May 1998, the *Guardian* obliquely commented on the SNP's lead in Scotland in the 'McPolls': silly names trivialize, but whether their object is a 'triviality' or not is not determined by this process. Williams's lecture, in its genteel way, was another contribution to a history of caricature.[41] W. E. Gladstone's emerging view of the United Kingdom as a multi-national state, visible in his later career (whether or not taken up for internal party reasons), 'was a major turning point in the description and imagery of the United Kingdom':[42] unfortunately and remarkably, almost all subsequent British political leaders ignored it in favour of a determined British organicism, which forced Scotland, Wales and (tragically) Ireland into a mould based on the assertion of a central type of Anglo-imperialist value as universally 'British'. As Lord Rosebery remarked to the students of Edinburgh University in 1882, 'England's wealth, power and population "make her feel herself to be Great Britain, with Ireland and Scotland as lesser gems in her diadem"'. India was, of course, in tellingly similar language, 'the Jewel in the Crown'.[43]

The view of Wales, Scotland and Ireland as colonies, whose internal culture was systematically downgraded, those who celebrated it infantilized and caricatured in unbecoming and trivial stereotypes like so many other 'foreigners', is thus a tempting one. Culturally speaking, it has a certain power; but it requires to be balanced with a degree of complicity in the celebration of a permitted imperial localism (Gladstone's 'local patriotism, which in itself is not bad, but good'), paradoxically visible in comments such as John Buchan's support of 'Scottish Nationalism' *'for the sake of Britain and the Empire'*. Such localism allowed (and to a considerable extent allows) groups such as the Protestants of Northern Ireland to adopt 'an elaborate series of communitarian emblems and rituals' of their own while claiming to conform to Britishness, a claim stretched to breaking point even in sympathetic eyes by the events of the 1998 Drumcree protest.[44] In Wales, sympathetic commentators such as the *Saturday Review* spelt out the terms on which imperial localism could be successful: 'Kept within proper limits, the worship of Welsh nationality is a harmless one, and may incidentally preserve some useful qualities from merging in the dead level of English society.'[45] 'Proper limits' was the key: local colour accentuated the glory of the Empire through stressing how many cultures it contained, and was welcome; nationalist irridentism was quite another matter. Thus imperial localism was a powerful manifestation of an idea we have met already: the acceptance of ethno-cultural difference which offered no political challenge, while rigorously resisting claims to territorial, national difference. Such was the regionalism of Sir Samuel Ferguson in Ireland.

Imperial localism in the British Isles was like yet unlike that found elsewhere, because the localities were themselves deeply implicated in the imperial mission, and had long been in this position. Welshmen had developed a colony in Newfoundland called Cambriol in the seventeenth century, while the beginnings of colonization in Nova Scotia dated from the same period. Unlike other parts of the Empire, the British Isles was held to be (for the purposes of that unitary imperial identity into which the British localities were drawn) an indissoluble, organic whole: hence the Irish Unionist argument that 'the counting of heads or votes ... ceases to have any meaning' 'when it comes to questions which go to the very roots of a Constitution, questions of national existence'.[46] The passionate anti-democratic organicism of these century-old arguments itself shows how very British some at least of Irish society was: Ireland was part of the 'national existence' as surely as Shropshire. Home Rule was 'a sick man's appetite', as Matthew Arnold, citing Shakespeare, put it: distempered and contrary to organic order.[47] Yet almost at the same time, in 1900, the revised Union Flag bore a 'cross of St Patrick' to stand for Ireland's organic participation in the Union, which itself was a badge of the colonizing Fitzgerald/Geraldine family.[48] So deeply were organicism and colonialism intertwined.

Externally, Scottish troops, long used to action in the wars of Europe, were deployed in the colonies as early as 1680, when the Royal Scots were sent to Tangier.[49] In the 1730s, 160 Mackintoshes were recruited by the Jacobite-leaning General Oglethorpe to defend frontier territory in Georgia.[50] By the late eighteenth century, Scots colonists represented 15 per cent of the population of Pennsylvania, Virginia and North Carolina: in the Revolutionary War, they tended to support the British Government, though Philadelphia Scots merchants raised companies for the American forces. During the war, the Georgian House of Assembly expressed its special distrust for the Scots, and a Philadelphian gentleman remarked 'These [Highlanders], with a few Episcopalians from the same county, who are to a man Jacobites, are all that favour the cause of slavery and oppression [George III].' Not only in the British Army, but also in the colonies, Jacobites were being transmuted into Empire loyalists: for them any king was better than none.[51]

In the nineteenth century, this loyalism developed, becoming ever more essentially British. Important Scottish generals led the fray at moments of imperial crisis: Major-General David Baird defeated Tipu Sultan at Seringapatam in 1799, Lieutenant-General Sir John Moore died at Corunna ('for England') in 1805, Field Marshal (as he was to become) Lord Clyde crushed the Indian Mutiny in 1858.[52] At the same time, there is plenty of evidence that Scottish troops, though officially partners in Empire, suffered as if they were expendable colonial auxiliaries. Of the 3 million or so men who served in the Scottish regiments (a good number of whom, it is true, were not Scots), 50 per cent have been killed or wounded.[53] Scots suffered grotesque casualties in the Seven Years War, four times the Anglo-American rate, with the Black Watch alone haemor-rhaging 650 from 1,300 at Ticonderoga, a rate they almost repeated at Magesfontein in the Boer War.[54] In the Indian Mutiny, Scots were heavily used in storming duties,[55] while in World War I their casualty rate was double the English level (incidentally, such disproportionate losses were repeated among other 'white' colonies: the ANZACs in particular grew to resent their dreadful casualties at Gallipoli, while Scots regiments tended to take pride in their slaughterhouse record).[56] Yet there is some evidence that used internally (against Irish insurgents for example), Gaelic-speakers in particular were less than wholehearted in suppression,[57] while in the colonies, Scots abroad could rescue compatriots sold into slavery, as the Jacobite gentlemen of Maryland did for a cargo of transportees at the sale of 22 July 1747.[58] Irish troops were less active in imperial engage-ments, frequently continuing what had been the Scottish tradition of fighting for other powers, for France and Spain in the eighteenth century, for Confederate and Union forces in the American Civil War, for Mexico, Brazil and the Boer Republic. Montserrat, to which Irish transportees were sent in the 1650s, was reported to be Irish-speaking until the end of the eighteenth century; elsewhere, Welsh and Scots Gaelic-speaking parts of the Empire were more likely to derive from emigrants (admittedly sometimes forced) and colonists than political exiles. As late as 1982, Plaid Cymru objected to the use of Welsh troops in the Falklands War against Argentina because they might meet Patagonian Welsh in combat.[59]

At the same time, complaints about the exploitation of the Celtic lands by outsiders date both back beyond and forward after the heyday of land-lordism and clearance in the eighteenth and nineteenth centuries. As early as the reign of Charles II, 'speculation' by 'strangers' in Flintshire land was regarded as 'undoing the country' by 'making land dear to the natives'.[60] Michael Hechter's early postcolonial text, *Internal Colonialism* (1975), popularized the terms 'core' and 'periphery', and made much of the differential rate of economic development as a structural component of colonialism on the periphery: the status of speculation in Flintshire land in the 1670s and holiday cottages in North Wales in the 1990s could be seen in these terms as part of the same process, just as the so-called 'white settler' moves into Scotland in the 1980s and 1990s are linked with the regeneration by incomers of the Highland economy. Typically, as true descendants of Arnold, many of these incomers both romanticize the locals as 'Noble Savages' or denigrate them as 'sly rustics, backward and degenerate roughs'. In keeping with their own experience, the economic regeneration they provide is often linked to tourism:

> the majority of cosmopolitans who visit or dwell in rural Scotland are attracted by their experience of the scenery as romantic, and they will, naturally enough, not wish their 'view' to be spoiled by rustic louts, and so they will be more likely to people the scenery with romantic figures ... It is a short step from being a consumer of tourism looking for facilities to becoming a producer for other tourists. So guest houses, hotels, restaurants, inns, craft shops, boat charter businesses, and the like, come to be owned by people who previously used them, that is, tourists and holiday makers.[61]

As frontiersmen and women, such people often treasure ethno-cultural Scottishness, while reacting virulently to even the mildest political expressions: in the *Aberdeen Press and Journal* in the 1990s one woman claimed that 'the use of the Saltire [Scotland's national flag, flown widely by tourist agencies and multinationals] was akin to the use of the Eire flag by the IRA'. Extreme reactions also abound: the idea that 'the extirpation of the Celtic race' will come about from incomers settling in the Highlands is not only doubtfully ethnic, but chooses to ignore the complicity of many in Scotland with a process of self-denigration. Nonetheless, the tension caused by the primarily recreational use of landscape preferred by incomers is a real one, dating back at least to the Clearances, some of which had much the same end in view: more than 3,000 square miles were given over to deer forest in Scotland by the time of the Napier Commission.[62]

As indicated in Chapter 2, the Irish experience in the early twentieth century increased the degree to which some Scots and Welshmen began to view the plight of their countries as a 'colonial' one. While the Jacobite period and the early nineteenth century had continued to provide evidence of close Scots-Irish sympathies (Sir Walter Scott calls in his quasi-nationalist *Letters of Malachi Malagrowther* (1826), for 'a league offensive and defensive ... brothers of Erin', against all such measures as 'tend to the suppression of any just right in either country'),[63] sectarianism and Irish immigration into Scotland, together with the high noon success of the British Empire, helped to force the two countries apart in the Victorian period: the *North British Daily Mail* for example attacking the 'simian Irish Celt' but sympathizing with the 'indigenous Gael'.[64] Irish nationalism also had a stronger and longer history, which meant that when the Celtic revival did something to re-establish commonality, its organizations in late nineteenth-century Wales and Scotland (e.g. *Cymru Fydd* ('Young Wales')) were timid in their demands compared to their Irish counterparts: T. E. Ellis was not untypical in stating that 'the more Wales has the power of initiative and decision in her own affairs, the more closely will she be bound to the very texture of the imperial fabric'.[65] Some scholars however, such as Cecile O'Rahilly, have argued for a greater identity of purpose between the Wales of the 1880s and the Ireland of Parnell.[66] The Irish events of 1916–21 provided encouragement to a militant minority, while arguably setting back the cause of milder forms of Home Rule: resentment in South Wales towards heavy Irish immigration did not help.[67] While the Irish expatriate community fed on a sense of injustice,[68] Scots expatriates in particular tended to downplay even forced emigration as a matter of shame to be forgotten:[69] they thus provided no external support for a domestic politics levelled at British injustice, whereas Irish-Americans were critically important in their support of a distinctively Irish politics. That Scots appear to have suffered little discrimination in North America after 1800 is probably important too: discrimination against the Irish in the USA ('No Blacks, No Irish') served rather to consolidate a sense of grievance. 'Who does not know', preached the *Chicago Tribune* in 1855, 'that the most depraved, debased, worthless, and irredeemable drunkards and sots which curse the community are Irish Catholics?'[70]

The Depression of the 1930s, together with the incipient metropolitan bias of the electronic media and the first signs of decay in the British Empire, served to move Scotland and Wales, albeit very slowly, in the direction of a distinctive national politics. Mostly respectable, it was nonetheless this decade which saw the first outrages of Welsh extremism, and the creation of quasi-paramilitary youth movements in Scotland. Although these were still small minorities, they attracted the attention of the Nazis, who (fruitlessly) sought to use them as a fifth column in much the same way as the Kaiser had used Ireland in World War I. The same process occurred in Brittany.

It was the collapse of Empire, linked to declining heavy industry, which in the 1960s brought Scottish and Welsh nationalism alive again, the former in a moderate, potentially popular form; the latter, linguistically and sometimes even violently extreme, as the voice of a regionally-based and largely rural defensively Cymrophone community. A 'Celtic League' was founded in 1961; in 1966, Gwynfor Evans, its President, was elected to Parliament for Plaid Cymru. Even in Cornwall there was some activity, with Cornish Nationalists (principally Mebyon Kernow) achieving some reasonable votes in parliamentary seats and obtaining the odd councillor.[71]

Although still largely fringe politics, the connections with Irish militancy which had spilt over into Scotland and Wales in the 1920s and 1930s were still present. In 1966, the Free Wales Army marched down O'Connell Street to mark the 50th anniversary of the Easter Rising: subsequently they acquired all the arms (what there were of them) of the Official IRA. Neither Plaid Cymru nor the SNP showed any interest in capitalizing on the Troubles after 1969 (the SNP in particular maintains an exemplary record of expelling militants and extremists), but the Provisional IRA nonetheless accepted a degree of Celtic commonality in 1972 by 'excluding any action in other Celtic countries': it has been speculated that the role of Sean MacStiofain, PIRA's Chief of Staff and a pan-Celt, was influential in this.[72] It was accompanied by rhetoric such as the statement that the PIRA 'stands with our Celtic brothers and other subject nations of Europe'.[73] Hence there have been no PIRA outrages in Wales or Scotland, a fact studiously ignored by the British media, and even neglected by hard-headed insurance companies, who in the early 1990s raised premiums in Glasgow in response to bomb attacks in the City of London.[74]

Others began in the 1990s to identify the same links on a larger stage. In 1995, the US film *Braveheart* portrayed William Wallace's struggle against Edward I as Third World resistance to a colonizing arrogance which was also internally corrupt, underlining its postcolonial alignment of Scotland with the resonant Irish experience by introducing an Irishman who saves Wallace's life and a Scots-Irish rapprochement at the Battle of Falkirk. Two years earlier, an Irishman, Liam Neeson, had been chosen to play the lead role in *Rob Roy*, as he was to do in *Michael Collins*. Hollywood's populist postcolonialism was beginning to merge the Scottish and Irish experiences. Educated opinion in Scotland was sneeringly sceptical of *Braveheart*, but in its crude way it was closer to Wallace's iconic (if not his strictly historical) role than some of Scotland's more limited and provincialized commentators imagined. For the Romantic Southey, the Wallace of his 1798 poem was an icon of liberty and defender of 'patriot blood' against Plantagenet tyranny; for Wordsworth, he served much the same role.[75] The Revd William Anderson (1796–1872) likened Wallace to Garibaldi;[76] in 1915, Wallace had been used as a 'justification for the black nationalist revolt in Nyasaland'. Wallace was a democratic icon for the nationalist Douglas Young in the 1940s, and was compared to Pearse by Sydney Goodsir Smith, while his capacity to irritate British opinion was once again confirmed in 1946, when the *Guardian*'s leader asked (in the context of the Nuremberg Trials), 'Could any Englishman doubt that justice was done ... when Wallace was executed?'.[77] The Wallace of world culture rather than Scottish history is much closer to the depiction offered by *Braveheart*, itself of course an offering from and to that culture.

So is the experience of the Celtic countries a 'colonial' one? There are too many tempting parallels to the imperial experience elsewhere to dismiss the argument. The contempt shown for the Celt and Celtic except at the level of local colour (and sometimes not even with this exemption) is only too redolent of imperial attitudes elsewhere. Indeed, in the 1850s, there was considerable support for the idea that Indian education should conduct itself along native lines with native subjects of study: such a possibility (although in the end not adopted) would have been unthinkable in Ireland and Wales, or in a Scotland where even today children are drilled in English history as if it were their own (in this context, the 'suppression' of the 1998 'Scottish Culture and the Curriculum' report for apparently political reasons by the education authorities in Scotland was a significant example of continuing resistance to the idea of informing children about their own country).[78] In literary and historical terms, the postcolonial impulse to regain a native voice is one found in the Celtic countries as well as the overseas colonies. Padraig Pearse's views on Irish literature would find a welcome echo in African writing (the attack on African writers for using English also has its Irish echo): 'The rediscovery of this buried ... literature ... will make it necessary for us to re-write literary history. And it will mean not only a re-writing of literary history, but a general readjustment of literary values.'[79] Here Pearse is an avatar of contemporary literary criticism, challenging the canon and the canonical concept of 'literary values' half a century before postcolonialism's (and other theories') role in doing the same.

The colonial analysis of the Celtic experience thus has its merits when it comes to analogies with the wider Empire and the literary and cultural renewals attending decolonization. But it has marked limitations also. While the idea of 'Britishness' on a domestic workaday level may always have been rarer outside England than some would choose to believe, there is little doubt of its force in time of crisis and war: and of course the Empire was won and defended by war. In this context, the exclusion of Catholics from commissioned rank until the later eighteenth century, and the preference of many Irish and some Scots to serve foreign powers once again limits Britishness: but the greater use and integration of Scottish soldiers after 1760 and Irish ones in the nineteenth century restores the concept's credibility once more. The Irish Party's support for World War I in the end destroyed them, but without the provision of conscription in 1918 and the clumsy shootings of 1916 (carried out under military jurisdiction) it is doubtful whether their desire to participate in a common British struggle would have been so heavily punished at the polls. Scottish troops suffered severe casualties in this, as in so many other wars: it is arguable that they have been used expendably, despite their strong support for the imperial mission. The opportunities for Scots and Irish administrators in the Empire appear, however, less vexed in the questions they raise. Here there were more opportunities for 'Britons' than for 'colonials': yet even this is undercut by the less favoured status of Catholics, when most British Catholics were Irish. Paradoxically of course, this sustained British views of Irish separateness at the same time as the country was regarded as organically linked to the rest of Britain.

Ireland, then, has the strongest case to be described as a colony: but it is *only the religious question which endorses it as one.* The Welsh were held in almost equal contempt; had they been Catholics, and the 22 per cent of Welsh inhabitants of English birth in the nineteenth century Protestants, the case for Wales's colonial status would be much stronger. The fact that there were Protestant nationalists in eighteenth-century Ireland does not set it apart either; for there were plenty of Protestant nationalists in Scotland in the Jacobite period. Even the indifferent attitude of the British authorities during the Famine of 1845–8 does not set Ireland apart; as Tom Devine has shown, similar sentiments were expressed towards Hebridean West Highlanders when they experienced crop failure during the same period. Their hardships were not nearly so great: but the circumstances in Ireland which brought about such terrible starvation were particularly unfavourable ones.[80] Yet again, the difference between Wales, Scotland and Ireland is one of degree rather than kind, except where the religious issue is at stake (see Figure 16). The romanticization of Celtic landholding customs in Scotland and Ireland at the end of the nineteenth century only endorses this underlying similarity.

The 1707 Union between Scotland and England does, however, suggest

FAMINE

Figure 16 *Famine*, 1763. 10″ × 8″. The Scot as starvation and poverty personified. In the 1690s, Scotland's population was ravaged by famine, blamed by some
on disloyalty to the Stuarts, and there were further very poor years in the 1740s.
A visual reminder that the Irish experience, though more recent and more
marked in degree, does not necessarily altogether differ in kind.

the presence of a strong differentiating factor: unlike the Welsh Union of
1536 or even the Irish one of 1800, it was, nominally at any rate, a free
partnership between two countries. Yet the last phrase shows the Scottish
bias of the author, for from the beginning the common English attitude
was far closer to the idea that Scotland had been 'added to the English
Empire' as Daniel Defoe put it.[81] The rhetoric of the Union was one thing
its reality often another. Nevertheless, it was a different kind of settlement: it enabled a certain section of Scottish society (Presbyterian Unionist gentry mostly) to enjoy partnership in Britain at a relatively early date.
The children of this elite gradually moved out of Scotland for their edu-

cation and career: yet here too there are parallels with the Irish Ascendancy and Welsh gentry at an even earlier period. Once again, the question is a vexed one, though it might be fair to say that Scots who displayed little public difference or eccentric departure from English norms stood a greater chance of being accepted in Britain than did their Irish or Welsh counterparts. The social prestige of the educated Scottish accent remained high even in the early twentieth-century drive towards received pronunciation in English, at a time when British benefits trickled down to the Scottish middle class. Ironically, it was the challenge to the local hegemony of the Scots bourgeoisie by the increasing appointment of non-Scottish candidates with little knowledge of the country to positions of authority in arts, culture, education and the public sector, which helped to serve (as in the case of economic development in the Highlands, discussed above), to turn many in the Scottish middle class away from Britishness. As perhaps was the case in Ireland in the late nineteenth century, the more British Scottish society became (and it remained deeply distinct until the 1960s), the more irritated it became with Britishness. This was the local manifestation of the recognized tendency of globalization to increase nationalism.

In summary, the answer to the question of whether Ireland, Wales or Scotland were 'colonies' must remain a mixed one, largely answered in terms of degree rather than kind. Aspects of colonialism and colonial attitudes can be found in all three countries; but so can participation in a Britishness held by many (and not just in England) to be organic. 'Breaking up Britain' has, from the days of Gladstone's Home Rule crisis to the present, always carried emotive resonance far beyond that found in the wider Empire, where colonies were relinquished with a readier recognition of political divergence. At the same time, British organicism often carries an undertone of colonial assumption: perhaps it is the case that the present identity of England is bound up with Britain to a greater degree than is often acknowledged, and that the periphery, particularly the periphery within the same island, must be incorporated to maintain that identity. A renewal and re-examination of English identity, perhaps even its modernization, are thus more likely where its assumption of historic rights to control Britishness are challenged: hence the growth of interest in the subject of English identity following the 1997 referenda in Scotland and Wales. British symbols of monarchy, state and nation survive, though in a weakened condition: they now appear to be increasingly bolsters for a certain kind of Englishness, with (except in Northern Ireland) limited appeal elsewhere. The Union Flag is decreasingly flown in

Scotland and attitudes to the monarchy are more sceptical; nor is this only the correlative of nationalism. The unifying symbols of Empire (with the exception of the monarchy) can appear colonial outwith England's boundaries. Britishness, designed for external use, functions more erratically when reduced to its island limits. But the organic thesis is enduring: and the denial of Irish Britishness, in which Britain and Ireland have both long been happily complicit, suggests that organic violation was survivable, even in an earlier and more politically immobile age. The conclusion must be that to describe the Celtic countries as colonial possessions is tendentious, but to describe them as inherently 'British' is equally so, as the oft-forgotten Britishness of Ireland shows.

Speak that I may see thee

'Language most shows the man. Speak, that I may see thee.'

Ben Jonson, Discoveries

Among the subjects of our discussion, Wales is the country where language has had the largest part in defining national identity. English took a long time to penetrate a society where as early as the late seventeenth century, linguistic difference was the prime means of stating nationality. Welsh cultural nationalism was based on the Welsh language from 1700 on, and to a great extent remains so: of all the countries of the 'Celtic fringe', Wales most closely reflects the centre's premiss of an ethno-cultural rather than politico-territorial basis for Celtic identity. From the days when Edward Morris feared that 'Britain's bright tongue today despised ... unrewarded and unprized' was under threat, Wales has sought to defend its Welshness primarily through language, through a Welsh press and Welsh-language publication.[82]

In the late eighteenth century, the rise of Methodism in Wales was closely connected to Welsh-speaking, as the Church of England's failure to install Cymrophone clergy in livings led to a general decline in the reputation and status of Anglicanism in the Principality. Marriages could not be conducted in Welsh until 1837,[83] and when a Cymrophone Welsh bishop was preferred to St Asaph in 1870, it was the first such appointment in 150 years, even though Welsh Bibles had reached a sale of 70,000 in 1867 alone, and the circulation of Welsh periodicals was 120,000.[84] This process of English clerical neglect was symbolized by the case of Dr Thomas Bowles, who in 1766 was appointed to a living in Ynys Mon (Anglesey), where only 1 per cent of his parishioners spoke English:

The Cymmrodorion Society and local dignitaries fought for his removal in a case at the Court of Arches, where Bowles's attorney argued that 'Wales is a conquered country; it is proper to introduce the English language, and it is the duty of the bishops to promote the English, in order to introduce the language'. The judge declared the Welsh plaintiffs right in principle, but Bowles kept his living.[85]

'The Honourable Society of Cymmrodorion', founded in 1751, was one of a number of eighteenth-century societies devoted to the support of Welsh language and culture; these were on the whole sympathetically treated by contemporary British antiquarians, since they had no political manifestations. Indeed, Cymmrodorion has been accused of possessing 'snobbish and anglicizing tendencies'. In 1819, the 'annual *Eisteddfod* or bardic meeting was revived ... after centuries of abeyance',[86] and went on to become a major feature of Welsh life. Welsh links with Brittany were renewed no later than the 1830s, and an Association Bretonne was formed in 1843, with a 'Comité de Preservation du Breton' and 'Union Regionaliste Bretonne' following later in the century.[87] Attempts to found an *Eisteddfod* in Brittany were less successful: it was banned as subversive in 1866, the Association having already been banned eight years earlier. It was in fact not until the 1980s that the French Government's dislike of Breton culture as a challenge to unitary Frenchness abated to any marked degree: when it did, 'the Lorient Inter-Celtic Festival' in the province began to attract up to 250,000 visitors every year.[88]

The Welsh language also benefited from the Celtic revival, with a 'Society for Utilising the Welsh Language' founded in 1885,[89] but the Victorian period as a whole saw increasing struggles between the language and a rising English hostility, which had replaced the contemptuous neglect of an earlier period. As communications improved and progress became the dominant watchword in metropolitan culture, the presence of an antique language in a country 'stuck at the bardic or poetic stage in the process of civilisation' became an increasing irritant. The infamous 1847 'Blue Book' report commissioned by Sir James Kay-Shuttleworth presented the Welsh as

fierce, laggardly, unreliable, dishonest, dirty, universally unresourceful and lacking any methodicality, their womenfolk little better than slatterns and 'universally unchaste', their children bastards more often than not ... The reports drew the conclusion that a state-funded system of education should be introduced to teach English and introduce the Welsh to the world of English progress and civilisation.[90]

Dispensing with the language did indeed for many (though the report had formidable opponents) seem the answer. William Williams, MP for Coventry, observed (inaccurately) that 'if the Welsh had the same education as the Scotch, they would, instead of appearing a distinct people, *in no respect differ from the English*'.[91] Language was the badge of difference, and its removal would destroy Wales's primitive society by removing its antiquated ethno-cultural identity.

This process was substantively endorsed by the 1870 Education Act, which 'made the English language compulsory in all Welsh schools' (although it remained true, as it had since the 1830s, that there were further education colleges where the language could be studied, and 'by the 1880s Welsh was offered as a paper for bursaries at several of the Welsh universities'.[92] Nonetheless, Welsh's exclusion from schools and its second-class social status were bound to cause long-term damage. This situation was painfully and slowly reversed over the next century, with the first Welsh-medium primary school opening in Aberystwyth in 1939 and the equal status of Welsh and English in Wales recognized at last by the 1967 Welsh Language Act: even so, it took a threatened hunger strike to obtain a Welsh-medium television station in the 1980s. By this time, the strength of the language had deteriorated considerably, although the initial impact of the 1870 Act appears to have been limited: in 1901, 46 per cent of the Welsh population still spoke the language, with 14 per cent of these monoglots. By 1961 (the year before the foundation of the Welsh Language Society), this had dropped to 26 per cent; by 1971, 21 per cent, and by 1981 19 per cent, and there to some extent it stabilized.[93] By the 1991 Census, there were still 508,100 Welsh speakers, almost 20 per cent of the population.[94]

The close alignment between linguistic, cultural and (now more emergent) political identities could be seen in the 1997 Referendum on Welsh devolution. Three hundred years earlier, when 90 per cent of the population spoke the language, it and the identity it stood for was strongest 'in the rural counties of north and west Wales'. This essential structure had not changed, though the proportion of Cymrophones was much reduced: it was noticeable that Wales divided in a straight east–west split in 1997, with the counties adjoining England voting No, the west (with the exception of the Pembrokeshire south coast) voting Yes, and large majorities being racked up in the north-west, the heartland of Plaid Cymru support. Research has shown that language was the key factor in the pro-Assembly vote: Cymrophones voted 7–2 in favour; English-speaking Welsh only 3–2, and voters born in England 2–1 against. The traditional bounds of

Welsh linguistic and cultural identity continue to make themselves felt in the political map of the Principality today.[95]

The politics of Irish Gaelic took rather longer to emerge, and did not begin to form a major feature of cultural nationalist claims of identity until towards the end of the nineteenth century: coincidentally, this was also the time when Irish nationalism passed irreversibly out of the hands of Anglophone Protestant patriots such as Fitzgerald, Tone, Emmet and Parnell. Irish was apparently in a strong position, with more than 300,000 monoglots in 1850 and 1.1 million speakers in total in 1870: yet despite the strong politicization of the country in comparison with Wales, it suffered a calamitous decline, through 700,000 in 1891 to only some 100–140,000 native speakers and fluent learners by the mid-1960s, though thanks to the government's policy of compulsory Irish, more than half a million others knew something of the language.[96] How enthusiastic they were in its use is open to doubt, however: even in the late 1950s, 'only 1 per cent listened to the news in Irish at 6.00pm (as against 41 per cent to the 6.30 English language news) while less than 0.5 per cent tuned in to the 7.30–8.30 slot in which a play in the Irish language was broadcast'.[97]

Despite this decline, the politicization of Irish was an important feature of the late nineteenth and early twentieth centuries. National tensions helped protect it from the same educational fate as Welsh. The Gaelic Union of Ireland was founded in 1880,[98] and within little more than a decade Douglas Hyde's lecture to the National Literary Society on 'The Necessity for de-Anglicising Ireland', accompanied by William O'Brien's article on 'The influence of the Irish language on Irish national literature and character' in *United Ireland*, paved the way for the development of the Gaelic League, launched in 1893. The League secured the position of Irish Gaelic in primary schools and successfully resisted its exclusion from secondary education. In 1909, Hyde, who had begun life as the son of a Church of Ireland rector, 'led the victorious campaign to include Irish as a compulsory subject for matriculation in the newly-established National University'.[99] This growth in Irish language use no doubt helped to provoke the reaction of 1905, in which the Post Office insisted that 'all letters and packets should be addressed in English only'.[100]

Linguistic patriotism undoubtedly played a significant part in Irish nationalism in the early 1900s, with growing cultural pressure on patriots with the most English names to adopt Irish forms for public use even where they could not speak the language. After the establishment of the Free State, compulsory school Irish followed on from this impetus, and there was enthusiasm for yet further developments in the public use of

Gaelic: Yeats responded, 'If I am attacked by a footpad and wish for protection how can I call for that protection by using words that I cannot
pronounce?'. Despite wishing 'to see the country Irish speaking', the poet
was deeply conscious of the rootless hyperbole of some Gaelic activism,
stating in the Senate in 1923 that

> I wish to make a very emphatic protest against the histrionics which have
> crept into the whole Gaelic movement. People pretend to know a thing they
> do not know and which they have not the smallest intention of ever learn-
> ing. It seems to me to be discreditable.[101]

Yeats's instincts were right. The truth of the view that informed enthusiasm for the Irish language was the obsession of a vanguard only was
clear for all to see with the heavy decline of the Gaelic League's popularity in the 1920s. Many had clearly supported the linguistic cause for
nationalist reasons: unlike Wales, where the language almost was the
nation, Ireland was always more important than Irish. Despite the
manner in which some theorists of nationalism point towards language
as a crucial sign of difference, it could be argued that the intensity of linguistic nationalism in Wales hampered other forms of national identity
rather than promoting them, while in Ireland the end was greater than
the means that language provided.

Scottish Gaelic, unlike its Irish and Welsh counterparts, had been in a
position of decline since the Middle Ages, when it had ceased to be the
preponderant language of Scottish identity, though the country's place
names still indicate its near ubiquity at an earlier date. Nonetheless, it is
more than likely that Gaelic contributed significantly to the lineaments of
Scottish thought and imagination in other fields: William Ferguson's
1998 study *The Identity of the Scottish Nation* persuasively demonstrates
the centrality of the Gaelic influence in Scottish culture and identity.[102]
Like its Irish counterpart, Gaelic suffered from an association with political disaffection in the seventeenth and eighteenth centuries, and was
regarded with considerable distrust and hostility: as in Ireland (but
largely wrongly in Scotland's case), it was associated with Catholicism. A
vernacular (Protestant) preaching tradition did however develop in the
eighteenth-century Gaeltachd. Nevertheless, by 1891, Gaelic's area of
strength had contracted to the north-west Highlands and Islands, with a
few pockets elsewhere: it had 254,000 speakers, around 6 per cent of the
Scottish population.[103] In the twentieth century it lost three-quarters of its
remaining numbers and territory, although as in the case of Welsh, there
was a tendency to stabilize from the 1960s.

Considerable Gaelic-speaking groups were also to be found in the colonies of the British Empire, principally in North America, although their decline here seems to have been just as steep as it was at home. Eighteenth-century Jacobite and post-Jacobite emigration to the United States helped to ensure that Mississippi and North Carolina retained Gaelic speakers into the nineteenth century. Nova Scotia's 33,000 speakers in 1939 had more than quartered by the 1950s, although as late as 1971 there were still 18,500 Gaelic-speakers in Canada as a whole.[104]

Like its Irish counterpart, Gaelic participated in a late nineteenth-century revival. Periodicals such as *The Celtic Magazine* and *The Celtic Monthly* spoke in twee defiance of 'Mo naire air a'Bheurla' ('my shame on the English tongue'), while societies such as the Gaelic Society of Inverness (founded 1871) promoted the interests of local worthies while doing some good on the side.[105] One of the most important of such good works was An Comunn Gaidhealach (founded 1899), which grew out of the activities of the Society.[106] An Comunn's programme and level of activism was mild: it was both less politicized than its Irish neighbour and also the tongue it promoted could no longer claim to be a national language. Perhaps partly as a result, it remained 'very guarded with respect to pronouncements concerning Gaelic in public affairs'.[107]

There was nonetheless some progress, despite the continuation of strong prejudices. Although Gaelic was totally excluded by the 1870 Act (a position which worsened the situation already existing in Gaeltachd schools, where the language was still taught),[108] the Education Act of 1918 allowed for 'adequate provision for teaching Gaelic in Gaelic-speaking areas'. Gaelic-medium further education had to wait until the 1970s,[109] while Gaelic units and Gaelic teaching in schools outwith the Gaeltachd developed a profile more recently still. By the 1950s, there was a small amount of Gaelic broadcasting, which has continued to increase: but there is very little sign that the greater desire to treat Gaelic with politeness, consideration and cash can improve its position in any sustained way, despite efforts to legitimize its use in the Scottish Parliament. Many Scots have inherited prejudices against the language and its use, disliking the politesse of bilingual signs where they occur outside the Gaeltachd, and denying the tongue's central role in Scottish history. Attitudes such as this are by no means majority ones, but they are still common, and remove Gaelic further than ever from any opportunities it might have had to be regarded as a national, or even a secondary national language.[110]

Cornish remained a literary language well into the Middle Ages, but by the sixteenth century was experiencing a steep decline, aided no doubt by the 1549 Act of Uniformity, which banned all languages but English from church services. By 1800, Cornish had disappeared altogether as a spoken language, though fragments of it and set pieces were understood and recited for at least sixty years longer. At the end of the nineteenth century, the county experienced its own faint echo of the Celtic revival in the shape of Henry Jenner (1848–1934), who became the leader of the Cornish language movement, following the foundation of the Cornish Celtic Society in 1901, two years after its Manx counterpart. Certain features of a perceived common Celtic culture were promoted by Cornish enthusiasts, including the wearing of the kilt. Jenner went on to become President of the Old Cornwall Society (1920) and First Grand Bard (1928–34), but apart from odd grammar books produced as curiosities, it was not until the latter part of the twentieth century that there was any noticeable kind of revival in the numbers learning the language. Even in the Duchy, there was a small nationalist flurry, and Mebyon Kernow's 1964 aim 'to maintain the Celtic character of Cornwall' was fulfilled to a limited extent by the development of Cornish in a few schools.

Manx survived rather better: it was said of Man in 1656 that 'few speak the English tongue', and in 1874 25 per cent of the population spoke it, though this had declined to only 8 per cent by the turn of the century. The community of native speakers did not finally disappear until the postwar period, and there were monoglots as late as the 1920s.[111] In recent times, as in the case of Cornish, interest in the language has revived: but given the conventional insistence on the crucial qualities of linguistic difference in promoting nationalism, what emerges here as in the more widely spoken Celtic tongues, is the lack of a direct and powerful link between linguistic and national patriotism.

Only in the case of Wales is there a strong confluence between these elements, and here the almost solely linguistic quality of Welshness is likely to strike the onlooker as constricting as much as liberating. Welsh nationalism's inability to cross the boundaries of language has clearly limited its potential for development, in contrast to the case in both Scotland and Ireland. At the same time, it is notable that opponents of political Welshness have often attacked the language as a synecdoche for politico-territorial ambitions in Wales. During the debates on the 1974–9 Labour Government's devolution proposals, Neil Kinnock averred that in a school in Ynys Mon children were forced to ask to go to the lavatory in Welsh or 'suffer the consequences', describing pro-Welsh linguistic policies as 'warfare against children'. Reference was made by another speaker to the 'natural loquacity' of the Welsh, while Daniel Abse commented that 'millions' were 'being spent in Gwent upon silly road signs'. Linguistic identity's homogeneity with politicization called forth savage political opposition. Sir David Renton opined that 'The Welsh have never had it so good since the days of the Tudors', while other MPs suggested that a Welsh Assembly would be a 'Frankenstein monster' , that the Scots had 'spent far more time fighting one another than they did fighting the English' and that 'the [Welsh] Assembly could *accidentally* [my italics] end up with a substantial number of nationalist members' (presumably owing to the innate stupidity of its electorate: the same argument was heard in Scotland in 1998). Various contributors to the debate declare such reasoned views as evidence that 'We English are a very tolerant people ... we ... have debates about Scotland and Wales, that seem to go on for ever' (Eric Heffer) and contrast this measured tolerance with 'the sniggers, the sneers and the active hatreds of all things English have been generated in Wales' (Fred Evans). Reading Hansard's record of these debates is a good way of seeing the arguments of this book in action: most of the contributions quoted above came, of course, from Labour MPs.[112]

Political culture or cultural politics

One of the key themes of my argument has been the tension which exists between cultural and politico-territorial notions of identity, particularly the manner in which the core British state has accepted the first as a manifestation of localist particularism, while historically viewing the second as a threat to organic unity. Ireland was a perpetual irritant because its cultural nationalism tended to be very closely linked to political action, and, even worse, because some of its leaders (Tone and Parnell, for example) tended to view cultural nationalism as expendable entirely: their aims were totalizingly political. When Wolfe Tone famously remarked (of a 1792 harpists' gathering) 'Strum, strum and be hanged', he was articulating a politico-territorial purity ('sever the connection with England, the never-failing source of all our evils') which had its root in deep-seated economic and structural grievances that rendered the sickly revivals of Romantic Primitivism an irrelevance. It was also relevant that Tone and Parnell were Protestants: Gaelic culture was not their culture, and hence perhaps their sympathies were limited towards manifestations of a native Irishness which rendered them uneasy. When cultural nationalism finally became wedded to the campaign for political change after Parnell's fall, the forces it released were colossal, and finally successful. Irishness in Irish politics was ultimately an appeal which transcended Redmondite calls for a more flexible British politics based on Home Rule. Easter 1916 would not have been possible without this new marriage of cultural and politico-territorial nationalism: and while it is well said that it was preparation for conscription in 1918 and not the 'martyrs' of 1916 that led to Sinn Fein's election victory, what is noteworthy is that this was a clash between old British and new Irish politics. Why should conscription not be extended to Ireland as elsewhere in Britain? Redmond and his nationalists supported the war. The key was that by continuing to do so, they revealed themselves as British politicians at a time of crisis. But Sinn Fein's politics were Irish politics: as Arthur Griffith had pointed out to Yeats long before, his national theatre was worth many victories on the battlefield. The long, sterile but ultimately respectable efforts of the Irish Party at Westminster were supplanted overnight by uncompromising cultural and political Irishness. The dynamic ferocity of Sinn Fein's Irish agenda brought both victory and civil war, as the inevitable compromise of the Treaty deeply shocked the Diehards who had spent twenty years absorbing a poetic, political and cultural rhetoric which abhorred rapprochement. That abhorrence created the abhorrent, as it was always prone to do.

In Ireland, it proved impossible to cultivate cultural nationalism at the expense of its political equivalent. In many respects, Wales presents a contrary picture. The diminution of the Welsh appetite for political prophecy in the seventeenth century was rapidly succeeded by concerns about Welshness primarily centred on the Welsh language, such as those discussed earlier in this chapter:[113] the movement from the relics of political identity to emergent fears over language and culture appears to have fully taken place by the latter part of the seventeenth century. It was not until the late nineteenth century that there was any sign of a realignment between political and cultural Welshness: given that this was relatively weak in national terms, it is at least arguable that Welsh political identity would barely have surfaced but for the insensitive and hostile manner in which Cymric language and culture were frequently treated. (The symbiosis between the two which resulted is described above.) As it was, political identity in Wales was always compromised in any territorial ambitions by its very status as the defence mechanism of a contracting cultural base. While political nationalism in Ireland did not succeed without its cultural correlative, it nonetheless flourished; its equivalent in Wales could not have existed. Had Britain prized and encouraged Welsh localism instead of diminishing it, there might have been very little Welsh nationalism. In the nineteenth century, the Conservatives articulated the view that 'there was no such place as Wales';[114] in 1995, a leading Tory could still appeal to a thousand years of British common language while publicly and conspicuously displaying an apparent lack of knowledge of Welsh. Such views feed what they ignore.

Quite possibly it was the strong survival of the Welsh language which helped to create a reluctance in Britain to endorse Welsh local habits and customs, when elsewhere Romantic primitivism and nineteenth-century revivals of popular sports, folkways and pastimes were viewed with benignity and encouragement. Queen Victoria's patronage effectively secured the development of the whole Highland Games industry after 1848,[115] but in Wales no support on such a scale was forthcoming. True, Gaelic was still spoken in the Highlands, but for historical reasons it could not express Scottish national identity in the same terms as those in which Welsh functioned; and, moreover, mass emigration was heavily diminishing its stock of native speakers. In these contexts, a gradual incorporation of an idealized and romanticized Highlands, strong in local colour while loyal to Crown and Parliament, was completed as the nineteenth century progressed.

The very popularity of Scottish cultural iconography helped render it suspect to many twentieth-century radicals. James Leslie Mitchell (Lewis Grassic Gibbon) described it as 'genteel hobbies', and ironically remarked that 'I like the thought of a Scots Catholic kingdom with Mr. Compton Mackenzie Prime Minister to some disinterred Jacobite royalty'.[116] There were those among the Irish revivalists who would have seen this as a perfectly respectable possibility. On the other hand, the (perhaps Scots-derived) strain of Celtic Communism, which found its Irish advocates among James Connolly and others of the men of 1916, was widespread in Scotland, and not only among figures like MacDiarmid and Ruaridh Erskine of Mar. John Maclean (1879–1923), the Communist revolutionary who was in many respects Connolly's Scottish equivalent, began to advocate 'a Scottish Socialist Republic', which he (a guest of honour in Ireland who shared a mass meeting platform with Countess Markievicz) at least on occasion saw as a Scots-Irish project: 'Further intercourse between Ireland and Scotland, between the forces of Labour in particular, and concerted action for common ends, will help the workers of both countries- and the Belfast worker is the natural link.'[117] In *All Hail, the Scottish Workers' Republic!* (1920), Maclean, who that year chaired the sexcentenary celebrations of the Declaration of Arbroath, argued in the language of Skene and Connolly that 'the communism of the clans must be re-established on a modern basis ... carrying forward the tradition and instincts of the Celtic race'.[118]

This kind of nostalgic, romantic politics was nonetheless only tangentially cultural, in that it imagined its culture rather than acknowledging, defining and seeking to defend it: Maclean was, as even his sympathizers admit, rather ignorant of Scottish history. The more typical nationalist response was a distrust of artists,[119] even though it was the writers of the Scottish Renaissance who tended to articulate (as in the work of Neil Gunn, Fionn MacColla, Edwin Muir and Hugh MacDiarmid) the plight of Scotland in nationalist terms (see Chapter 2). With the exception of Gunn, these figures were treated, not with the contempt reserved by Wolfe Tone for the harpists, but with a distrust which reflected their perceived eccentricity and extremism. Partly this distrust was justified (as in the case of MacDiarmid); but it also bore witness to growing reservations concerning the politico-cultural symbiosis of Irish politics, and its expression through violence. Early positive comparisons of Yeats and MacDiarmid (e.g. by W. H. Hamilton in *Scots Independent* V:2 (1930), 28–9) diminished as time progressed. Nonetheless, as discussed in Chapter 2, the nationalist youth movements of the 1930s owed something to those of Sinn Fein and Countess Markievicz: Clan Scotland, for example, 'the *Political Army* of the National Party', sported 'as its insignia two crossed broadswords and a targe'.[120] Augusta Lamont, writing in 1931 in a piece for the *Scots Independent* on 'Boy Scouts and a Gaelic Tradition', Pearse-like invoked the adoption of Fionn/Fingal as a hero and exemplar, while Neil Gunn too wrote articles on Pearse for the *Scots Independent*, where H.C. MacNeacail remarked that 'as Cuchulain … defended the marches of ancient Uladh, so Wallace … defended his native land'.[121] At the same time, however, suspicions of the kitsch quality of Scottish culture at large were undermining the case of cultural nationalism to be taken seriously:

> This 'Highland' cult is amusing, and it is exasperating. Like British Israelism it gives no heed to history, anthropology, or philology. Originating about a century ago, fathered by Sir Walter Scott and Stewart of Garth (mother unknown), it has been fostered ever since by our military and feudal caste, tartan kilt-makers, sellers of souvenirs and advertisers of whisky.[122]

One novelist, Eric Linklater, stood as the National Party of Scotland's candidate in the East Fife by-election of 1933 on a cultural agenda, devising

> a policy for Scotland based upon a model combining the Court of King James IV with Edinburgh in the eighteenth century, incorporating certain Norse and Celtic values, and ignoring 'the cultural blight of Presbyterianism

and the industrial revolution' ... During his discussions ... he had found himself more than once quoting a dictum of the German critic and poet Herder: 'Study the superstitions and the sagas of the forefathers.' That was what Yeats and Synge had done.[123]

As John Coakley has shown, it was not only Yeats and Synge, but the ideas of Pearse himself which followed the dicta of Herder.[124] Notwithstanding such distinguished avatars, Linklater fared badly, and turned on his Nationalist sponsors. When in the following year (1934) the more determinedly cultural Scottish Party merged with the National Party of Scotland to form the modern SNP, the new organization, 'committed to tackling the Scottish heartland rather than the Celtic fringe', gave the culturalists short shrift. As H. J. Hanham observed, 'So far as the S.N.P. is concerned the Scottish renaissance might never have occurred'.[125] Harsh as this verdict is, there was an element of truth in it, at least up to the 1980s. Middle-class cultural nationalism expressed itself through organizations such as the National Trust for Scotland (1931) and the Saltire Society (1936), which (particularly in the NTS's case) were vehicles for unionist localism. By contrast, the SNP (with notable exceptions, such as that of John MacCormick) for many years attracted activists from the provincial lower-middle classes of Scotland, a Poujadiste tendency which frequently expressed an ignorant hostility towards a state whose operations and political processes it did not understand. When large numbers of such people were elected (as in 1968), they did a disservice to the cause they espoused.

It could be argued that Scottish political nationalism based on economic grievance and structural inequity could never function as effectively as its equivalent in Ireland. The absence of a cultural dimension helped to reduce the SNP to the pleading of the provincial pressure group on more than one occasion, though in its defence it must be said that, according to one poll at least, only 6 per cent of Scots prioritized cultural matters. It was not until the 1980s that the nationalists began to catch up with the cultural dimension, and by then Scottish culture was again developing in a second or third phase of the 1920s Renaissance, a development which was able increasingly to find its international correlative in the European Union which the nationalist luminary William Power had called for in the 1940s (a longstanding idea held by Renan nearly a century earlier).[126]

Many might think that cultural self-definition would of necessity play a key role in the attempts of Celticism and Celtic identities to gain recognition for themselves within the British Isles. The Celtic cult, Celtic revival and brief pan-Celticism of the late nineteenth century appear to lend support to this argument, as do several more recent developments. Yet the internal dynamic in the relationship between cultural and political nationalism has been very distinct in Wales, Scotland and Ireland. In Ireland, cultural revival lent the crucial dimension to political nationalism, rendering it both more intense and more narrowly sectarian; in Wales, cultural politics have always occupied a prominent place, limiting rather than enhancing the scope for political nationalism. Scotland provides, here as elsewhere, a middle ground, where territorial politics have survived, if not flourished, while keeping a suspect culturalism at arm's length. More recently, signs of a closer contiguity between cultural and political nationalism, and the return of artists and writers as nationalist spokesmen in numbers for the first time since the 1930s, have provided a faint echo of the Irish revival of the previous *fin de siècle*. In the last chapter, I shall turn to some of the implications for Celtic identities as they appear in the fluctuating loyalties and political conditions of the world since the 1960s, habituated and yet unused to change.

Chapter 4

The 'imagined community'

Terror and Totems

I heard the Poor Old Woman say
'At break of day the fowler came
And took my blackbirds from their songs
Who loved me well through shame and blame ...
In Derry of the little hills'.

Francis Ledwidge, 'The Blackbirds'

despite its sympathies, still saying
'I think these natives human, think their code,
though strange to us, and farther from the truth,
only a little so – to be redeemed
if they themselves rise up against the spells
and fears their celibates surround them with'.

John Hewitt, 'The Colony'[1]

The Imagined Community is a phrase deriving from Benedict Anderson's influential study, *Imagined Communities: Reflections on the Origin and Spread of Nationalism*, first published in 1983. Like all 'one stop shop' solutions to the complex issues raised by nationalism, it is found wanting in several areas, some of which have been touched on in earlier chapters.[2] Sociological approaches to nationalism often display severe limitations in the blithe simplicity with which they theorize the depth and variety of the history which generates and absorbs us all: many of the theorists of nationalism do not seem to care overmuch for historical detail or counterfactual evidence. For this reason, as discussed in Chapter 3, the more flexible ideas of writers such as Anthony Smith, who stress continuity and ancestry more than 'invention' or 'imagination', are to be preferred. As William Ferguson rightly points out, 'invention' as a totalizing concept is 'superficial and unscholarly'. The idea that identities are mainly chosen, invented or dreamt up is, like the teleological and sometimes Marxian history whence it derives, a judgement on the past in the terms of a present agenda: 'be whatever you want to be' may be a sentiment understood by our posterity; but it was inaccessible to our ancestors.[3] Flowery it may be, but there is still much to be said for the essential approach of *ur*-texts such as Ernest Renan's 'Qu'est-ce qu'une nation?':

> The nation, even as the individual, is the end product of a long period of work, sacrifice and devotion ... our ancestors have made us what we are ... To have common glories in the past, a common will in the present; to have accomplished great things together, to wish to do so again, that is the essential condition for being a nation. A nation is a grand solidarity constituted by the sentiment of sacrifices ...

Here the 'sentiment' may be 'imagined' in Anderson's terms, but the sacrifices are 'essential' and real. Renan's definition clearly fits the development of nationalisms in Ireland, Finland and Egypt among many others. It can be deconstructed as 'romantic' by modern theorists: but if Renan can be historicized, so can they: and it is he who emphasizes the significance of history and the historical as the real grounds for shared imaginings.[4]

Nonetheless, Benedict Anderson's contribution is a major, and in some areas a deeply appropriate response to a key problem of nationalism where what is shared is isomorphic with what is contested. In this chapter I shall argue that it is in Northern Ireland, where the contestation of imagined identity lies at the heart of the conflict, that ideas of the 'imagined community' work best in the British Isles: here the sound of 'ancestral voices' has been forcibly and continuously projected through imaginative writing, literature and cultural representation which lie at the heart of its generative power, whether for good or ill. In Northern Ireland, uniquely in the British Isles, this imaginative dynamo is not simply the property of protest against a central state: it is divided against itself, with mutual incomprehension between the communities, not only because they have different myths, but also because they squabble over the same ones. The 'imagined community' is riven by incompatible imaginings, rendered more dangerous by a history of violence which ensures that the vocalization of the past is in terms of a narrative of crises: as Walter Benjamin points out in a more general context, the past is articulated by seizing 'hold of a memory as it flashes up in a moment of danger'. This is particularly (and indeed on occasion tragically) true in the marching season, where 'moments of danger' (cf. Richard Kirkland's recent study) are orchestrated to crystallize the thrill and terror of ancient conflict. There are little other than such moments in the imagination of Northern Ireland's past: yet even in the ferocious divisions that surface through them, a curious commonality is present as mythic images of one past are frequently competed for in an irreconcilable present.[5]

Cuchulain is a prime example of one such image, and an important one because of the issues of gendering the Celt which are still in the foreground in the imaginative conflicts of the north. For twentieth-century Republicanism in the wake of Pearse, Cuchulain has been an undiluted idol of Celtic heroism: thus in one Derry mural of 1988, 'the dying Cuchulain' is portrayed alongside 'busts of seven signatories of the 1916 Proclamation [of an Irish Republic]'; in another of 1981 the dying Cuchulain is portrayed alongside the names of 25 dead local IRA Volunteers. Yet the masculine Gaelic hero (unless one counts Cuchulain as a Pict, as Ian Adamson's Unionism and other traditions imply[6]) has a more uneasy role in the North than was the case in 1916 Dublin. The re-masculinizing of the Celt was an important feature of the Irish Renaissance in both its cultural and political dimensions; yet in the North it has to contend with the strongly masculinized self-image of the Unionist community, elements in which have been determined both to postulate a pan-Ulster identity for the two-thirds of the old province incorporated in the North, and to point out Cuchulain's mythic role as defender of Ulster. UDA targets in the Republic may have included 'the Cuchulain statue in the Dublin GPO',[7] but in the North a different Cuchulain has appeared in 'a place of honour on a prominent … UDA mural in East Belfast … ancient defender of Ulster from Irish attacks'.[8]

The masculinity of 'Unionist Ulster' has a long history, 'proud, protestant and northern, and male'.[9] In deference to its partly Scottish heritage, it utilized the heroic Celt in its defiance of the Home Rule bills: a cartoon of 'The Ulster Scot' from early this century shows a 'stereotypical kilted Highland warrior, complete with claymore' and the following verse in Scots:

This land oor heritage by richt
Priest ridden saints may grudge us
Three hunner years we hae been here
An Deil th' fit they'll budge us.

As one commentator remarks, 'the irony of an image popularly associated with Jacobite rebelliousness being used to promote the Unionist cause seemed to escape the propagandists'.[10] Indeed, the use of the heroic Highlander as an icon by the descendants of the Covenanters is itself ironic, while being suggestive of the extent to which the Ulster Unionist tradition has expressed itself through the imaginative imagery claimed by its oppo-

nents. Cuchulain as Orangeman and Jacobite as Unionist alike are examples of Protestant Ulster's attempts to seize and contest the validity of the
'imagined community' projected by Unionism's opponents, and to claim
it as their own: to be the 'Cuchulain / bellowing against / the Scarlet
Whore' rather than the sacrificial Celtic Catholic hero of Pearse.[11]

By contrast, although Cuchulain has had great potency as a nationalist
image, it is arguable that the image of the feminized Ireland as
oppressed/ravished/abused/neglected retains a strong hold in the same
community, a hold much diminished outside the North. Disguised
images of the Sean Bhean Bhocht are continually present in the northern
nationalist imagination: Seamus Heaney's 'Bog Queen', for example. The
sacrificial qualities of Pearseite nationalism have a continuing undertow
in the implicit portrayals of Ireland/Cuchulain as Christ and Mother Ire-
land/the Sean Bhean Bhocht in association with the Blessed Virgin in
Republican murals. One in Rockmount Street in 1981 portrayed the
Virgin above a dying hunger striker with the motto 'Blessed are those',
alluding both to the Magnificat ('Of all women you are the most blessed')
and also to Christ's words to Thomas, ('Blessed are those who have not
seen, and yet believe').[12] Another from the hunger strike year showed an
image of the Union Jack as the cross on which Ireland hangs beside
another of Ireland carrying the cross.[13]

The call for 'womanly times', and the 'new lease of life in Northern
Republican ideology' enjoyed by figures such as 'Maeve the warrior-
queen' also point in the direction of a continuing role for Mother Ireland
imagery.[14] At the same time, writers such as Paul Muldoon mock the continuing potency of such images: in 'Aisling' he asks whether the beautiful
woman he encounters was 'Aurora, or the goddess Flora ... or Anorexia',
a bitter allusion to the hunger strikers of 1981 and the sacrificial politics
they continued to represent.[15] Heaney's Bog Queen appears on the surface
to be a similar image, undermining the glory and beauty of the ideal with
imagery of death, darkness and ugliness: 'the plait of my hair / a slimy
broth-end / Of bog ...'; yet in the end the living quality of the feminine
landscape celebrated elsewhere by Heaney (e.g. in 'Act of Union') can be
held to provide a compellingly ugly image of resurrection for the Sean
Bhean Bhocht in a new Republican generation: 'I rose from the dark,
hacked bone, skull-ware.' The poet's doubts remain however: in Heaney's
'Aisling' the writer is not, as in Yeats's 'Hound Voice', part of the excited
blood hunt, with its 'chants of victory', but rather aware of the 'high
lament' of 'The stag's exhausted belling', unable to divorce himself from
the victim.[16]

Attempts by the Unionist community to contest Irish nationalist icons appear to derive from two main underlying aims. First, there are signs of a desire to create an Ulster identity for the six counties of the North by acts which 'foreclose Ulster's past' by assuming the uncontested distinctiveness of its present: the Ulster Museum has a 'commitment to the Education for Mutual Understanding programme', but its very title (cf. also the University of Ulster) is indicative of a shared 'Ulster' identity which is designedly oblivious of the artificial border of Partition which splits the historic province's nine counties. Secondly, the creation of such an Ulster identity bolsters the self-belief of a Unionism which can no longer unreservedly align itself with a Britishness which often now regards it as a quaint curio, if not simply another example of mad Irishness.[17] The imperialist iconography of Loyalist murals and their habits of referring back to the sacrifices of Unionism for the Empire or on the Somme are more attuned to the days of the Orange Card and the Curragh Mutiny than the priorities of modern British government: in one 1988 Shankhill Road mural, 'Ulster' is portrayed as a woman calling men to arms in 1914, while holding a Winchester rifle. The unusual femininity of Ulster identity here is of course undermined both by the fact that it is men who are called to arms (cf. *Cathleen Ni Houlihan* and the Sean Bhean Bhocht tradition), and also possibly through echoes of the famous *Women of Britain, Say Go!* poster of World War I, which displays British unity across all classes in a common war effort. So important is such Orange iconography to the Unionist tradition that it remained possible as late as the 1950s to earn a 'living solely as a painter of Orange banners'.[18]

The very acts of contestation which operate dynamically within Northern Ireland are inimical to the construction of a settled polity, either British or Irish. In particular, the manner in which Unionist iconography simultaneously displays anachronistic features of Britishness while using imagery which (under the guise of Ulster identity) effectively bolsters its own Irishness, simultaneously alienates it from both Britain and Ireland. At the same time, nationalist imagery has until recently adopted a Pearseite (or even hyperPearseite) line in sacrificial memorialization which has become increasingly detached from the postwar Irish Republic's mixture of sympathetic nostalgia and ironic distance towards the imagery of the Celtic revival. In particular, the gendering of politics in the North has perpetuated a contestation effectively resolved in the rest of Ireland many years earlier. Pearse's manly Gael Cuchulain has in part been recruited by a Unionist community defined by warrior males from Cromwell to Carson by way of claymore-wielding Celts, while the feminized images of

Ireland have received a new and complex lease of life in the nationalist community, without necessarily turning their emblems of deprivation, ravishment and oppression into anything more positive. If the political settlement of 1998 holds, the image of Northern Ireland as a statelet annexed by Unionist rape will be as untenable as the view of it as a heroic male bastion against the insinuating 'Bog-Wog',[19] but the contestation runs so deep that only a postmodern irony towards the cultural contents of the 'imagined communities' can rob them of their need for strife. The mode for both the construction and preservation of identity in Northern Ireland is contestation: that contestation will either have to become a game, or be otherwise decoupled from its outward manifestation in open strife for the communities to live together. That, or one side must win: and such an aim, much more in common with the deep history of the North's identities than their reduction to irony or jouissance, is unsurprisingly the aim both of Sinn Fein and the Ulster Unionists. It may be enough on its own for a peace which shares means but not ends, which in its turn of course depends on how close or achievable these ends appear.

Independence in Europe?

In 1994 the present author was interviewed by a Ph.D. student from the London School of Economics who was working on a thesis on Scottish Nationalism, and had come to the conclusion that the European Union and the development of the European idea had a key role to play in the growth of modern nationalist consciousness in Scotland. In this she was almost certainly right. 'Europe' has increasingly become an ideological counterweight to 'England' in Scottish opinion. In the 1980s, increasingly apparent English xenophobic and milder scepticism towards the EU and the European ideal has run in tandem with an increasingly pro-European nationalist left in Scotland, not only in the SNP but in elements of the Labour Party. The idea that Scotland is a more outward-looking, international and European nation than England has gained great ground: it can be found on the pages of minority interest articles on Scottish culture, and was heard in the Paris pubs during the 1998 World Cup (indeed, it may not be too fanciful to speculate that the improving behaviour of Scottish football fans abroad after 1980 has arisen in part from a wish both to be different from the English and more internationalist).[20] As such, the European dimension forms the greatest distinction between the Scottish nationalism of the 1970s (when only Jim Sillars's Scottish Labour Party showed any interest in pro-European policies) and that of the

1990s. In the EEC referendum of 1975, where the SNP was the only main-stream party campaigning 'for withdrawal',[21] Scotland voted in favour of membership by a significantly smaller margin than was the case south of the Border, and provided the only districts in any part of the UK which voted No. Scotland was still inward-looking and post-imperial: its nationalists had articulated their difference from England, but many still thought of the nascent EU as alien, irrelevant or other in what was arguably a fundamentally British way. This was to change.

A vein of pro-Europeanism had been evident in Scottish nationalism for many years. In the 1940s, William Power had supported European integration, and in the 1950s George Dott could write that 'We are a Euro-pean people, and instinct and interest alike should align us with our European kindred … let us create a European authority.' Yet on the other hand, there was a marked British strain, 'a strong element of anti-Catholic bigotry and anti-Irish racism'. The 1934 merger of the Scottish Party and the National Party of Scotland had as one of its bases an agreement to share the 'rights and responsibilities' of Empire, and this kind of attitude was present into the 1980s: the 'association of states of the British Isles' policy of 1969 was on this reading simply a post-imperial updating of this 1930s position. In addition, whether pro- or anti-Empire, the so-called 'fundamentalists' of the SNP arguably consistently displayed a 'British' approach to sovereignty: totalizing, indivisible, nationally exalting and ultimately chauvinistic; anti-English comments at conferences from the 1950s to the 1990s have frequently come from this wing of the party.[22] The irony is that the most anti-British politicians in Scotland have tended to be those whose concept of nationality is essentially a British one. Thus both moderate and fundamentalist Scottish nationalism shared certain aspects of a 'British' outlook.

The rise of the SNP and Plaid Cymru in the 1960s is conventionally, and no doubt rightly, attributed to the decline of Empire overseas and to the attrition of heavy industry at home. There are also other factors which are less well explored, such as the provincialization of Scotland after 1945 as it ceased to have 'junior partner' status in the Empire, its exclusion from portrayal in the expanding British electronic media, and the weak-ening control exercised by the Scottish middle class over its own institu-tions. In the age of Empire, Scotland's leading novelist was taught in many English schools and selected parts of Scottish history were far more visible in British education than they subsequently became: Flora Thompson's *Lark Rise to Candleford*, one among many examples, demon-strates the depth of influence the poetry and prose of Sir Walter Scott had on the education of rural Oxfordshire at the turn of the century. At the same time, educated Scots graduating from Scottish universities had a statistically higher chance of reaching the highest British political and public sector offices than did graduates of England's provincial universities. After 1945, this gradually changed, and the status of Scotland appeared to many increasingly provincialized. It was not only Scottish difference which was stigmatized; Scottish Britishness also found its domestic control challenged and its opportunities outwith Scotland curtailed. Scottish loss of opportunity and autonomy was symbiotic with imperial decline.

As a result, the upsurge in 1960s and 1970s nationalism in Scotland was, in its own way, very British, representative of the growing failure of Britain to sustain its Scottish component's status. Its vision of sovereignty as a unique, total and absolute good which could be held in the same way and to the same extent by small nations as superpowers had far more in common with British constitutionalism and Tory Euroscepticism than would be the case today. If Scottish nationalism was anti-British, it wasn't clearly very much in favour of anything else: indeed, as will be argued below, its Nordic bias was in its own way also a British one. There are still signs of this: the SNP's somewhat sentimental attachment to the Scottish regiments of the British army is one; but much has changed since the last anti-EU election campaign of 1987. 'Independence in Europe' as a campaigning theme was launched to undermine for ever the credibility of 'trenches along the Border' and 'customs posts at Berwick' which had haunted the isolationist arguments of earlier 'separatists'. It altered the focus of Scottish nationalism, and neatly combined itself with the contemporary opening of a rich seam of sentimental recollection of the history of the Auld Alliance and Scots abroad among a wider section of Scottish society.

The Europeanness of Scotland, its long history of internationalism and openness, is thus a consolidating image for the country of very recent date, however true it may have been of a past now remote: Scotland's modern identity has, partly as a result, a continuing problem in coming to terms with the real historicity of Scottish complicity in the British Empire (this is not to agree with Anderson's full claims, only that they are relevant in certain developments – see above) . In many respects this new European internationalism can appear a myth, a piece of manufactured selfhood from a country where fewer school-leavers take a foreign-language Higher today than in the narrow nationalist 1970s. Heavily reliant on (often factually rather fuzzy) memorials and representations of the

'Auld Alliance' with France, Scottish Europeanism has been further boosted by the evident success of Ireland within the European Union. The rapid economic growth of the so-called 'Celtic Tiger' exerts increasing pressure on the imagination of a Scotland experiencing the end of its heavy industries and a collateral decline in sectarianism. Marketing themselves as 'the young Europeans' and with a pleasing postmodern juxtaposition of Ogham script and internet cafés in their planning development, the Irish have successfully cast off what appeared to many to be the backward-looking imagery of the Celtic Revival. *The Scotsman*'s recent verdict on Ireland was that 'perhaps we in Scotland, imbued by the vote for devolution with a similar sense of adventure, can also learn to look further ahead'.[23] *Also?* The term would have been unthinkable before 1980, but in important respects the modernizing of Ireland is a sign of an underlying pattern of change from which Britain has largely been excluded. In common with other European countries (but significantly unlike both Scotland and Britain), Ireland's planned building and other developments contributed to the 'imaging' of the country: the use of certain shapes, images or themes (cf. the 'Green Heart' of the environmentalist Netherlands) to evoke national identity and priorities. Strategic planning and marketing was lifting Ireland the brand into fresh geopolitical significance, in common with the cultural policy of other non-British EU countries. Nationalism in Scotland eventually responded. In 1988, the SNP moved definitively to a pro-European policy; by the mid-1990s, Ireland was being used freely by Scottish nationalists as an exemplar of what an independent Scotland could be like. By mid-1998, Alex Salmond, the SNP leader, appeared to be linking Scotland's relationship with Ireland to the 'Council of the Isles' to be developed under the terms of the 1998 Peace Settlement in Northern Ireland. Symbiotically, the sharing of advisory powers in the Council among 'the people of these islands' brought to life the historic metropolitan response: 'a guillemot has been elected' from Rockall sneered the *Guardian*.[24]

European identity projected along a Scots-Irish axis offered a contrast to the SNP's previous rhetoric. In the 1960s and early 1970s, the UK had been involved in the looser European Free Trade Association (EFTA) rather than the EU. EFTA was strongest in the Nordic countries, and this is perhaps one of the reasons that the SNP used Norway (admittedly also a country with strong oil revenues) as its normative exemplar of an independent future during this period (and indeed for some time after it). Norway, still outside the EU, is now downgraded as a comparator: the use of Ireland, now that circumstances have made it possible, is potentially more effective. The development of Scottish Europeanism in the context of Irish Europeanism is perhaps more genuinely 'independent' than the use of Norway as an exemplar for Scotland in an era when the UK as a whole had closer Nordic alignments. The anti-EU, EFTA-style agenda of Scottish nationalism was British in a way the Irish one is not. Ireland is, whatever it once was, a definitively anti-British state, its *raison d'être* being to throw off the identity which once possessed it. Hence Scottish alignment with Ireland, besides renewing and exploring old links of Celtic commonality (real or imagined), provides an axis of cultural, economic and political interest which is fundamentally un-British. Comparisons between Scotland and Ireland spring up at every level: the 1999 Scottish Office/Dublin support for the Celtic Studies Centre in Bonn, the 1997 Gaelic language initiative by the Scottish Office and the government-backed 1995 Irish-Scottish Academic Initiative between the universities of Aberdeen, Strathclyde and Dublin being only two examples of a new search for understanding between the two countries, one perhaps amplified by the (apparently at least) un-English focus of the proposed new 'Council of the Isles'. The imagining of Scotland in connection with Ireland is happening at much more profound and politicized levels than its Celtic revival predecessors of a century ago. The political and cultural developments of the EU offer it a more favourable context than could ever have been the case in 1900; and the intense imagining of Europe and Europeanness in relation to the Scottish experience helps sustain this contextualization. The internationalism of Scotland is seen as an external counterpart to the erosion of internal differences and divisions in the country. For example, according to a poll in *The Universe*, 35 per cent of Scottish Catholics were preparing to vote for the SNP in the 1992 election, many times the number who were prepared to support it in the 1970s, when the 'British' qualities of Scottish nationalism were more evident.[25] Whether such findings are reliable or not (and the 1994 Monklands by-election provided divergent evidence, admittedly in an exceptional context), these indicators are part of a changing mood among a community which had once suspected (not always unjustly) the SNP of representing only a version of British Protestant identity. Naturally enough, this change of mood can only make the task of using Ireland as a model for Scotland an easier one for nationalist internationalists. Polls on identity bear out the changing mood: in 1994, 64 per cent of Scots felt more Scots than British (one-third more than the Welsh, and more than twice the English figure), while a majority of SNP and Labour supporters also identified themselves as Scottish and European to some degree.[26]

Even as such shifts began to occur, however, British satire often remained levelled at targets which had been moved on. *Punch* once observed that 'leave the Scots alone and they splinter immediately; the only thing that unites them deeply is the auld enemy, England', and such sentiments continued to be expressed into the 1990s.[27] The extent to which such statements were true has been undermined by the slowly growing symbiosis between an imagined internationalist solidarity and the vision of Scotland which is its necessary counterpart at home. The British elements of a shared past have been significantly replaced by a Europeanism which puts the accent on Ireland (and Scotland) as representatives of a mainstream from which England (through xenophobia, Euroscepticism, football violence in Europe, etc.) is excluding itself. The sharing of Celtic roots and the anti-British elements of Scottish history are now increasingly to the fore. Britain is seen as irrevocably linked to an England in denial about its national decline, which in turn is being accelerated by isolationism. Rather than focusing on England to preserve unity of purpose and keep internal divisions at bay, the diminution of internal divisions in Scotland runs in tandem with focusing elsewhere.

If internationalism is powerfully emphasized, so also is its domestic correlative and community and commonality. Claims are made about Scotland's lack of racism vis-à-vis England as indicative of the absence of xenophobia in the united community, while the SNP's development of 'Scots Asians for Independence' and 'New Scots for Independence' backs up this cosy civic ideal. Misleading and overstated as it may be in practice, it contains a grain of truth made all the more likely to swell into a pearl of wisdom by irritations like the *Guardian*'s view that 'the Scots are too busy hating the English to abuse ethnic minorities'.[28] Similarly the opinion expressed by a Conservative minister that if Scotland became independent, 'England, Wales *and Ireland*' (my italics) would be the successor state only reinforces charges of isolationist and nostalgic imperialism.[29] The European dimension and Scotland's now famed internationalism provide the external counterpart to such claimed internal cosiness: one seen as modern and advancing, while England/Britain stagnates and declines. As Winnie Ewing put it during the 1992 General Election, the choice is to 'remain second-class Britons instead of first-class Europeans'.[30] Such projections may be simplistic, and many in Scotland hold limited or no allegiance to this emergent international identity: but its growth, whether or not marketed by outright nationalists as 'Independence in Europe', is a significant development of our times. Indeed, by the mid-1990s, Conservative spokesmen were 'using the SNP as a cipher for Brussels' to express 'visceral hostility to European Union'.[31]

Beyond the European dimension, the Irish exemplar offers even broader international horizons. Irish and Scottish industries such as tourism appeal to expatriate or ex-expatriate markets in the former Empire, chiefly the United States: thus they can be directly compared to the detriment of Scotland in (say) cinema and tourism, because of its lack of independent policy-making and submergence within general British marketing efforts.[32] At the same time, it is clear that North American attitudes and outlooks offer significant benefits to Scotland if it can be seen as a kind of new, second or lesser Ireland, one of two countries in a symbiotic relationship with 'a great bond between them', as L/Cpl Ian Muncie (serving in Northern Ireland) recently pointed out.[33] The link between Scotland and Ireland made in *Braveheart* (1995) and elsewhere shows how potent this new identity is in the context of historic North American sympathies and the North American marketplace. Rising interest in contemporary Scotland in the United States can only be reinforced (and to some extent has been engendered) by the Irish connection, while links between Canadian, Scottish and Breton Celtic festivals are increasingly evident.[34] Imagined or not (and there is of course a considerable shared history between the two countries), Celtic commonality is a potent force in cultural representation and its political implications.

The strength of these developments to some extent derives from their underlying substratum of buried experience: in short, Scotland and Ireland have had a good deal in common in a history often hidden by religious division. The weakness of Anderson's notion of the 'imagined community' is that it implies that one can imagine at will, and choose an identity as the postmodern consumer chooses a lifestyle product. Indeed, this is arguably present in the Hegelian antecedents of Anderson's theory, with their philosophic stress on abstraction in contrast with the shared historic substance of our lived subjective autobiographic selves imagining their being in the more objectivized (and indeed objective) biographic community, the supplied, irremovable grounds of our story. In reality, one of the most powerful features of such communal imagining is the sense of discovery, of laying bare what has been hidden: few invented traditions can sustain themselves on fantasy alone. As this book has made clear, 'imagined' Scots-Irishness, like 'imagined' Celticism, cannot be held to be the spurious hype of a marginal agenda. It rests on much that is common, and recognized as common, in experience, concerns and history. Wendy Wood's and Gwynfor Evans's protest fasts of the 1970s and 1980s may have been imitations of their more potent Irish forerunners and successors: but the Irish example was imitated for a reason, that of a believed and perceived underlying commonality.[35] From Fionn to James Connolly, there is a strong case for that commonality, particularly as it existed between Scotland and Ireland. Its appearance in the light of day is a stimulus for a community born of the discovery of the sources for the images of its own imaginings.

In short, then, one of the major features of Celticism today is its internationalism and Europeanism, in Ireland's case achieved, in Scotland's aspirational. To some extent this new dimension of experience and identity is based on the realities of underlying history and experience: to some extent it is projected and imagined. Enthusiasm exaggerates the balance between these factors in one direction, prejudice in another. But beliefs, whether more fact than myth or the reverse, have their effects. Celticism in its broadest sense has moved away, at least to some extent, from defining itself in terms of its oppositionalism to ownership by English experience. In Scotland's and Ireland's case, such centripetal obsessions with the Britain from which they wished to differentiate themselves led to narrowness and a reactive quality in the assertions of identity which a more centrifugal Europeanism promises to deliver them from. In significant contrast, moreover, those with a strongly Anglo-British identity see Brussels and Strasbourg as centripetally constraining rather than centrifugally liberating. Thus Celtic internationalism celebrates itself in terms which contrast with British nationalism without being constrained into simple reaction to it. Projected or not, imagined or not, such cultural representations are very distinct from those of the Celtic revival, which struggled so often to define what was right with the Celt as being what was wrong with the Saxon, or vice-versa. Celticism's present manifestations are more multifaceted and various, less driven by ideas (though these are present) and more by images. Suitable, that is, to this age, where a politics of representation and sentiment has great potential. Scottish internationalism is the 'Motherhood and Apple Pie' of Scottish identity in the present generation: yet Scotland itself is mature enough to have sceptics, and motherhood is an enduring truth, however contingent it is on any particular culinary imagining: in any case, better its apple pie than the vampiric demands of the Mother Ireland of an earlier generation. The 'Celtic Fringe' has projected itself into the heart of the international family.

Unity in diversity?

These developments in Scotland have, like the stronger ones in Ireland of a century ago, taken the rhetorics of Britain and Britishness by surprise. To a great extent, the centrality of Englishness and English experience in notions of Britishness has entrenched a failure, often a total failure, to conduct cultural dialogue with the other countries of the British Isles. Indeed, the extent to which English identity has found its recent historic expression only through notions of Britishness emphasizes the degree to which the Celtic margins are organically important in confirming, through their own marginality, the English possession of that Britishness: it is no coincidence that English qua English identity is now being more closely examined in the aftermath of Scotland's (more especially than Wales's) 1997 referendum. The knee-jerk hostility often visible to what some see as Scotland's special pleading for a difference greater than Yorkshire's is often, on close examination, seen to be an anger at perceived theft. Scotland has made claims for its own territoriality: and as Britons, many English believe that Scotland belongs to them.

History has told us so. In the nineteenth century, the Saxon Englishman was seen as possessing the feminized marginal Celt in just this way. Such a characterization of Saxon/Celtic relations was at one with 'the ideology of imperialism' with its 'assertion of masculinity'.[36] As Denis Judd has pointed out, 'in a host of histories, words and ... school textbooks, Anglo-Saxon racial superiority was not merely taken for granted, but vehemently asserted'.[37] The associated gendering of the Celt had important consequences in confirming a discourse of English protective ownership (cf. the masculinity of Northern Irish Protestantism). In this sense, the masculinization of the Celt in the latter stages of the Irish Celtic revival was a significant challenge to British identity and spelled the beginning of the end for Irish Britishness throughout most of the island. Ireland's organic place in Britain, once extolled as necessary and inevitable, was largely airbrushed out of British accounts after 1922, while it remained as an initially ignored and subsequently embarrassing survival in the festering snakepit of Northern Irish politics, to which Britain clumsily returned in 1969, when government policy showed that they had learnt and Northern Irish response that they had forgotten, nothing. The British Government, the Unionists and the IRA made one perfect Bourbon between them.

Such intrinsic clumsiness is fed not only by the history of British development and its paradigmatic assumptions, but also by the media which inherited them. The BBC in particular can clearly be seen to continue its allegiance to Reithite *de haut en bas* educative centralism in significant areas of underlying policy. Even in news and current affairs programmes, it can be strongly monologic in its portrayal of Britain and Britishness. For example, despite the New Labour imprimatur attaching to the 1997 devolution referenda, BBC treatment of the issue (and this was particularly true of its London coverage) was biased towards sceptical, hostile and outright Unionist opposition to constitutional change to the extent that one of their own watchdogs reproved the corporation. Likewise, even after the referendum, in a *Question Time* broadcast from Scotland, an automatic place was preserved for the Conservative Party representative (with no parliamentary seats), but not granted the Scottish Nationalists: politics cannot be different in different parts of Britain, because then it would not be British politics, seems to be the assumption. Yet, while viewers and listeners in Middle England would be up in arms if they were fed a diet of shinty, in-depth reporting on the Highers results in schools and organizational changes in the Scottish legal system, the same irrelevancies in reverse are pumped endlessly into Scottish homes.[38]

This failure of dialogue has also had far more serious consequences. In the context of the 1994 IRA ceasefire and the subsequent peace negotiations, neither the BBC nor ITN has, in news bulletins or more focused current affairs programmes, shown much interest in the question of decommissioning Loyalist (as opposed to Republican) weapons. Yet not only did Loyalist killers match the IRA murder rate in the early 1990s, but there is a long history of tens of thousands of legally held firearms in Northern Ireland, mostly in the hands of the Unionist community. To say this is not to offer apologetics for the Provisional IRA's miserable trail of mayhem: it is simply to point out that as long as Britain and the British media expresses the priorities of a settlement in this way only, so long will they be under the deepest suspicion from those they mean to convince, and worse, even from more moderate quarters. Dialogue in Northern Ireland has been a considerable achievement: but it could arguably have come earlier if Britain's elites had not developed such a profound habit of only talking to themselves, based on the premiss that only they had anything of worth to say. Broadcasting, like the Millennium Dome and many other examples from defence procurement to the Eurostar link and London weighting, is an unacknowledged subsidy to south-east England: a deliberate reinforcement of the marginal qualities of being elsewhere which has been only lightly touched by the repositioning of Celticism into internationalism. More fundamentally, it casts a shadowy question-mark over the re-emergent questions of English identity through the implicit contempt for diversity and regional metropolises which the policy whose formulation it exemplifies reveals. In T. S. Kuhn's terms, we have seen what the paradigm enables us to see: the dominant paradigm of Britishness has generated and reinforced a fish-eye view of the demography, culture and geography of these islands.[39]

As has been remarked on earlier, the deep-seated ruralist quality frequently expressed in appeals to Englishness is also, while non-metropolitan, overwhelmingly southern, often evoking rolling downs and good weather in the process of opening its 'deep vein of rural nostalgia', whether present in Kipling's Sussex, Baldwin's Worcestershire or Kent as 'the garden of England'. Even the British Left has its peasant version of this ideal, the 'populist face of the rural myth' as it has been called.[40] This envisioning strongly emphasizes a different dimension of community, one which seeks to account totalizingly for the nature of Britishness in terms which are geographically limited and by definition experienced only by a minority. Aspirational British images are thus frequently monologic also, even if not always so comically so as in John Major's evocation of the rural idyll in his 1993 Mansion House speech (see Introduction). Hence it is no coincidence that the Demos-led rebranding of Britain, whether as 'Cool Britannia' or otherwise, has accompanied the first major redefinitions of Britishness in three-quarters of a century. But the structural monologism outlined above continues and indeed develops in a democratic centralism always congenial to the British Left and more recently so to the Right: hence neither Manchester nor Belfast can confidently respond that 'Cool Britannia, she loves us still', to paraphrase an ironic Irish Republican song. Bereft of the military masculine gear of the imperial age Britannia may be, but the expression of the Celtic identities with which this book has been concerned, and the exploration of English identity which will doubtless be the consequence of the changes on which it comments, alike have over centuries shown that 'Britons never never shall be slaves' is a historic sentiment of imperial Protestant identity which functioned externally in ruling the waves, not internally through understanding each other. Less than ten years after the Scot, James Thomson, wrote these lines, his compatriots were being sold into slavery in the American colonies for bearing arms in the cause of 'Prosperity to Scotland and no Union', the badge on their Jacobite blades.[41]

Notes

Introduction

1 N. Davies (1997 (1996)), 55.
2 Lord (1994), 96.
3 *The Herald* (6 August 1997), 12.
4 Chapman (1992), 251–2.
5 *FT Weekend,* 14/15 June 1997.
6 Anderson (1983, 1991).
7 P. Curtis (1971).
8 Discussed in Brown, McCrone and Paterson (1996), 195–6.
9 J.S. Bratton in Mackenzie (1986), 74–93 (80); cf Wiener (1981) for a discussion of the ruralist phenomenon.
10 Osmond (1988), 157.
11 Larkin (1990 (1988)), 190.
12 Greenhalgh (1988), 64, 122–3; Samuel (1989), III:xii.
13 Osmond (1988), 157; Bratton in Mackenzie (1986), 74–93.
14 Newbolt (1914 (1898)), 54, 56, 67.
15 J.A. Mangan, 'The Grit of Our Forefathers', in Mackenzie (1986), 113–39 (115, 117 ff., 134); cf. Colls and Dodd (1986).
16 *Examination Decrees and Regulations* (1997–8), Honour School of Modern History.
17 Lord (1994) 139 ff.
18 D. Jenkins (1975), 132; cf. Osmond (1988).
19 Rolston (1991), 32.
20 Adamson (1982); Osmond (1988), 110 ff.
21 Hobsbawn and Ranger (1983).
22 R.R. Davies (1994), 1–20 (3); J.E. Lloyd (1931), 55.
23 R.R. Davies (1994).
24 Lloyd (1931), 46.
25 Geoffrey of Monmouth (1968 (1136)), 54; Tolkien and Gordon (1946 (1925)), 1.
26 Roger Mason, 'Scotching the Brut', in Mason (1983).
27 Gwyndorf in Alanquist *et al.* (1987), 413–51 (436).
28 Geoffrey of Monmouth (1968 (1136)), 10, 218–19, 258, 261; Ferguson (1998), 14.

29 Ellis (1993 (1985)), 78.
30 Gwyndorf in Alanquist *et al.* (1987), 437.
31 E. Jenkins (1975), 167.
32 Brinkley (1932), vii; Ferguson (1998), 121.
33 Mason (1983): 'Scotching the Brut'.
34 Skene (1880), 94; Ferguson (1998), 304.
35 MacInnes in Alanquist *et al.* (1987), 101–30 (105); Ferguson (1998), 305.
36 Lord (1994), 104.
37 Yeats (1977), 52, 61.
38 Brinkley (1932), 2.
39 Lloyd (1931), 31.
40 Brinkley (1932), 8, 21, 23; Pittock (1997), 13–15.
41 E. Jenkins (1975), 168.
42 Brinkley (1932), 108.
43 E. Jenkins (1975), 169.
44 Enright (1976), 31; Ferguson (1998), 123 for discussion of *Macbeth* and the Stuarts.
45 *Scottish Historical Review* 3, 261 ff.
46 Brinkley (1932), viii, 116, 143, Aeneas is of course Arthur's ancestor in the terms of the Brutus myth.
47 Kidd (1993), 248
48 Taylor and Brewer (1983), 3, 15, 21 ff.
49 Pittock (1997), chs 1 and 2.

Chapter 1

1   Cf. Cannon (1994), 215 ff., 217; Hutchinson and Smith (1994), 45.
2   Cited in Newman (1987), 54.
3   Cited in Hutchinson in Boyce and O'Day (1996), 100–19 (110).
4   R.R. Davies (1994), 3, 7.
5   Hary (1998), 6.
6   Hutchinson and Smith (1994), 47.
7   *The Compact Edition of the Oxford English Dictionary* (1971), Vol. 2.
8   Reproduced in Hutchinson and Smith (1994), 137–8
9   *Ibid.*, 276.
10 Cairns Craig, 'Scotland and Ireland: Imagined Communities, Invented Traditions', unpublished seminar paper to Scots-Irish Research Network, University of Strathclyde, 3 December 1998.
11 Hutchinson and Smith (1994), 178, 306, 317; cf. Anderson, reproduced 89–96 (94).
12 Singer (1996), 309–37.
13 Kennedy Index IX:61, 362, Aberdeen City Archives.
14 David Ditchburn in Dukes (1996), 89–100 (89–90, 91); Cowan (1998), 13.

21 Lloyd (1987), 6.

22 Borrow (1928 (1862)), 8–9.

23 Bromwich (1965), 17.

24 Cairns and Richards (1988), 46.

25 Renan (1896 (1860)), xxii, 4, 7, 8.

26 Yeats (1977), 269, 492.

27 Howes (1998 (1996)), 25, 72.

28 Bromwich (1965), 6.

29 Cairns and Richards (1988), 47, 50, 53; Howes (1998 (1996), 106.

30 O'Rahilly (1924), 89.

31 Quoted in Gibbons (1996), 149, 150.

32 Pittock (1993), 106; Sharp and Matthay (1896), lii.

33 Foster (1997), 237.

34 *The Evergreen* (1895–6).

35 Macgillivray (1911), 3, 4.

36 *The Celtic Magazine V* (1880), 345–7.

37 *The Evergreen* (Spring 1895), 9, 131, 133.

38 Saddlemyer in Skelton and Saddlemyer (1965), 19–21 (20, 21).

39 Cf. *The Fiery Cross 15* (1904), 8.

40 Housman (1995 (1896)), 58; Housman (1928 (1922)), 1, 3.

41 Conan Doyle (1993), xxviii.

42 *Exhibition of the Royal House of Stuart* (1889), 7.

43 Cf. Pittock (1986; 1993); Fletcher (1987).

44 Macdonell (1896), 188.

45 *The Royalist 1:2* (1890), 22; *7:3* (1896), 41–6; *8:1* (1897), 10–14.

46 Cf. Pittock (1993), 97 ff.; Fletcher (1987), 83–123.

47 Pittock (1991), 130.

48 *The Fiery Cross 17* (1905), 2.

49 *The Fiery Cross 1:1* (1901), 2, 3, 5; *1:3* (1901), 4, 8; *6* (1902), 5; *11* (1903), 2;
    12 (1903), 2.

50 *Ibid.*, *1:2* (1901); *10* (1903), 5.

51 James Joyce, in Deane (1991), III:7.

52 Oscar Wilde, 'The Irish Poets of '48', in Wilde (1982), 373–8 (374).

53 Young (1995), 48; Skene II:134; Dewey (1974), 30–70 (33, 42, 43, 50, 52, 54,
    55, 64).

54 Dewey (1974).

55 *Ibid.*

56 Hutchinson (1987), 125; Boyce (1991(1982)), 302.

57 Michael Collins, quoted in Coogan (1990), 422.

58 Deane (1991) II:984.

59 A. Morgan (1988), 16, 19, 23, 26, 193.

60 James Connolly, in Deane (1991), II:985–6.

61 Foster (1997), 71.

62 Edwards (1977), 31–4.
63 *The Evergreen IV* (1896–7), 101–5 ff.
64 Bradley (1998), vii, 25.
65 R.F. Foster (1997), 156, 166.
66 Bradley (1998), 42–3; Coogan (1990), 176.
67 Coogan (1990), 77.
68 Yeats (1970), 43.
69 Cairns and Richards (1988), 51, 52, 53.
70 Deane (1991), II:279.
71 Cairns and Richards (1988), 49.
72 Foster (1997), 180.
73 Yeats (1970), 36–7 and passim.
74 Foster (1997), 84.
75 *Ibid.*
76 Yeats (1977), 52.
77 *Ibid.*, 61.
78 Zimmerman (1969), 185–97 (188).
79 Yeats (1977), 290, 394.
80 Yeats, quoted in R.F. Foster (1997), 250.
81 Yeats (1953), 20–1.
82 MacBride (1974 (1937)), 227; White *et al.* (1992), 489n.
83 Yeats (1953), 86; Howes (1998 (1996)), 60.
84 R.D. Edwards (1977), 117; Howes (1998 (1996)), 36.
85 Thompson (1967), 95; Howes (1998 (1996)), 17.
86 Foster (1997), 262; Yeats (1977), 632.
87 Arthur Griffith, quoted in Hutchinson (1987), 193.
88 Yeats (1961), 173–88 (185, 186–7).
89 Foster (1997), 313, 314.
90 Frayne (1970), 55.
91 Sheridan Gilley in Obelkovich *et al.* (1987), 479–97 (482).
92 Foster (1997), 405; Boyce in Boyce and O'Day (1996), 163–87 (171).
93 Gilley in Obelkovich *et al.* (1987), 482.
94 Philip O'Leary in Koch and Rittmueller (1983), 21–38 (21, 31).
95 Coogan (1990), 71, 298.
96 Patrick Rafroidi in MacDonagh *et al.* (1983), 137–48 (142).
97 Cf. Boyce in Boyce and O'Day (1996), 216–38 (228).
98 Hutchinson (1987), 145.
99 Foster (1987), 3, 73, 308–9.
100 Pearse (1952), 24, 26; Yeats (1961), 509–26 (515); Lyons (1982 (1971)), 337.
101 Boyce (1991 (1982)), 307, 308.
102 Edwards et al (1968), 204; Yeats (1977).
103 Yeats (1953), 695.
104 Cairns and Richards (1988), 91.

105 Gilley in Obelkovich *et al.* (1987), 482.
106 Hutchinson (1987), 117.
107 R.D. Edwards (1977), 1; Boyce (1991 (1982)), 215, 238, 240.
108 James Joyce in Deane (1991), III:7–10 (7).
109 Boyce (1991 (1982)), 323, 351, 354.
110 Longley (1994), 75, 189.
111 Wood (1994), x.
112 Longley (1994), 72; Pittock (1991).
113 Finlay (1994), 31, 32.
114 Cf. Pittock (1991), 134 ff.
115 Thuente (1980), 198.
116 Finlay (1994), 29–31, 37, 39, 84.
117 MacGill-Eian/MacLean (1977), 162.
118 Cf. in particular *Sunset Song* (1932). There is a Gibbon visitor centre at Arbuthnot in the Mearns.
119 Price (1991), 46.
120 *The Herald* (14 January 1999), 4.
121 MacColla (1984 (1932)), 216.
122 Gunn (1943).
123 Cf. Pittock (1995), Chs. 1 and 2. I am indebted to Professor Michael Lynch, President of the Society of Antiquaries of Scotland, for the information on James's marriage.
124 McCrone *et al.* (1995), 51.
125 Prebble (1988b), 118, 121.
126 *The Herald* (10 April 1998), 3.
127 Quoted in Barrow (1976 (1965)), 428.
128 Sheehy (1980), 6, 95, 96, 116, 147 ff., 189.
129 *Ibid.*, 13.
130 Yeats (1977), 621.
131 Sheehy (1980), 92.
132 *The Evergreen* (Spring 1895), 33 and passim.
133 *Ibid.*, (Summer 1896), 7; Boardman (1978).
134 Scott and Macleay (1990), 118.
135 Banham *et al.* (1991), 177.
136 Glendinning *et al.* (1996), 356, 358; Macmillan (1990), 273.
137 Glendinning *et al.* (1996), 358.
138 Cf. the holdings of the Hunterian Museum and Art Gallery, University of Glasgow.
139 Kelvingrove Museum and Art Gallery, Glasgow; Macmillan (1990), 282.
140 Aberdeen City Museum and Art Gallery collections.
141 Kelvingrove Museum and Art Gallery, Glasgow.
142 Lord (1994), 72.
143 Banham *et al.* (1991), 177

Chapter 3

1 N. Davies (1997 (1996)), 650; Linda Colley, British Society for Eighteenth-Century Studies Annual Lecture, St John's College, Oxford, 5 January 1999.
2 N. Davies (1997 (1996)), 23–6.
3 Butterfield (1931), 3, 16.
4 Morris and Morton (1998), 88.
5 Cairns and Richards (1988), 47–8.
6 Coogan (1995), 550, 556, 557.
7 Fasel (1988), Introduction.
8 Arnold (1891), 10.
9 Edmund Burke, quoted in O'Brien (1992), 322.
10 Pittock (1991), 116
11 Ian Campbell Ross, unpublished address to the Strathclyde University English Studies Graduate Seminar, 26 February 1998.
12 Boyce in Boyce and O'Day (1996), 183.
13 Gibbons (1996), 171, 172, 180.
14 Colley (1992); cf. Bradshaw and Morrill (1996).
15 Morrill in Bradshaw and Morrill (1996), 1–38 (7).
16 N. Davies (1997 (1996)), 650.
17 Ferguson (1998), 303.
18 Haldane (1990), 282; Bradley (1998), 76–7.
19 Cf. Ellis (1993 (1985)), 50
20 Chapman (1992), 103.
21 Foster (1987), 203.
22 Quoted in Cairns and Richards (1988), 51.
23 Curtis (1986), 10.
24 Cf. Morris and Morton (1998), 12 ff, 128.
25 Opie (1985), 13; Hobsbawm and Ranger (1983).
26 D. Jenkins (1975), 132; Osmond (1988), 127.
27 Nairn (1977), 266.
28 Morgan in Brockliss and Eastwood (1997), 93–109 (93).
29 Cf. Morris and Morton (1998), 80; Ferguson (1998), 301.
30 Ferguson (1998), 177, 196–7, 304–5; G.H. Jenkins (1987), 224.
31 Campbell and Thomson (1963), xiii.
32 Ferguson (1998), 197; Hechter (1975); Morris and Morton (1998), 107 ff.
33 Chapman (1992), 2–3, 207.
34 Curtis (1986), 11.
35 Ellis (1993 (1985)), 200.
36 Cited in Morris and Morton (1998), 110.
37 Colls and Dodd (1986), 294, 312.
38 Osmond (1988), 168
39 Morris and Morton (1998), 94.
40 Boyce in Colls and Dodds (1986), 230–53 (249).

41 G.A. Williams (1979), 6, 14, 15, 23.
42 Boyce in Colls and Dodd (1986), 230–53 (235).
43 Hugh Cunningham in Colls and Dodd (1986), 283–307 (293).
44 Nairn (1977), 152, 234.
45 *Saturday Review*, 4 September 1867; cited by Morgan in Brockliss and Eastwood (1997), 93–109 (93).
46 Colls in Colls and Dodd (1986), 29–61 (33, 41).
47 Arnold (1891), viii ff.
48 Osmond (1988), 174; Colls in Colls and Dodd (1986), 29–61 (42).
49 Mileham (1996 (1988)), 66.
50 Donaldson (1966), 61.
51 Graham (1954).
52 S. Wood (1987), 46.
53 Mileham (1996 (1988)), 7.
54 Hill (1986), 168; S. Wood (1987), 76.
55 Mileham (1996 (1988)), 156.
56 Judd (1996), 245 shows that the death rate among troops from Canada, Australia, New Zealand and Newfoundland was also significantly higher than the English rate; cf also S. Wood (1987), 85 ff.
57 Cf. Ellis (1993 (1985)), 191.
58 Smith (1947), 201.
59 Ellis (1993 (1985)), 166–7, 176.
60 Dodd (1971), 19.
61 Hechter (1975); Jedrej and Nuttall (1996), 15, 17.
62 Jedrej and Nuttall (1996), 34, 81n; Pittock (1991), 108.
63 Scott (1981 (1826)), 83, 85.
64 Kidd in Brockliss and Eastwood (1997), 110–26 (117).
65 Osmond (1988), 125.
66 O'Rahilly (1924), 89.
67 K.O. Morgan (1980), 68.
68 Cf. K. Miller (1985) for a discussion of this phenomenon.
69 Cf. the recent work of Margaret Bennett in this area, particularly as unveiled in her unpublished study at the 'Highland History and Highland Myth' conference, Research Centre for Scottish History, University of Strathclyde, 14 September 1996.
70 Seenan and James, 'irish highs beguiling', *The Herald Magazine*, 14 March 1988, 14–16 (15, 16).
71 Ellis (1993b), 112, 116, 126.
72 Ellis (1993a (1985)), 114; (1993b), 99; cf. Coogan (1995), 333, 548–50.
73 Coogan (1995), 548.
74 Pittock (1997), 52.
75 Southey (1845).
76 Kidd in Brockliss and Eastwood (1997), 110–26 (118).

77 Marinell Ash in Samuel and Thompson (1990), 83–94 (83).
78 *Scottish Culture and the Curriculum: A Report to Scottish CCC from the Scottish Culture Review Group* (June 1998), Appendix 2; cf. 'Anger at suppressed report on Scots culture', *Scotsman* (26 June 1998); 'Report on Scottish culture buried', *Times Educational Supplement (Scotland)* (26 June 1998).
79 Pearse, 'Some Aspects of Irish Literature', *Collected Works* (Dublin, Cork, Belfast, 1916), 332–3; citation in O'Driscoll (1982 (1981)), xviii. 77.
80 Tom Devine, opening address, 'Highland History and Highand Myth' conference, Research Centre in Scottish History, University of Strathclyde, 14 September 1996.
81 Cf. Pittock (1994), ch. 1.
82 G.H. Jenkins (1987), 222, 252.
83 Ellis (1993a (1985)), 80.
84 K.O. Morgan (1980), 8, 9, 33.
85 Pittock (1997), 123–4.
86 N. Davies (1997 (1996)), 829; J. Davies, 1993 (1990), 305.
87 Ellis (1993a (1985)), 59.
88 Ellis (1993b), 12, 66; *Carn* (Spring 1998), 7.
89 *Ibid.*, 71.
90 Prys Morgan in Brockliss and Eastwood (1997), 93–109 (98–9).
91 *Ibid.*, 99–100; my italics.
92 Durkacz (1983), 198.
93 Ellis (1993a (1985)), 81, 85, 89, 95, 96; Glanmor Williams (1979), 30.
94 Ellis (1993b), 41.
95 G.H. Jenkins (1987), 220; *Carn* (Summer 1998), 11.
96 David Greene in Ó Tuama (1972), 9–19 (12); Breandan S. MacAodhe, *ibid.*, 20–30 (25, 26); Ellis (1993a (1985)), 117.
97 Gibbons (1996), 76.
98 *The Celtic Magazine VI* (1881), 248.
99 Lyons (1982 (1971)), 229; Ellis (1993b), 69, 71; (1993a (1985)), 118.
100 Ellis (1993a (1985)), 119.
101 *The Senate Speeches of W.B. Yeats* (1961), 57, 59.
102 Ferguson (1998), passim; esp. 300 ff.
103 Durkacz (1983), 13, 14; Maclean (1902), 10.
104 Ellis (1993a (1985)), 183–5.
105 *The Celtic Monthly 20* (1912), 67; Ellis (1993a (1985)), 50.
106 Ellis (1993a), 50.
107 MacKinnon (1977), 2.
108 Durkacz (1983), 162.
109 Ellis (1993a (1985)), 50, 53.
110 MacKinnon (1977), 2; *Carn* (Spring 1998), 4.
111 Ellis (1993b), 71; (1993a (1985)), 142, 147, 153, 157; Maclean (1902), 10; *Carn* (Summer 1998), 23

112 *Hansard* 5th series, Vol. 945 (1978), 487, 517, 547, 551, 556, 572, 578, 678, 704, 705, 725, 1435, 1436.
113 Prys Morgan in R.R. Davies *et al.* (1984), 199–215 (214).
114 Kenneth O. Morgan in R.R. Davies *et al.* (1984), 232 ff (239).
115 Kightly (1986), 138.
116 MacDiarmid and Gibbon (1934), 52, 139–40.
117 Young (n.d. [1995]), 200.
118 Bold (1988), 319
119 Glen (1964), 53.
120 Pittock (1991), 147.
121 *Scots Independent V:5* (1931), 77; *VI* (1932), 151–8.
122 L.M.G., 'The "Elusive Gael"–and the Highland delusion', *Scots Independent II:6* (1928), 94–5.
123 Parnell (1984), 123.
124 Boyce in Boyce and O'Day (1996), 228.
125 Hanham (1969), 145, 150, 155, 157, 180.
126 Pittock (1991), 144; Ernest Renan, cited in Hutchinson and Smith (1994), 18.

Chapter 4

1 Boland (1996), 141–2 for the poem and a discussion; Ormsby (1992), 12–13.
2 See Chapter 3 in particular.
3 Ferguson (1998), 177.
4 Ernest Renan, quoted in Hutchinson and Smith (1994), 17–18.
5 Kirkland (1996), 1: *Moments of Danger* is, appropriately, the subtitle of his book.
6 Rolston (1991), 35, 80, 86.
7 Coogan (1995), 600.
8 Wood (1994), ix–x.
9 Heaney (1975), 51.
10 Graham Walker in Wood (1994), 97–115 (107).
11 Ormsby (1992), 35.
12 New Jerusalem Bible: Luke 1:42; John 20:29.
13 Rolston (1991), 32, 88.
14 Longley (1994), 189.
15 Ormsby (1992), 147.
16 Heaney (1975), 32–4, 48–50.
17 Kirkland (1996), 1, 2, 20.
18 Rolston (1991), 20–1, 27, 32.
19 Coogan (1995), 556.
20 Cf. Radio Scotland's World Cup preview, 8 June 1998 (10 p.m.).
21 Mitchell (1996), 213.

22 *Ibid.*, 181, 183, 194, 202, 207.
23 Alan Crawford, 'Celtic connections', *The Scotsman*, 15 April 1998 (*Interactive Supplement*), 8–9.
24 Keith Hayton, unpublished seminar paper, Strathclyde Devolution Workshop, University of Strathclyde, 17 June 1998; 'Pass notes: Richard Caborn', *Guardian*, Section 2, 2 February 1999, 3.
25 *Guardian*, 23 March 1992, 4; cf. Mitchell (1996), 291.
26 Morris and Morton (1998), 98; Brown *et al.* (1996), 211.
27 Kington (1977), viii; *Guardian*, 11 March 1992, 18.
28 *Guardian, ibid.*
29 *Ibid.*, 21 March 1992, 6.
30 *The Herald*, 16 March 1992, 5.
31 Ian McWhirter, 'Forsyth fails to impress with rashly Pict words', *Scotland on Sunday*, February 2, 1997, 16.
32 Dorothy Grace-Elder, 'Rattling the cages', *ibid.*, 14.
33 *The Big Issue Scotland*, 5–12 February 1998, 25.
34 *Celtic Connections*, 13–30 January 1999.
35 Scott and Macleay (1990), 59.
36 Mackenzie (1986), 6.
37 Judd (1996), 146.
38 The journalist Ruth Wishart made these points repeatedly in her support for the campaign for an independent Scottish Six O'Clock news in 1998.
39 Kuhn (1962), 115.
40 Wiener (1981), 50, 57, 118.
41 Cf. Norman (1996), 11 (backsword no. 1:18: inscribed 'Prosperity to Schotlandt and no union').

Bibliography

Primary sources

Aberdeen City Archives. Kennedy Index I, IX.

Adamson, Ian. *The Identity of Ulster.* Ulster: Ian Adamson, 1982.

Arnold, Matthew. *On the Study of Celtic Literature and Other Essays.* London: Everyman, 1910.

——. *Irish Essays and Others.* London: Smith, Elder & Co., 1891.

Ashton, John. *Chapbooks of the Eighteenth Century.* London, 1882.

The Big Issue (Scotland). 5–12 February 1998.

Boland, Eavan. *Object Lessons.* London: Vintage, 1996.

Borrow, George. *Wild Wales.* London: Oxford University Press (World's Classics), 1928 (1862).

Brooke, Charlotte. *Reliques of Irish Poetry.* Dublin: George Bonham, 1789.

Buchan, John. *Witch Wood.* Edinburgh: Canongate, 1988 (1927).

Carlyle, Thomas. *Selected Writings.* Ed. Alan Shelston. London: Penguin, 1988 (1971).

Carn. Spring/Summer 1998.

Celtic Connections. Festival programme, 13–30 January 1999.

The Celtic Magazine. 1876–.

The Celtic Monthly 20 (1912).

The Oxford Conan Doyle: His Last Bow. Ed. Owen Dudley Edwards. The Oxford Sherlock Holmes. Oxford and New York: Oxford University Press, 1993.

The Poems of John Davidson. Ed. Andrew Turnbull. 2 vols. Edinburgh: Scottish Academic Press, 1973.

Dublin University Calendar, 1856, 1887.

Durcan, Paul. *Daddy, Daddy.* Belfast: Blackstaff Press, 1990.

Evans, Gwynfor. *Wales Can Win.* Llandybie, 1973.

——. *A National Future for Wales.* Swansea, 1975.

The Evergreen I–IV (1895–7).

The Poems of Samuel Ferguson. Ed. Padraic Colum. Dublin: Allen Figgis ,1963.

The Fiery Cross, 1901–12.

The Financial Times. Weekend, 14/15 June 1997.

Geoffrey of Monmouth. *Historia Regum Britanniae: The History of the Kings of Britain.* Translated by Lewis Thorpe. Harmondsworth; Penguin, 1968 (1966, 1136).

Gibbon, Lewis Grassic. *A Scots Quair.* Harmondsworth: Penguin, 1986 (1932–4).

Gregory, Augusta Lady. *Gods and Fighting Men.* Gerrards Cross: Colin Smythe, 1970 (1904).

Guardian. 11, 21, 23 March 1992; 19 May 1998; 2 February 1999.

Gunn, Neil. *The Silver Darlings.* London: Faber, *c.*1990 (1943).

Hansard. 5th series, Vol. 945 (Session 1977–8). London: HMSO, 1978.

Hary, Blin. *The Wallace.* Tr. William Hamilton of Gilbertfield. Ed. Elspeth King. Edinburgh: Luath Press, 1998.

Heaney, Seamus. *North.* London: Faber, 1975.

——. *The Government of the Tongue.* London: Faber, 1988.

The Herald. 16, 21, 23, 25 March 1992; 9 April 1992; 6 August 1997; 14, 16 March and 10 April (Good Friday) 1998; 21 August 1998; 14 January 1999.

Housman, A.E. *Last Poems.* London: Richards Press, 1928 (1922).

——. *A Shropshire Lad.* Introduced by Ian Rogerson. Cambridge: Silent Books, 1995.

Kington, Miles, ed. *Punch on Scotland.* London: Punch Publications, 1977.

Larkin, Philip. *Collected Poems.* London: Faber/Marvell Press, 1990 (1988).

MacBride, Maud Gonne. *A Servant of the Queen.* London: Victor Gollancz, 1974 (1937).

MacColla, Fionn. *The Albannach.* London: Souvenir Press, 1984 (1932).

MacDiarmid, Hugh and Gibbon, Lewis Grassic. *Scottish Scene.* London: Jarrolds, 1934.

Macdonell, A.C. *Lays of the Heather.* London: Elliot Stock, 1896.

MacGill-Eain, Somhairle. *Spring Tide and Neap Tide: Selected Poems 1932–72.* Edinburgh: Canongate, 1977.

Macgillivray, Pittendrigh. *Memories of the '45* n.p., 1911.

Macpherson, James. *The Poems of Ossian.* Ed. Howard Gaskill with an Introduction by Fiona Stafford. Edinburgh: Edinburgh University Press, 1996.

Miller, David W., ed. *Peep O'Day Boys and Defenders.* Belfast: Public Record Office, 1990.

Muir, Edwin. *Scott and Scotland.* London: Routledge, 1936.

National Library of Scotland ACC 9290 (Archie Lamont papers).

Newbolt, Sir Henry. *The Island Race.* London: Elkin Mathews, 1914 (1898).

Ó Rathaille, Aoghan. *The Poems of Egan O'Rahilly.* Ed. Patrick S. Dinneen. London: Irish Texts Society, 1900.

Opie, Iona and Peter. *The Oxford Dictionary of Nursery Rhymes.* Oxford: Oxford University Press, 1992 (1951).

The Compact Edition of the Oxford English Dictionary. Oxford: Oxford University Press, 1971.

Oxford, University of. *Examination Decrees and Regulations.* 1997–8.

The Patriot. Spring 1998.

Pearse, Padraic H. *Political Writings and Speeches.* Dublin, 1952.

Renan, Ernest. *The Poetry of the Celtic Races, and Other Studies.* Tr. William G.

Hutchinson. London: Walter Scott, 1896 (1860).

The Royalist. 1890–.

Scotland on Sunday. 2 February 1997.

The Scots Independent. 1926–.

The Scotsman. 15 April 1998 (*Interactive* Supplement); 26 June 1998.

Scott, Sir Walter. *The Letters of Malachi Malagrowther.* Ed. Paul Scott. Edinburgh, 1981.

——. *The Two Drovers and Other Stories.* Oxford: World's Classics, OUP, 1987.

'Scottish Culture and the Curriculum. A Report to Scottish CCC from the Scottish Culture Review Group'. June 1998.

Sharp, E.A. and Matthay J., eds. *Lyra Celtica.* With an Introduction and Notes by William Sharp. 2nd edn Edinburgh: John Grant, 1924 (1896).

Sinclair, John, Master of. *Memoirs of the Insurrection in Scotland in 1715.* Ed. Messrs MacKnight and Lang, with notes by Sir Walter Scott, Bart. Edinburgh: Abbotsford Club, 1858.

Southey, Robert. *Poetical Works.* London: Longman, 1845.

Swift, Jonathan. *The Drapier's Letters and Other Works 1724–5.* Ed. Herbert Davis. Oxford: Oxford University Press, 1941.

Thomas, Edward. *Collected Poems.* London: Faber, 1974.

Times Educational Supplement (Scotland), 26 June 1998.

Tolkien, J.R.R. and Gordon, E.V, eds. *Gawain and the Green Knight.* Oxford: Clarendon Press, 1941 (1925).

The Annotated Oscar Wilde. Ed. H. Montgomery Hyde. London: Orbis, 1982.

The Collected Plays of W.B. Yeats. London: Macmillan, 1953.

The Variorum Edition of the Poems of W.B. Yeats. Ed. Peter Allt and Russell K. Alspach. New York: Macmillan, 1977.

——. *Essays and Introductions.* New York: Macmillan, 1961.

——. *The Senate Speeches of W.B. Yeats.* Ed. Donald Pearce. London: Faber, 1961.

——. *Uncollected Prose Volume 1.* Ed. John Frayne. London: Macmillan, 1970.

——. *Memoirs.* Ed. Denis Donoghue. London: Macmillan, 1972.

——. *The Gonne–Yeats Letters 1893–1938.* Eds. Anna MacBride White and A. Norman Jeffares. London: Pimlico, 1992.

——. *Writings on Irish Folklore, Legend and Myth.* Ed. Robert Welch. Harmondsworth: Penguin, 1993.

Secondary sources

Alanquist, Bo, O'Cathan, Seamas and O'Healain, Padraig, eds. *The Heroic Process.* Dun Laoghaire: Glendale Press, 1987.

Alexander, J.H. and Hewitt, David, eds. *Scott in Carnival.* Aberdeen: Association for Scottish Literary Studies, 1993.

Anderson, Benedict. *Imagined Communities.* London: Verso, 1983. 2nd edn. 1991.

Ash, Marinell. *The Strange Death of Scottish History.* Edinburgh: Ramsay Head

Press, 1980.

Banham, Joanna, MacDonald, Sally and Porter, Julia. *Victorian Interior Design*. New York: Crescent Books, 1991.

Barrow, Geoffrey. *Robert Bruce*. 2nd edn. Edinburgh: Edinburgh University Press, 1982 (1976, 1965).

Barry, Michael Joseph, ed. *The Songs of Ireland*. Dublin: Duffy, 1869.

Boardman, Philip. *The Worlds of Patrick Geddes*. London, Henley and Boston: Routledge and Kegan Paul, 1978.

Bold, Alan. *MacDiarmid*. London: Murray, 1988.

Bonner, Elizabeth. 'French Naturalization of the Scots in the Fifteenth and Sixteenth Centuries'. *Historical Journal* (1997), 1085–116.

Boyce, D. George. *Nationalism in Ireland*. 2nd edn. London and New York: Routledge, 1991 (1982).

Boyce, D. George and O'Day, Alan, eds. *The Making of Modern Irish History: Revisionism and the Revisionist Controversy*. London and New York: Routledge, 1996.

Bradley, Joseph. *Sport, Culture, Politics and Scottish Society: Irish Immigrants and the Gaelic Athletic Association*. Edinburgh: John Donald, 1998.

Bradshaw, Brendan and Morrill, John, eds. *The British Problem 1534–1707*. Basingstoke: Macmillan, 1996.

Breatnach, R.A. 'The Lady and the King'. *Studies* 42 (1953), 321–36.

Brinkley, Roberta Florence. *Arthurian Legend in the Seventeenth Century*. Baltimore: The Johns Hopkins Press, 1932.

Brockliss, Laurence and Eastwood, David, eds. *A Union of Multiple Identities: The British Isles c.1750–c.1850*. Manchester and New York: Manchester University Press, 1997.

Bromwich, Rachel. *Matthew Arnold and Celtic Literature: A Retrospect*. Oxford: Clarendon Press, 1965.

Broun, Dauvit. 'The Birth of Scottish History'. *Scottish Historical Review* (1997), 4–22.

Brown, Alice, McCrone, David and Paterson, Lindsay. *Politics and Society in Scotland*. Basingstoke: Macmillan, 1996.

Butterfield, Herbert. *The Whig Interpretation of History*. London: G. Bell & Sons, 1931.

Cairns, David and Richards, Shaun. *Writing Ireland: Colonialism, Nationalism and Culture*. Manchester: Manchester University Press, 1988.

Campbell, J.L. and Thomson, Derick. *Edward Lhuyd in the Scottish Highlands 1699–1700*. Oxford: Clarendon Press, 1963.

Cannon, John. *Samuel Johnson and the Politics of Hanoverian England*. Oxford: Clarendon Press, 1994.

Chapman, Malcolm. *The Gaelic Vision in Scottish Culture*. London: Croom Helm, 1978.

——. *The Celts: The Construction of a Myth*. Basingstoke: Macmillan, 1992.

Clark, David R. *W.B. Yeats and the Theatre of Desolate Reality.* Dublin, 1965.

Clements, Alan, Farquharson, Kenny and Wark, Kirsty. *Restless Nation.* Edinburgh and London: Mainstream, 1996.

Colley, Linda. *Britons.* New Haven: Yale University Press, 1992.

——. 'Looking for Ourselves: Uses and Abuses of the Heritage Idea'. *Times Literary Supplement,* 2 May 1997, 8–9.

Collie, Michael. *George Borrow: Eccentric.* Cambridge: Cambridge University Press, 1982.

Colls, Robert and Dodd, Philip, eds. *Englishness: Politics and Culture 1880–1920.* London: Croom Helm, 1986.

Connolly, S.J. *Religion, Law and Power: The Making of Protestant Ireland 1660–1760.* Oxford: Clarendon Press, 1992.

Coogan, Tim Pat. *Michael Collins.* London: Arrow, 1990.

——. *The IRA.* 4th edn. London: Harper Collins, 1995 (1971).

Corkery, Daniel. *The Hidden Ireland.* 2nd edn. Dublin: M.H. Gill and Son, 1925.

Cowan, Edward. *Scottish History and Scottish Folk.* Inaugural Lecture, Chair of Scottish History and Literature, University of Glasgow, 15 March 1995. Glasgow: Department of Scottish History, 1998.

Craig, Cairns. *Out of History.* Edinburgh: Polygon, 1996.

Cramb, Isobel. 'Francis Peacock, 1723–1807'. *Aberdeen University Review* XLIII (1967–70), 251–61.

Crawford, Robert. *Devolving English Literature.* Oxford: Oxford University Press, 1992.

Cullan, Patrick. 'The Political War Ballads of Sean O'Casey, 1916–18'. *Irish University Review* (1983), 168–79.

Curtin, Nancy J. *The United Irishmen.* Oxford: Clarendon Press, 1994.

Curtis, Tony, ed. *Wales: The Imagined Nation.* Bridgend: Poetry Wales Press, 1986.

Curtis, Perry, Jr. *Apes and Angels: The Irish Man in Victorian Caricature.* Washington, 1971.

Davies, John. *A History of Wales.* London: Penguin, 1993 (1990).

Davies, Norman. *Europe: A History.* London: Pimlico, 1997 (1996).

Davies, R.R. 'The Peoples of Britain and Ireland, 1100–1400, Identities'. *Transactions of the Royal Historical Society* 4 (1994).

——. 'The Peoples of Britain and Ireland 1100–1400: II Names, Boundaries and Regnal Solidarities'. *Transactions of the Royal Historical Society* 5 (1995).

Davies, R.R., Griffiths, Ralph A., Jones, Ieuan Gwynedd and Morgan, Kenneth O., eds. *Welsh Society and Nationhood.* Cardiff: University of Wales Press, 1984.

Deane, Seamus, ed. *The Field Day Anthology of Irish Writing.* 3 vols. Derry: Field Day, 1991.

Dewey, Clive. 'Celtic Agrarian Legislation and the Celtic Revival: Historicist Implications of Gladstone's Irish and Scottish Land Acts 1870–1886'. *Past and Present* (August 1974), 30–70.

Dickson, David, Keogh, Daire and Whelan, Kevin, eds. *The United Irishmen.*

Dublin: Lilliput Press, 1993.

Dijkstra, Bram. *Idols of Perversity: Fantasies of Feminine Evil in Fin-de-Siècle Culture.* New York and Oxford: Oxford University Press, 1986.

Dixon, Wilmott. *The Jacobite Episode in Scottish History and its Related Literature.* Edinburgh, Glasgow and London, 1874. MacBean Collection, Aberdeen University Library.

Dodd, A.H. *Studies in Stuart Wales.* Cardiff: University of Wales Press, 1971 (1952).

Donaldson, Gordon. *The Scots Overseas.* London: Hale, 1966.

Donaldson, William. *The Jacobite Song.* Aberdeen: Aberdeen University Press, 1988.

Donnachie, Ian and Whatley, Christopher, eds. *The Manufacture of Scottish History.* Edinburgh: Polygon, 1992.

Dukes, Paul, ed. *Frontiers of European Culture.* Lampeter: Edwin Mellen, c.1996.

Dunn, Douglas, ed. *Two Decades of Irish Writing – A Critical Survey.* Cheadle Hulme: Carcanet, 1975.

Durkacz, Victor Edward. *The Decline of the Celtic Languages.* Edinburgh: John Donald, 1983.

Du Toit, Alexander. 'William Robertson'. *Scottish Literary Journal* 26:1 (1999), forthcoming.

Dwyer, John, Mason, Roger and Murdoch, Alexander. *New Perspectives on the Politics and Culture of Early Modern Scotland.* Edinburgh: John Donald, n.d. [1983].

Edwards, Owen Dudley, Evans, Gwynfor, Rhys, Ioan and MacDiarmid, Hugh. *Celtic Nationalism.* London: Routledge and Kegan Paul, 1968.

Edwards, Ruth Dudley. *Patrick Pearse.* London: Gollancz, 1977.

Ellis, Peter Berresford. *The Cornish Language and its Literature.* London and Boston: Routledge and Kegan Paul, 1974.

——. *The Celtic Revolution.* Talybont, Ceredigion: Y Lolfa, 1993a (1985).

——. *The Celtic Dawn.* London: Constable, 1993b.

Enright, Michael J. 'King James and his Island: An Archaic Kingship Belief'. *Scottish Historical Review* 55 (1976), 29–40.

Evans, E.D. *A History of Wales 1660–1815.* Cardiff: University of Wales Press, 1976.

Fasel, George. *Edmund Burke.* Boston: Twayne, 1988.

Ferguson, William. *The Identity of the Scottish Nation.* Edinburgh: Edinburgh University Press, 1998.

Fielding, Steven. *Class and Ethnicity: Irish Catholics in England 1880–1939.* Buckingham: Open University Press, 1993.

Filbee, Marjorie. *Celtic Cornwall.* London: Constable, 1996.

Finlay, Richard. *Independent and Free? The History of the Scottish National Party to 1945.* Edinburgh: John Donald, 1994.

Fletcher, Ian. *W.B. Yeats and His Contemporaries.* Brighton: Harvester, 1987.

Foster, John Wilson. *Fictions of the Irish Literary Revival.* Syracuse: Syracuse University Press, 1987.

Foster, R.F. *Paddy and Mr Punch*. Harmondsworth: Penguin, 1995 (1993).

——. *W.B. Yeats: A Life*. Oxford: Oxford University Press, 1997.

Fraser, Angus M. 'George Borrow's Wanderings in Quest of Manx Literature'. *Proceedings of the Isle of Man Natural History and Antiquarian Society* VIII(3) (1980), 296–314.

Freshwater, Peter, ed. *Sons of Scotia Raise Your Voice!* Edinburgh: Edinburgh University Library, 1991.

Garvin, Tom. *Nationalist Revolutionaries in Ireland 1858–1928*. Oxford: Clarendon Press, 1987.

Gerrard, Christine. *The Patriot Opposition to Walpole*. Oxford: Oxford University Press, 1994.

Gibbons, Luke. *Transformations in Irish Culture*. Field Day Essays. Cork: Cork University Press, 1996.

Gibson, A.J.S. and Smout, T.C. *Prices, Food and Wages in Scotland 1550–1780*. Cambridge: Cambridge University Press, 1995.

Glen, Duncan. *Hugh MacDiarmid and the Scottish Renaissance*. Edinburgh and London: W.R. Chambers, 1964.

Glendening, John. *The High Road: Romantic Tourism, Scotland, and Literature, 1720–1820*. Basingstoke: Macmillan, 1997.

Glendinning, Miles, MacInnes, Ronald and MacKechnie, Aonghas. *A History of Scottish Architecture*. Edinburgh: Edinburgh University Press, 1996.

Gold, John R. and Margaret M. *Imagining Scotland: Tradition, Representation and Promotion in Scottish Tourism Since 1750* Aldershot: Scolar Press, 1995.

Graham, Ian Charles Cargill. 'Colonists from Scotland: Emigration to North America 1707–1783'. *William and Mary Quarterly* (1954).

Greenhalgh, Paul. *Ephemeral Vistas*. Manchester: Manchester University Press, 1988.

Haldane, Katherine Jean. 'Imagining Scotland: Tourist Images of Scotland 1770–1914'. Unpublished Ph.D. thesis, University of Virginia, 1990.

Hampton, David and Hill, Myrtle. *Evangelical Protestantism in Ulster Society 1740–1890*. London and New York: Routledge, 1992.

Hanham, H.J. *Scottish Nationalism*. London: Faber, 1969.

Hechter, Michael. *Internal Colonialism*. London: Routledge and Kegan Paul, 1975.

Henderson, Charles. *Essays in Cornish History*. Edited by A.L. Rowse and M.I. Henderson. Oxford: Clarendon Press, 1935.

Hewison, Robert. *The Heritage Industry*. London: Methuen, 1987.

Hill, James Michael. *Celtic Warfare 1595–1763*. Edinburgh: John Donald, 1986.

Hobsbawm, Eric and Ranger, Terence, eds. *The Invention of Tradition*. Cambridge: Cambridge University Press, 1983.

Holmes, Ronald. *The Legend of Sawney Bean*. London: F. Muller, 1975.

Howes, Marjorie. *Yeats's Nations: Gender, Class and Irishness*. Cambridge: Cambridge University Press, 1998 (1996).

Hutchinson, John. *The Dynamics of Cultural Nationalism: The Gaelic Revival and the Creation of the Irish Nation State*. London, in association with the London School of Economics: Allen and Unwin, 1987.

Hutchinson, John and Smith, Anthony D., eds. *Nationalism*. Oxford and New York: Oxford University Press, 1994.

Jedrej, Charles and Nuttall, Mark. *White Settlers*. Australia, UK: Harwood Academic, 1996.

Jenkins, Daniel. *The British, Their Identity and Their Religion*. London: SCM Press, 1975.

Jenkins, Elizabeth. *The Mystery of King Arthur*. London, 1975.

Jenkins, Geraint H. *The Foundations of Modern Wales*. Oxford: Clarendon Press, 1987.

Jenkins, J. Geraint. *Life and Tradition in Rural Wales*. London: J.M. Dent & Sons, 1976.

Jenkins, Philip. *The Making of a Ruling Class: The Glamorgan Gentry 1640–1790*. Cambridge: Cambridge University Press, 1983.

———. *A History of Modern Wales 1536–1990*. London and New York: Longman, 1992.

Jones, R. Bruley, ed. *The Anatomy of Wales*. Glamorgan: Gwairin Publications, 1972.

Judd, Denis. *Empire*. London: Harper Collins/Fontana Press, 1996.

Kidd, Colin. *Subverting Scotland's Past*. Cambridge: Cambridge University Press, 1993.

———. 'The Canon of Patriotic Landmarks in Scottish History'. *Scotlands* 1 (1994), 1–17.

———. '*The Strange Death of Scottish History* revisited: Constructions of the Past in Scotland, c.1790–1914'. *Scottish Historical Review* (1997), 86–102.

Kightly, Charles. *The Customs and Ceremonies of Britain*. London: Thames & Hudson, 1986.

Kirkland, Richard. *Literature in Culture in Northern Ireland Since 1965: Moments of Danger*. London and New York: Longman, 1996.

Koch, John and Rittmueller, Jean, eds. *Proceedings of the Harvard Celtic Colloquium III*. Cambridge, MA: Harvard University Press, 1983.

Kuhn, T.S. *The Structure of Scientific Revolutions*. Chicago and London: Chicago University Press, 1962.

Leerssen, Joep. *Mere Irish and Fior-Ghael*. Amsterdam and Philadelphia: John Benjamines, 1986.

Lloyd, David. *Nationalism and Minor Literature: James Clarence Mangan and the Emergence of Irish Cultural Nationalism*. Berkeley, CA: University of California Press, 1987.

Lloyd, J.E. *Owen Glendower*. Oxford: Clarendon Press, 1931.

Longley, Edna. *The Living Stream: Literature and Revsionism in Ireland*. Newcastle: Bloodaxe, 1994.

Lord, Peter. *Gwenllian: Essays on visual culture*. Llandysul: Gomer Press, 1994.

Low, Mary. *Celtic Christianity and Nature*. Edinburgh: Edinburgh University Press, 1996.

Lynch, Michael. Review of Macinnes (1996). *University of Edinburgh Journal* (1997), 118–19.

Lyons, F.S.L. *Ireland Since the Famine*. Bungay: Fontana, 1982 (1971).

McBride, I.R. '"When Ulster Joined Ireland": Anti-Popery, Presbyterian Radicalism and Irish Republicanism in the 1790s'. *Past and Present* (November 1997), 63–93.

McCarthy, Justin. *A History of the Four Georges*. 4 vols. London: Chatto & Windus, 1890.

McCrone, David, Morris, Angela and Kelly, Richard. *Scotland the Brand*. Edinburgh: Edinburgh University Press, 1995.

MacDonagh, Oliver, Mandley, W.F. and Travers, P. *Irish Culture and Nationalism*. London: Macmillan in Association with the National Humanities Research Centre, Australian National University, 1983.

MacDougall, Hugh. *Racial Myth in English History*. Montreal, Hanover and London: Harvest House/University Press of New England, 1982.

MacFarland, Elaine. *Protestants First: Orangeism in 19th Century Scotland*. Edinburgh: Edinburgh University Press, 1990.

Macinnes, Allan I. *Clanship, Commerce and the House of Stuart, 1603–1788*. East Linton: Tuckwell, 1996.

Mackenzie, John, ed. *Imperialism and Popular Culture*. Manchester: Manchester University Press, 1986.

MacKinnon, Kenneth. *Language, Education and Social Processes in a Gaelic Community*. London: Routledge and Kegan Paul, 1977.

Maclean, Magnus. *The Literature of the Celts*. London: Blackie, 1902.

Macmillan, Duncan. 'Scottish Painting Ramsay to Raeburn'. *Cencrastus* 17 (1984), 25–9.

——. *A History of Scottish Art 1460–1990*. Edinburgh: Mainstream, 1990.

Martin, Raymond. 'The Essential Difference Between History and Science'. *History and Theory* 36:1 (1997), 1–14.

Marwick, Arthur. *The Nature of History*. 3rd edn. Basingstoke: Macmillan, 1989.

Mason, Roger A., ed. *Scotland and England 1286–1815*. Edinburgh: John Donald, 1983.

——. *Scots and Britons: Political Thought and the Union of 1603*. Cambridge: Cambridge University Press, 1994.

Mercer, V. 'Swift and the Gaelic Tradition'. *Review of English Literature* 3 (1962), 69–79.

Mileham, Patrick. *The Scottish Regiments 1633–1996*. Staplehurst: Spellmount, 1996 (1988).

Miller, Delia. *Queen Victoria's Life in the Scottish Highlands Depicted by her Watercolour Artists*. London, 1985.

Miller, Kerby A. *Emigrants and Exiles: Ireland and the Irish Exodus to North Amer-

ica. New York and Oxford: Oxford University Press, 1985.

Mitchell, James. *Strategies for Self-government: The Campaigns for a Scottish Parliament*. Edinburgh: Polygon, 1996.

Moore, Dafydd. 'James Macpherson'. Unpublished M.Res. thesis, University of Strathclyde, 1997.

Morgan, Austin. *James Connolly*. Manchester: Manchester University Press, 1988.

Morgan, Kenneth O. *Wales in British Politics 1868–1922*. 3rd edn. Cardiff: University of Wales Press, 1980.

Morris, Angela and Morton, Graeme. *Locality, Community and Nation*. London: Hodder and Stoughton, 1998.

Morrison, David, ed. *Essays on Fionn MacColla*. Thurso, n.d.

Munro, Ailie. *The Folk Music Revival in Scotland*. London: Kahn and Averill, 1984.

Nairn, Tom. *The Break-Up of Britain*. London: NLB, 1977.

Newman, Gerald. *The Rise of English Nationalism: A Cultural History 1740–1830*. London: Weidenfeld and Nicolson, 1987.

Norman, A.V.B. *Culloden: Catalogue to the exhibition 16 April–20 September 1996, Supplement giving fuller details of the swords and daggers*. National Trust for Scotland, 1996.

The Norton Anthology of Poetry. Ed. Alexander Allison *et al.*, 3rd edn. New York and London: Norton, 1983 (1970).

O'Brien, Conor Cruise. *The Great Melody*. London: Minerva, 1992.

O'Connor, Ulick. *Celtic Dawn: A Portrait of the Irish Literary Renaissance*. London: Hamilton, 1984.

O'Driscoll, Robert, ed. *The Celtic Consciousness*. Portlaoise: Dolmen Press, 1982 (1981).

O'Halloran, Clare. 'Irish Re-creations of the Gaelic Past: The Challenge of Macpherson's Ossian'. *Past and Present* 124 (1989), 69–95.

Ó Mathuna, Diarmuid. 'A Late Aisling'. *The O Mahony Journal* 14 (1990), 15–22.

O'Rahilly, Cecile. *Ireland and Wales: Their Historical and Literary Relations*. London: Longman, 1924.

Ó Tuama, Sean, ed. *The Gaelic League Idea*. Cork and Dublin, 1972.

——, ed. *An Duanaire 1600–1900: Poems of the Dispossessed*. Tr. Thomas Kinsella. Dublin: Dolmen Press, 1994 (1981).

Obelkovich, Jim, Roper, Lyndal and Samuel, Raphael, eds. *Disciplines of Faith: Studies in Religion, Politics and Patriarchy*. London, 1987.

Opie, Robert. *Rule Britannia: Trading on the British Image*. Harmondsworth: Penguin, 1985.

Ormsby, Frank, ed. *A Rage for Order: Poetry of the Northern Ireland Troubles*. Belfast: Blackstaff Press, 1992.

Osmond, John. *The Divided Kingdom*. London: Constable, 1988.

Parnell, Michael. *Eric Linklater*. London: Murray, 1984.

Pennick, Nigel. *Celtic Sacred Landscapes*. London: Thames and Hudson, 1996.

Philpin, C.H., ed. *Nationalism and Popular Protest in Ireland*. Cambridge: Cambridge University Press, 1987.

Piggott, Stuart. *The Druids*. Harmondsworth: Penguin, 1977 (1968).

Pittock, Murray G.H. "'Falcon and Falconer": W.B. Yeats and Marvell's *"Horatian Ode"'*. *Irish University Review*, Autumn 1986.

——. *The Invention of Scotland: the Stuart Myth and the Scottish Identity 1638 to the Present*. London and New York: Routledge, 1991.

——. 'The Making of the *Jacobite Relics*', *Studies in Hogg and his World 3* (1992), 10–17.

——. *Spectrum of Decadence: The Literature of the 1890s*. London: Routledge, 1993.

——. *Poetry and Jacobite Politics in Eighteenth-Century Britain and Ireland*. Cambridge: Cambridge University Press, 1994.

——. *The Myth of the Jacobite Clans*. Edinburgh: Edinburgh University Press, 1995.

——. *Inventing and Resisting Britain*. Basingstoke and New York: Macmillan/St Martin's Press, 1997.

——. *Jacobitism* . Basingstoke and New York: Macmillan/St Martin's Press, 1998.

Pocock, J.G.A. 'British History: A Plea for a New Subject'. *JMH* 47:4 (1975), 601–21.

——. 'The Limits and Divisions of British History: In Search of a Unknown Subject'. *American Historical Review* 87 (1982), 311–36.

Pomper, Philip. 'Historians and Individual Agency'. *History and Theory 35:3* (1996), 281–308.

Porter, Roy, ed. *Myths of the English*. Cambridge: Polity Press, 1992.

Prebble, John. *The Clearances*. Harmondsworth: Penguin, 1963.

——. *The King's Jaunt*. London: Collins, 1988.

Price, Richard. *Neil M. Gunn*. Edinburgh: Edinburgh University Press, 1991.

——. 'Whose History, Which Novel? Neil M. Gunn and the Gaelic Idea'. *Scottish Literary Journal* 24:2 (1997).

Rafferty, Oliver. *Catholicism in Ulster 1603–1983*. London: Hurst & Co., 1994.

Reid, Harry. *Dear Country: A Quest for England*. Edinburgh and London: Mainstream, 1992.

Richards, Thomas. *The Commodity Culture of Victorian England: Advertising and Spectacle 1851–1914*. Stanford: Stanford University Press, 1990.

Rolston, Bill. *Politics and Painting: Murals and Conflict in Northern Ireland*. Rutherford, Madison, Teaneck: Fairleigh Dickinson University Press, 1991.

Said, Edward. *Culture and Imperialism*. London: Chatto and Windus, 1993.

Samuel, Raphael, ed. *Patriotism: The Making and Unmaking of British National Identity*. 3 vols. London and New York: Routledge, 1989.

——. *Theatres of Memory Volume 1: Past and Present in Contemporary Culture*. London: Verso, 1994.

Samuel, Raphael and Thompson, Paul, eds. *The Myths We Live By*. London and New York: Routledge, 1990.

Scott, Andrew Murray and Macleay, Ian. *Britain's Secret War: Tartan Terrorism and the Anglo-American State.* Edinburgh: Mainstream, 1990.

Scott, Paul H. *Defoe in Edinburgh and Other Papers.* East Linton: Tuckwell Press, 1995.

Scottish Historical Review 3 (1906). 'Ballads on the Bishops' wars'.

Seton, Sir Bruce, Bart. 'Dress of the Jacobite Army'. *Scottish Historical Review 25* (1928), 270–81.

Sheehy, Jeanne. *The Rediscovery of Ireland's Past: the Celtic Revival 1830–1930.* London: Thames and Hudson, 1980.

Sherry, Frank Andrew. *The Rising of 1820.* Glasgow: William McLellan, n.d. [1968].

Singer, Brian C.J. 'Cultural Versus Contractual Nations: Rethinking their Opposition'. *History and Theory* 35:3 (1996), 309–37.

Skelton, Robin and Saddlemyer, Ann, eds. *The World of W.B. Yeats.* Victoria, British Columbia: University of Victoria/Adelphi Bookshop, 1965.

Skene, William F. *Celtic Scotland.* 3 vols. Edinburgh: David Douglas, 1880.

Smith, Albert Emerson. *Colonists in Bondage: White Servitude and Convict Labour in America.* Chapel Hill: University of North Carolina Press, 1947.

Smith, G. Gregory. *Scottish Literature: Character and Influence.* London: Macmillan, 1919.

Stephens, Meic, ed. *The Bright Field: An Anthology of Contemporary Poetry from Wales.* Manchester: Carcanet 1991.

Swift, Roger and Gilley, Sheridan, eds. *The Irish in Britain 1815–1939.* London: Pinter, 1989.

Szechi, Daniel. 'Constructing a Jacobite: The Social and Intellectual Origin of George Lockhart of Carnwath'. *Historical Journal* (1997), 977–96.

Taylor, Beverley and Brewer, Elisabeth. *The Return of King Arthur.* Cambridge: Cambridge University Press, 1983.

Taylor, Miles. 'John Bull and the Iconography of Public Opinion in England c.1712–1929'. *Past and Present* 134 (1992), 93–128.

Thomas, R. George. *Edward Thomas: A Portrait.* Oxford: Clarendon Press, 1985.

Thompson, William Irwin. *The Imagination of an Insurrection.* New York: Oxford University Press, 1967.

Thomson, Derick. *An Introduction to Gaelic Poetry.* 2nd edn. Edinburgh: Edinburgh University Press, 1993 (1989).

Thuente, Mary Helen. *W.B. Yeats and Folklore.* Dublin: Gill and Macmillan, 1980/ Totowa, NJ: Barnes and Noble, 1981.

Trench, Charles Chevenix. *George II.* London: Allen Lane, 1973.

Watson, G.J. *Irish Identity and the Literary Revival.* London: Croom Helm, 1979.

Watson, Ian. *Song and Democratic Culture in Britain.* Beckenham, 1983.

Wells, Roger. *Insurrection: The British Experience 1795–1803* Gloucester: Alan Sutton, 1986 (1983).

Wiener, Martin J. *English Culture and the Decline of the Industrial Spirit 1850–1980.* Cambridge: Cambridge University Press, 1981.

Williams, Glanmor. *Religion, Language and Nationality in Wales*. Cardiff: University of Wales Press, 1979.

Williams, Gwyn A. *When Was Wales?* London: BBC, 1979.

Williams, Raymond. *The Country and the City*. London: Chatto & Windus, 1973.

Womack, Peter. *Improvement and Romance: Inventing the Myth of the Highlands*. Basingstoke: Macmillan, 1989.

Wood, Ian S., ed. *Scotland and Ulster*. Edinburgh: Mercat Press, 1994.

Wood, Stephen. *The Scottish Soldier*. Manchester: Archive Publications/National Museums of Scotland, 1987.

——. *The Auld Alliance: Scotland and France, The Military Connection*. Edinburgh: Mainstream, 1989.

Young, James D. 'Forging the Nation'. *Cencrastus 49* (1994), 40–1.

——. *The Very Bastards of Creation: Scottish International Radicalism 1707–1995*. Glasgow: Clydeside Press, n.d. [1995].

Zimmerman, G.D. 'Yeats, the Popular Ballad and the Ballad Singers'. *English Studies* (1969), 185–97.

Index

Aberdeen 22, 100
Act of Uniformity (1549) 122
Act of Union
    with Ireland 114
    with Scotland 19, 113
    with Wales 17, 114
Aisling poetry 46–8
Albert, Prince Consort 43, 62
America 140
    Civil War 108
    Scots and Welsh in 107
Ancient Britons, Society of 41
An Comunn Gaidhealach 122
Anderson, Benedict 6, 20, 102, 103,
        129 ff., 136, 140
Anglo-Saxonism 20, 104, 142
Antiquaries of Scotland, Society of 57
Arnold, Matthew 30, 37, 64–9, 96,
        107, 109
    and Celticism 64–5
    attitude towards Wales 64
Arthur, King 14–16
    and Alfred, Lord Tennyson 16, 19
    and James VI and I 17
    decline of as monarchical symbol
        18–19
Arthurianism 44–5
Art Nouveau 91–2
Arts and Crafts
    in Ireland 89
Auld Alliance 136–7
Austen, Jane 8
Austria-Hungary 23

Baird, Major-General David 108
Baldwin, Stanley 144
    and Englishness 8
Balmoral 42
Bard
    as icon 34, 61
    poetry of 45
    in Wales 40
    see also harpers
Barrie, J. M. 60
Bean, Sawney 31
Belfast 24, 144
Bhabha, Homi 22
de Blacam, Aodh 76
Blackie, John Stuart 75
Blake, William 81
The Blood is Strong (1988) 4–5
'Blue Book' 117
Borrow, George 69
Boru, Brian 15
Boswell, James 96–7
Bowles, Thomas 116
Braveheart (1995) 4–5, 111–12, 140
Le Braz, Anatole 72
Brest 3
Britain
    army of 45
        Scots in 107–8
    Englishness 115–16
    historic population of 19
British Empire 110
    and speakers of the Celtic languages
        108

British identity 4, 6, 7, 9–11, 14–16,
    17–18, 23–4, 52, 97, 101–2, 106
  and 'four nations' history 95
  in Ireland 98–9, 105
  and kitsch 41–3
  monarchy, symbols of 115
  rebranding as 'Cool Britannia' 102,
    144
  and Scotland 115, 143
British–Irish Council see 'Council of
    the Isles'
Brittany 3, 117, 140
Brooke, Charlotte 36
Bruce, King Robert 5
Brugha, Cathal 81
Brutus myth 13–15
Buchan, John 85, 106
Buchanan, George 103
Bull, John 101
Burke, Edmund 96
Burns, Robert 2
Burns, William 58
Butt, Isaac 63

Caledonian Antisyzygy 60
Canada 23, 121, 140
Carlyle, Thomas 58, 71
Carson, Sir Edward 133
Castle of Heroes 80–1
Cathleen Ni Houlihan 47, 70, 80
Catholic identity 45, 48–9
  and colonialism 113
'Celtic Communism' 75, 77, 125
  see also Collins, Michael; Connolly,
    James; Maclean, John; Skene,
    W. F.
'Celtic Connections' festival 3
Celtic festivals 140
Celtic identity 103–4
  and George Buchanan 103
  and Celtic Twilight 71
  and Cuchulain 131–3
  and dogs 89–90

  see also deerhound; dogs
  and femininity 61, 65–6
  and folk culture 101
  images of 76
  and religious sites 62
  and Charles Edward Stuart 68
Celticism
  and the British Empire 67, 72
  and chic 40
  and Darwinism 70–1
  and design 86, 89
Celtic League 111
Celtic Magazine 72, 121
Celtic Monthly 121
Celtic Revival 7, 117, 122, 137, 140
  see also separate country entries
Celtic Society 63
Celtic Twilight 58, 71
  see also Celtic identity
Charles II 18, 108
Childers, Erskine 7
Clan Albain 84
Clan Scotland 126
Clearances 109
Clyde, Lord 108
Collins, Michael 76, 111
  and 'Celtic Communism' 76
  compared to Cuchulain 81
  and removal of Stone of Destiny 77
colonialism 106–16
  internal colonialism 108–9, 112
Colorado
  Celtic festivals in 3
Combe, George 56
Comun nan Albanach 84
'Cool Britannia' 102, 144
Connolly, James 7, 76, 79, 125, 141
  and Scotland 77
Connolly, Sean ('the player Connolly')
    82
Cooper, James Fenimore 25–6
Cork 98
Corkery, Daniel 85

see also Gunn, Neil
Cornwall 1, 3, 14, 19, 111, 122
  and Cornish 121–2
  and Cornish nationalism 111, 122
Corunna, Battle of 108
'Council of the Isles' 137
Craig, Cairns 22
Craig, James 51
Crofters' Act (1886) 75
Cromwell, Oliver 26, 133
Cuchulain 13, 83, 131–3
  compared to Cathal Brugha and
    Michael Collins 81
  and Pearse 81–2
  and Yeats 81–2
Curragh Mutiny 133
Cymmrodorion Society 34, 41, 117
Cymru Fydd 110

Darwinism 70–1
Davis, Thomas 54
Davitt, Michael 78
Declaration of Arbroath (1320) 125
  and American identity 87
deerhound 90
  see also Celtic identity; dogs
Defenders 49, 54, 58
(London)Derry 24
Devine, Tom 113
devolution 1, 2, 23–4, 115, 118, 123
Die-hards 83, 124
dogs
  as Celtic symbols 89–90
  see also Celtic identity; deerhound
Doyle, Arthur Conan 73
Druids and Druidism 35, 40
Drumcree 106
Dublin 19
Duncan, John 90, 91, 92
Dwyer, Michael 47

Easter Rising (1916) 82, 124
Edinburgh 19, 37, 100, 106

Edward I 111
Edward VII 73–4
Egypt 130
Eisteddfodd 41, 117
Elizabeth, Queen 20
Emmet, Robert 47, 119
Empire Exhibition (1924) 41–2
England 5
  as synonym for 'Britain' 104–5,
    142–4
  English in Wales 113
  identity of 7–11, 24, 115–16, 142–3
Episcopalianism 45
Erskine, Ruaridh 83, 84, 125
Euroscepticism 10
Evans, Evan 36
Evans, Gwynfor 111, 140
The Evergreen 72, 77, 90
Ewing, Winnie 140

Falklands War 108
Fardd, Ieuan 34
Fenians 78
Ferguson, Sir Samuel 63, 78, 107
Ferguson, William 120, 129
The Fiery Cross 73
Finland 130
Fitzgerald, Lord Edward 119
Flintshire 108–9
Fionn 15–16, 45–6, 63, 86, 89, 141
Fraserburgh 100
Free Wales Army 111

Gaelic 1, 3
  discrimination against 100–1
  in Scotland and Ireland 46, 119–20,
    125
Gaelic Athletic Association 63, 78
  in Scotland 77
Gaelic League 64, 89, 119
  expansion and decline 82–3
Gaelic Union 119
Geddes, Patrick 72, 77, 90

Gellner, Ernest 20–1, 101, 102
Geoffrey of Monmouth 14
George III 96
George IV 42, 86
    and 1822 visit to Scotland 42
Gibbon, Lewis Grassic (James Leslie
    Mitchell) 85, 125
Gladstone, W. E. 106, 115
Glasgow 3, 22, 99, 111
Gloucestershire 24
Glyn Dŵr, Owain 13–17, 41
Gonne, Maud 7, 79, 80
    and Scottish nationalism 77
Gothic 40
    Patriot Gothic 34
Gray, Thomas 34
Great Exhibition (1851) 41
Gregory, Lady Augusta 80, 101
Griffith, Arthur 78, 80, 124
Gunn, Neil 60, 85, 126
    and Daniel Corkery 85
    and Fionn 86
    and Padraig Pearse 126

Hamilton, Ian 77
harpers 40, 123
Hary, Blin 20
Hastings, Adrian 102
Heaney, Seamus 24, 65, 132
Hechter, Michael 2
Henry II 14
Henry VII 14–16, 29
    and Welsh messianism 14–15
Henry VIII 15
Highlander (1984) 4
Highland Games 125
Highlands 42–4
    alienation from rest of Scotland 57
    and colonialism 25
    and famine 113–14
    Highland dress 63
    Highland societies 63
    image of the Highlander 62–3, 125

Hobsbawm, Eric 22
Hogg, James 57, 63
Hollywood
    and postcolonialism 111
Home Rule 115
Hornel, Edward 92
Housman, A. E. 72
Hyde, Douglas 119

Imperial localism 106–7
incomers 39, 108–9
India
    like Ireland and Scotland 106, 112
    Mutiny of 1857 108
IRA 83, 109, 111, 131, 142, 143
    and Pan-Celticism 111
    and postcolonialism 95
Ireland 1, 2, 3, 4, 19, 23–4, 39–40, 44,
    130
    and famine 113–14
    and Germany in World War I 110
    Irish soldiers abroad 108
    and 1798 Rising 40
Irish identity 45–54, 106–16, 132
    and Anglo-Saxonism 104
    and Ascendancy 115
    and Britishness 98–9, 105
    and colonialism 25, 49, 52, 106
    and femininity 64
    and Free State 83, 119, 124
    and immigration 110
    and Protestantism 49–51
    and stupidity 29, 33
    and Unionism 107, 130–4
Irish language 119–20
Irish Literary Society 64
Irish Party 113, 124
Irish revival 89–90
Irish-Scottish Academic Initiative 138
Irish Volunteers 82
Irish Wolfhound Club 89

Jacobitism 5, 25, 26, 42, 109, 144

and Irish Republicanism 48
neo-Jacobitism 91, 93
uniform in the Rising of 1745
    86
James VI and I 17, 55, 86
James VII and II 45
    as Irish hero 45
James VIII and III 29
Jenner, Henry
    and Celtic revival in Cornwall
    122
John, King 14
Joyce, James 74, 83, 101
de Jubanville, Henri d'Arbois 72

Kay-Shuttleworth, Sir James 117
King, Jessie M. 92
Kingsley, Charles 25
Kinnock, Neil 122
Kipling, Rudyard 8, 43, 144
Knox, Robert 56
Ku-Klux-Klan 5

Labour Party 134
    and devolution 123
    and land reform 76
Land League 75, 77–8, 84
Larkin, James 48
Larkin, Philip 8
Lauder, Sir Harry 87, 88
Lawrence, D. H. 71
The Legitimist Ensign 73
The Legitimist League 73
Lhuyd, Edward 103
Linklater, Eric 126–7
Lom, Ian 36
London 111
Londonderry *see* Derry

MacColla, Fionn 85, 126
MacCormick, John 127
MacDiarmid, Hugh (Christopher
    Grieve) 83–4, 85, 125, 126

MacDonagh, Thomas 82
MacGill-Eain, Somhairle (MacLean,
    Sorley) 85
Macgillivray, Pittendrigh 72, 92
Mackenzie, Sir Compton 38
Mackintosh, Charles Rennie 91
Maclean, John 93, 125–6
MacMhaighstir Alasdair, Alasdair 36
MacNair, Herbert 91
MacNeill, Eoin 76, 80
Macpherson, James 35–6, 56, 61–2,
    78–9
MacStiofain, Sean 111
Major, John 8, 144
Man 1, 3
    and Manx 122
Manchester 144
Markievicz, Countess Constance 81,
    83, 125, 126
Mathers, Samuel MacGregor 77
Mebyon Kernow 111, 122
Mitchell, James Leslie *see* Gibbon,
    Lewis Grassic
Montserrat
    Irish in 108
Moore, George 89
Moore, Sir John 108
Muir, Edwin 85, 126
Muldoon, Paul 132
murals 12, 131–2

Napier, Theodore 48, 73–5, 83
Napier Commission 58, 75, 109
National Association for the
    Vindication of Scottish Rights
    (NAVSR) 97
nationalism 102, 105–6
    Protestant 113
    theories of 1, 7, 11, 20–4
National Literary Society 119
National Party of Scotland (NPS)
    126–7, 135
National Tartan Day 87

National Theatre (Ireland) 89
National Trust for Scotland 127
Neo-Jacobitism *see* Jacobitism
Newbolt, Sir Henry 9, 66
Noble Savage 3, 6, 65, 69, 100, 109
Nordau, Max 66
Norman Yoke 17–18
Northern Ireland 2, 5, 12, 115, 130–7, 140
    Peace Settlement (1998) 134, 137
Norway 137
Nova Scotia
    Gaelic in 121

O'Casey, Sean 48
O'Connell, Daniel 46, 48, 51, 63
    and Scotland 58
O'Grady, Standish 70, 80, 83–4
    and Unionist politics 77–8
O'Heffernan, William Dall 84
Orange Card 133
Orangeism 49–51
    in Scotland 50
Ó Rathaille, Aoghan 47, 85
origin myths 13–15, 17–18, 55
Ossian/Oisin 16, 36
Ó Suilleabhain, Eoghan Rua 84

Pan-Celticism 74, 77, 83, 128
Parnell, Charles 70, 110, 119, 123
Paton, Sir Noel 72
Patriot Whigs 34
Peacock, Francis 40
Pearse, Padraig 7, 12, 77, 80–3, 92, 112, 131–3
    compared to African writers 112
Pennant, Thomas 17
Percy, Bishop Thomas 36
Pezron, Paul Yves 103
Pinkerton, John 56
Plaid Cymru 108, 111, 135
Plunkett, Sir Horace 66
Pocock, J. G. A.

    and Britishness 95
    and Scotland and Ireland 97–8
postcolonialism 94, 106–16
Powell, Enoch 102
Power, William 127, 135
primitivism 36–7, 39–44, 123

Quebec 23

Redmond, John 123–4
Referendum (1997) 1–2, 115, 142
Renan, Ernest 69, 130
Richard I 14
Rob Roy (1994) 4, 111
Romanticism 41, 123, 125
    and Celtic identity 3, 5, 6
Rowlands, Richard 55
The Royalist 73
Russell, George ('A. E.') 72, 81

Said, Edward 4, 70
    sees Ireland as colony 95–6
St Patrick, Cross of 107
Salmond, Alex 137
Saltire Society 127
Scoti 15
Scotland 1, 2, 3, 4, 5, 15, 16, 19, 20–1, 23–4, 39–40, 106–16
    and Ireland 15–16, 59, 110
    and popular culture 39–40, 126
    and tourism 37–9
Scots
    accent 115
    aristocracy 31
    in British Army 43–4, 107–8
    caricatured 26–8, 30–5
    colonials 42, 109, 111
    country dancing 40
    discrimination against 100–1
    disloyal 27
    and immigration 108, 110
    rising of 1820 58
Scots National League 84

Scott, Sir Walter 25–9, 42, 61, 75, 86,
        90, 109, 135
    and the Royal Visit of 1822 37–8
    and Scottish identity 56, 60
Scottish enlightenment
    and British identity 56–7
    and the Union 57
    and the Wars of Independence 57
Scottish identity 23, 44, 54, 106–16
    and anti-Englishness 22–3
    and Britain 115, 138–9
    and Catholicism 120
    and class politics 115
    and devolution 60
    and education 112
    and Empire 114–15, 120
    and English identity compared
        99–100
    and Gaelic 120–1
    like India 100
    and Irish identity compared 103,
        109, 111, 126, 137, 140–1
    and its origin myth 15, 17–18, 55
    and Protestantism 50
    like South Carolina 63
    and tartan 86–8
    and Teutonism 54–60
Scottish National Party 106, 111, 127,
        143
    and British Empire 135
    and Catholicism 138
    and Celtic revivalism 84
    cultural nationalism 127
    and EFTA 137–8
    and European Union 134–7
    first mention of 74
    fundamentalist wing 135
    and Irish nationality today 137
    rise of 111, 135–6
Scottish Office 138
Scottish Party 127, 135
Sean Bhean Bhocht 47, 70, 80, 83,
        132–3

Sectarianism 110
    see also Orangeism
Seringapatam 108
Seven Years' War 108
Sharp, William (Fiona MacLeod)
        71–2, 77, 80
Shetland 24
Shropshire 107
Sillars, Jim 134
Sinn Fein 2, 124, 126, 134
Siol Nan Gaidheal 91
Skene, W. F. 58, 75, 76, 84
    and 'Celtic Communism' 75, 77
    and Pearse 81
Smith, Anthony 102, 129
Sobieski Stuarts 43
Society for the Preservation of the
        Irish Language 63
Society for Utilising the Welsh
        Language 117
Southey, Robert 111
Stonehenge 35
Stuart Exhibition (1888) 73
Swift, Jonathan 25, 49, 54, 70
Swinburne, A. C. 19
Synge, J. M. 127

tartan 86–8
Teutonism 37, 54–60
Thomas, Edward 72
Thomson, James 144
Tipu Sultan 108
Tone, Wolfe 47, 119, 123, 126
Tonnies, Ferdinand 101
Traquair, Phoebe 92
Treaty of 1922 83, 124
    non-Irish links of Diehards 83

UDA 131
union see Act of Union
unionism 107
    in Northern Ireland 12, 131–4
    and Scots tongue 131–2

United Irishmen 40, 49, 54, 58

de Valera, Eamonn 83
Verstegan, Richard *see* Rowlands,
    Richard
Victoria, Queen 42, 73, 74
    Diamond Jubilee (1897) 41
    and Highlands 42–3, 62, 125
    statue of in Cork 98
    and tartan 86

Wales 1, 2, 3, 4, 11, 14, 15, 19, 23–4,
        39–40, 44, 45, 106–16
    images of Celticism 93
    and colonies 107
    holiday homes in 108–9
    inhabitants depicted as thieves
        29–30, 33
    Irish immigration 110
    in mediaeval period 13
    support for Charles I 17
Wallace, Sir William 5, 84, 97, 111–12
    cult of 97
    likened to Garibaldi and Pearse 112
War of Three Kingdoms 17
Welsh 1, 3, 116–19
    and Anglophone clergy 30
    and Brittany 117
    and Celtic revival 117

and politics 118–19, 122–5
Welsh nationalism 118–19, 122–5
    and militancy 110
    rise of 111
    see also Plaid Cymru
Wilde, Oscar 74
    as effeminate Irishman 66
Wilkes, John 31–3, 54, 62
William III and II (of Orange) 18
Wilson, Marion 92
Wood, John 35
Wood, Wendy 83, 140
Worcester, Battle of 26
Wordsworth, William 8
World War I 108, 110, 113

xenophobia 25

Yeats, Jack B. 89
Yeats, Lily 89
Yeats, W. B. 16, 47, 69–70, 77, 90, 101,
        124, 126, 127
    and Blake 81
    and the feminine Celt 79–80
    his Cuchulain an influence on
        Pearse 81–2
    and Irish language 120
    and Irish politics 78–81
Young Ireland 51